Red State Blues

Over the last quarter-century, a natioı [D0873357] :ive Republican Party made unprecedent ing control of 24 new state governments. Liberals and conservatives alike anticipated far-reaching consequences, but what has the Republican revolution in the states achieved?

Red State Blues shows that, contrary to liberals' fears, conservative state governments have largely failed to enact policies that advance conservative goals or reverse prior liberal gains. Matt Grossmann tracks policies and socio-economic outcomes across all 50 states, interviews state insiders, and considers the full issue agenda. Although Republicans have been effective at staying in power, they have not substantially altered the nature or reach of government. Where they have had policy victories, the consequences on the ground have been surprisingly limited. A sober assessment of Republican successes and failures after decades of electoral victories, *Red State Blues* highlights the stark limits of the conservative ascendancy.

Matt Grossmann is Director of the Institute for Public Policy and Social Research at Michigan State University and Senior Fellow at the Niskanen Center. A regular contributor to *FiveThirtyEight*, he has published analysis in the *New York Times*, *Washington Post*, and *Politico* and hosts the *Science of Politics* podcast. He is the author of *Asymmetric Politics* (with David A. Hopkins), *Artists of the Possible*, and *The Not-So-Special Interests*.

Red State Blues

How the Conservative Revolution Stalled in the States

Matt Grossmann
Michigan State University

CAMBRIDGE
UNIVERSITY PRESS

University Printing House, Cambridge CB2 8BS, United Kingdom

One Liberty Plaza, 20th Floor, New York, NY 10006, USA

477 Williamstown Road, Port Melbourne, VIC 3207, Australia

314–321, 3rd Floor, Plot 3, Splendor Forum, Jasola District Centre,
New Delhi – 110025, India

79 Anson Road, #06-04/06, Singapore 079906

Cambridge University Press is part of the University of Cambridge.

It furthers the University's mission by disseminating knowledge in the pursuit of
education, learning, and research at the highest international levels of excellence.

www.cambridge.org
Information on this title: www.cambridge.org/9781108476911
DOI: 10.1017/9781108569187

First published 2019

Printed in the United States of America by Sheridan Books, Inc.

A catalogue record for this publication is available from the British Library

ISBN 978-1-108-47691-1 Hardback
ISBN 978-1-108-70175-4 Paperback

For Norah and Ari

CONTENTS

List of Figures   *page* viii
List of Tables   ix
Acknowledgments   xi

1   Leviathan's Resilience   1

2   The Rise of Republican Rule   32

3   Sticky Liberal Policymaking   51

4   Conservative Dilemmas in Action   83

5   The Mostly Missing Results of Republican Policies   118

6   The Elusive Red State Model   152

References   173
Index   191

FIGURES

2.1   Republican control of state legislative chambers and governorships, 1992 and 2017   *page* 34

2.2   Average number of Republican state legislative chambers and governorships per state   35

2.3   Average proportion of house and senate seats held by Democrats over time   36

2.4   State Republican Party median conservatism in house and senate over time   46

3.1   State government expenditures over time   53

3.2   Annual state government employment   55

3.3   Average net liberal policy adoptions over time   57

3.4   Predicting net counts of policies expanding minus contracting scope of state governments   63

3.5   Predicting net counts of Democratic-preferred minus Republican-preferred policies   66

3.6   Predicting state government expenditures as a percentage of state economy   69

3.7   Predicting underlying dimension of state policy liberalism   72

4.1   Primary issue areas of state policy proposals   88

4.2   Author mentions of explanations for policy success or failure   88

4.3   Characteristics of proposals and policies adopted   89

4.4   Ideological positions of Wisconsin economic policy and economic public opinion   101

TABLES

5.1   Policy evaluations of Republican-initiated state policy
       changes   *page* 124
5.2   Evidence assessments of policies and programs by
       ideological perspective   136
5.3   Outcomes of partisan governance   141
6.1   Conclusions and implications of the book's evidence   157
6.2   Lessons for policy   158

ACKNOWLEDGMENTS

In an unanticipated move, I became Director of the Institute for Public Policy and Social Research (IPPSR) at Michigan State University in 2016. The Institute has a long-running role as the primary outreach vehicle connecting the state government in Lansing with the university three miles away. The distance between scholarly knowledge and political practice, of course, often seems quite a bit longer. IPPSR tries to reduce the gulf, connecting university researchers with policymakers as well as training candidates, state legislators, staff, and interns. I thus acquired a front-row seat for action in one state capital area during unified Republican control. That inspired this book, as I decided to take on a new scholarly venture on state politics and policy. Thanks to IPPSR administrators for helping me keep up with scholarship despite the new role, especially Arnold Weinfeld, Linda Cleary, Lin Stork, AnnMarie Schneider, Cindy Kyle, Iris Harper, and Milly Shiraev. The Lansing policymaking community, especially supporters of our Michigan Political Leadership Program, also helped orient my research to the on-the-ground concerns of state politics.

I entered state politics as a newcomer to the academic field and have been uniformly encouraged and assisted. The subfield is the most welcoming I have encountered, with scholars sharing ideas and data and working hard to integrate up-and-coming researchers. Thanks especially to Chris Warshaw, Alex Hertel-Fernandez, Jason Sorens, Devin Caughey, Frederick Boehmke, and Charles Barrilleaux, as well as everyone involved in the State Politics and Policy Conference. My research is always informed by my conversations with my Michigan State University colleagues in political science, including Ben Appel, Valentina Bali, Ryan Black, Eric Chang, Jeff Conroy-Krutz, Erica Frantz, Eric Gonzalez Juenke, Steve Kautz, Nazita Lajevardi, Ian Ostrander, Chuck Ostrom, Josh Sapotichne, Ani Sarkissian, Cory Smidt, and Jakana Thomas.

I had the special privilege of finishing this book on a year-long sabbatical in Cambridge, MA, where I had full access to resources but little to no actual responsibility as a Visiting Associate Professor in the Department of Political Science at the Massachusetts Institute of Technology and Visiting Scholar at the Institute for Quantitative Social Science at Harvard University. Thanks to all of my temporary colleagues, as well as the support staff in departments and libraries who made my research possible.

While researching this book, I also joined the Niskanen Center in Washington to produce a podcast on political science research. My colleagues there, trying to reshape conservative and libertarian predispositions in a dispiriting political age, have also influenced my thinking, especially Jerry Taylor, Steven Teles, Josh McCabe, and Will Wilkinson. I also thank Yuval Levin and Matt Spalding for early relevant conversations. I anonymously interviewed dozens of state capitol reporters for this book; well beyond the quotes I include, their observations informed it. I benefit from Twitter interactions as well, with political scientists and research-informed reporters. A surprisingly active Twitter community has arisen over the last five years, with researchers, practitioners, and laypersons all offering useful commentary on my early drafts and observations. I also presented the work at Boston University in the critical last moments, adding insights from Taylor Boas, Dino Christenson, Katherine Levine Einstein, Lauren Mattioli, and Spencer Piston.

I benefited from amazing research assistance in completing this book. Marty Jordan helped put together the initial Correlates of State Policy database and Zuhaib Mahmood was responsible for the legwork for many of the analyses I present. Emily Jenkins, Iris Robare, Babs Hough, and Jonathan Spiegler conducted compilations and analysis that I include in the book. My Cambridge University Press editor Sara Doskow and my independent editor Ken Barlow provided very useful comments on the full book.

My family has been quite supportive of my research. My father Larry Grossmann, who worked on state legislative campaigns in Missouri, and my mother Jan Grossmann, who runs a statewide women's leadership program there, were instrumental in developing my interests. My mother-in-law Ellen Reckhow and father-in-law Ken Reckhow, who are active in North Carolina politics, have also been influential. My wife, Sarah Reckhow, who is not only a loving life partner but also my colleague in political science, provided thoughtful comments on the project from initial ideas to finished manuscript. This book is dedicated to my daughter, Norah, and my son, Ari. They are daily life's inspiration – and also a constant reminder to take time to talk and play.

1 LEVIATHAN'S RESILIENCE

In the Spring of 2018, a movement for increased education funding arose in a curious constellation of Red states. West Virginia teachers walked out in protest over low wages and health costs, winning concessions from a Republican-controlled state government and sparking a broader wave of protest. Oklahoma teachers walked out as well, winning funding and staffing increases, while also sparking Republican primary challenges and Democratic general election victories in support of better-funded education. In a "Red for Ed" mass mobilization, Arizona teachers won raises and school funding from their Republican-controlled legislature. Kentucky teachers became successful candidates, protesters, and lobbyists, forcing significant changes to pension reforms. Protests in North Carolina and Colorado had more limited success but did help stimulate legislative and electoral backlash. In states like South Dakota, Kansas, and Georgia, preemptive concessions limited further teacher mobilization.

Most of these states had limited unionization (with some teachers only organized in associations without striking capacity), but nonetheless union officials and liberal activists nationwide were energized. Even without statewide collective bargaining, activists managed to organize teachers and convince the public and policymakers to support liberal policy positions, often impacting non-education debates by causing taxes to be raised, tax cuts to be scaled back, or state budgets to be revised.

In some ways, these mobilizations and their policymaking success were responses to significant rightward moves in state policy, which in turn stimulated a backlash by Democratic-leaning constituencies and voters. The upsurge came at the end of a long period of rising Republican and conservative dominance in the American states. In the eyes of their advocates, teachers were simply responding objectively to the reality they were faced with: that of a stingily funded education system. But the revolt's breadth and success also point to some inherent limits to conservative governance. Cutting back on the size and scope of government is popular in principle, but students being forced to attend underfunded schools without teachers is not popular in practice. The implications of reduced funding for state responsibilities, education and health care chief among them, create predictable repercussions for Republicans focused on cutting taxes and stimulating the private over the public sector.

The conservative movement that took power in the Republican Party in the twentieth century – and the party's politicians and activists that took control of American state governments in the 1990s, 2000s, and 2010s – wanted to overcome these constraints to enact a fundamental restructuring of government, but they have succumbed to the same limitations that have long bedeviled conservative governance. The more pessimistic predictions of liberals resisting increased Republican electoral success have also failed to come to pass. Even in Red America, liberal policy positions remain popular, and liberal movements are able to succeed with Republican politicians and voters. The teachers' uprisings provide an opportune moment to evaluate just what Republicans have managed to achieve in state governments with their increased control, as well as examining why their legislative and policy ambitions have not been fulfilled to the extent many had anticipated.

Republican Renaissance or Disappointment?

By the early 1990s, Republicans had been the minority party in the American states for decades. Since the 1930s, aside from a few brief mid-century periods, they had controlled a minority of state lower (house) and higher (senate) chambers, as well as having a minority of legislators in every year – usually by large margins. Since then, though, they have experienced a sharp electoral rise. From 1990 to 2016, Republicans gained 813 state house seats, 360 state senate seats, and

23 governorships – moving from full control of just three states to full control of 23 states.

The Republican Party arose in the 1990s not through moderating its positions or adapting to local circumstances, but by becoming a full-throated national conservative party responsive to an activist base. Its call was to roll back decades of liberal advances and remake America into a country of traditionalist values and limited government. Just as Newt Gingrich led a 1990s Congressional Republican resurgence with a detailed agenda, promising a new "Contract with America" and an attendant series of policy reforms, 29 state Republican parties also began the 1990s by committing themselves to comprehensive action plans for conservative government.[1] Proposals from conservative think tanks, activists, and state legislators ripened into a full plate of policies to address education, crime, welfare, health, housing, family decline, the environment, taxes, government spending, gambling, privatization, torts, and political reform.[2] Republicans, as the more nationalized of the two major American parties, had developed mature institutions – such as think tanks, state legislator associations, and grassroots networks – to promote conservative goals. With an extensive array of conservative policy proposals on the table and big promises made, voters were now granting them the power to enact their agenda.

Republicans moved into power as conservatives advanced the objective of making the states the primary sites of their policymaking renaissance. Congressional Republicans sought to devolve power away from national government and toward the states. In his first speech as Senate Majority leader in 1995, Bob Dole said "we will continue in our drive to return power to our states and our people." New Speaker Gingrich declared "we are committed to getting power back to the states." Even President Clinton agreed, claiming government should "ship decision-making responsibility and resources" to lower levels, including states.[3] Reporters largely bought the story, claiming that the political action would soon move to state capitols, where the Republican revolution would make its true mark.

What do Republicans have to show for their electoral gains and conservative policy advances? Political scientists Theda Skocpol and Alexander Hertel-Fernandez see a "persistent imbalance between right and left in state-level organizational prowess" with "right-wing political networks [achieving] striking victories."[4] Republican governors like Wisconsin's Scott Walker and Kansas's Sam Brownback, according to both their admirers and critics, are said to have fundamentally changed their states. Liberals are now seeking to emulate what they see as conservative success, building equivalent organizations and refocusing on state politics.

When it comes to policy, however, Republican success is overstated. I argue that the Republican Party's widespread gains in state legislative and gubernatorial elections over the past quarter-century have resulted in only limited success in changing state policy direction or affecting social and economic outcomes. Despite a more conservative and ascendant national party, Republican-controlled state governments have not reduced the size or scope of state governments, overcome long-standing state idiosyncrasies in policy and practice, reversed prior liberal gains, or enacted a substantive policy agenda that advances conservative values and goals.

That is not to say that Republicans have had no successes. Instead, Republicans have slowed liberal gains in the states. They have also advanced several important policies, some of which have achieved their proximate goals. Most strikingly, they have been remarkably effective at staying in power. However, both the impact Republicans have had on policy as well as the impact their policies have had on the social and economic life of the states has been surprisingly constrained.

As we shall see, the limited success Republicans have had in translating their electoral gains into impactful policy victories is the product both of inherent governing challenges facing conservative parties worldwide, as well as the dependence of US states on federal policy and national socio-economic trends. Sustained conservative policymaking is difficult: the scope of government tends to expand over time and programs are rarely dislodged, with social changes more often codified than reversed. Of the policies that do come into being, the effects on real-world outcomes such as economic growth and societal well-being tend to be small; conservative policies are limited by design and then tend to be diluted or counteracted by bureaucracies that implement them. This adds up to two critical limits to Republican policy results: policy goals that are often not achieved and policies that pass but fail to have broad social and economic impact. Both make it difficult to translate Republican electoral victories into lasting change.

Polarization and Power Without Results

Republican and Democratic politicians now present completely different visions of government. Voters have increasingly joined them, splitting along partisan lines across many issues and behaving as if team players in support of their preferred party. Citizens expect positions articulated in election campaigns to translate into real results when a party has an opportunity to govern. But the Republican Party has long had trouble translating its broad campaign messaging into tangible policy results.[5] Its goals of reducing the size and scope of government and limiting social change are inherently hard to achieve. Conservative policy change is difficult worldwide, but even so the Republican Party stands out in the distance between its professed agenda to roll back government's advance and its actual results in office. Both conservative activists and critics from the left complain that Republicans have failed to carry out their promises when in power – at least at the federal level. The American states, at the center of a recent massive political shift to the right, offer a good opportunity to properly assess Republican rule.

Looking at the political map in 2017 compared to 1992, Republicans had gained full control of 23 new states, controlling both houses of the state legislature and the governor's office in states they did not previously control, without losing control anywhere.[6] Policymakers in the states are now much more conservative than their predecessors and Republicans now hold much larger legislative majorities in most states. Some argue that their control has yielded results, pointing to roll-backs in union power and electoral rules that advantage the party. Portraits of the Koch brothers' network even claim that Republicans have transformed the states, urging liberals to copy their tactics in order to compete effectively.[7]

What, though, has the Republican revolution in the states yielded in terms of policy change and real-world results? The picture is mixed. For the most part, Republican-controlled states are not innovating in new policy adoptions or overturning prior Democratic policies. They have made progress on some social issues such as abortion and gun control, but these policies have not had broad social or economic effects and are counter-balanced by nationwide liberal gains in other social-issue areas such as gay rights and drug policy. Republicans have made even less progress in scaling back the size and scope of government; long-standing state differences in policy priorities and government's breadth remain while nearly all states are continuing to increase government's share of economic activity. Where conservative policies have passed, there is little evidence that they have made a difference in important outcomes such as economic viability, health, innovation, or quality of life. In determining the relative standing of the states, the limited policy gains made have proved no match for broad regional and national demographic and socio-economic trends.

The results of this book challenge established views of politics and policy. In public debate, Republicans are portrayed as state capitol conquerors, with Democrats protesting against what they see as the exercise of unprecedented Republican power. Academics claim that party control of legislatures matters more than ever for the liberalism of state policy; that although state parties used to adapt to regional cultures, they now pursue and achieve nationalized agendas. All this presents a distorted picture. It is the (few remaining) Democratic majorities that have been more successful than their Republican counterparts in advancing new policies. Neither party has significantly altered state trajectories, but Democratic majorities have continued to expand government's scope at a faster rate.

The results suggest that the conventional policy trade-offs attributed to liberal and conservative policies are no longer evident. There is no clear choice between growth and equality – the normal outcomes supposedly associated with smaller and larger governments – or between economic protection and innovation (as few industries can be effectively protected or stimulated). Policies can work to marginally impact these outcomes, but not to meaningfully alter state trends. Despite regular claims that Texas or California are modeling "Red state" or "Blue state" successes or failures, most state outcomes are the product of either non-political factors or long-standing differences. Newly Republican states have not shifted their policies enough to stimulate socio-economic or cultural change.

Why Republican Electoral Gains Don't Translate into Conservative Policy Results

As early as the nineteenth century, German economist Adolph Wagner proposed that the size and scope of government expand over time in response to economic and social change, political pressure, and path-dependent historical development (the phenomenon is sometimes known as Wagner's Law). Libertarian Robert Higgs outlined the many reasons for this built-in pressure for expansion. These include:

- modernization, economic transformation, and urbanization creating new social problems;
- tax collection and program administration becoming increasingly feasible;
- progressive social impulses and democratization leading to new policy proposals;
- wars and economic downturns creating crises, increasing state power without fully reverting;
- political and policymaking activity becoming routinized, making it available for facilitating action;
- new agencies and legal precedents enabling fresh claims for rights or benefits;
- past policies creating bureaucrats and experts who push for new and expanded policies;
- social organizations such as businesses and interest groups enlarging over time, facilitating larger bureaucracy;
- popular expectations adjusting to broader government roles in society.[8]

Early state development is thus path dependent, with increasing returns to continuing down the same path; the large fixed costs involved in the set-up of programs – plus learning, coordination, and adaptive expectations by beneficiaries and implementers – make it unlikely that program development is reversed or past policy regimes are overturned.[9] Because prior government benefits and regulatory regimes create constituencies, programs and roles are difficult to undo. Even in moral and cultural issues, conservatives tend to fight losing battles in their role as protectors of traditional norms facing social change.[10] Americans have collectively liberalized social norms, become more socially tolerant, and grown progressively less constricted over 200 years.[11] As a result, conservative policy achievements are less frequent than liberal victories, and are usually paired with expansions of government and accelerations of social change in other domains.[12]

Though all policy is difficult to enact, the retrenchment of existing policies is thus more difficult than other types of political action. If a health care program is established, it creates or expands the community of beneficiaries, administrators, and experts who are aligned with the policy's goals, and who gain directly from its continuation and expansion. It also makes all actors, even those who might prefer an alternative, accustomed to it, with the public and policymakers taking its continued presence for granted when making decisions. Social norms and other programs may also evolve to interface with it. Medicaid, for example, was not initially embraced by every state and was not nearly as expansive as it is today. Now all kinds of actors – from nursing homes to hospitals to short-term employers – are heavily invested in it, and the policy has become overwhelmingly popular. Some states may refuse to expand it (as 14 states did recently), but few actively contract its scope (and as voters in Utah, Idaho, Nebraska, and Maine have shown, voters may eventually demand their preferred expansion). It is a common story of social programs everywhere: they are difficult to create but even more difficult to contract.

Governors, as overseers of state bureaucracies as well as policymaking participants, tend to be wary of cutting programs, curtailing benefits, or taking on their underlings. That matters for conservative policy success because governors are consistently more influential in guiding budgetary choices than other policies. Studies of gubernatorial agendas announced in State of the State addresses show that they obtain about 70 percent of the size of their budget requests, and that successful budget requests account for a large share of the 41 percent of their proposals that legislatures enact.[13] However, these requests are not driven by ideology: 65 percent of requests made by Democratic governors are for increasing spending, but then so are 57 percent of the requests made by Republican governors. A plurality of governors (even in public speeches) also call for tax increases, rather than cuts. In addition, governors are more focused on education and economic development than on social issues or political reforms, but successes in the areas they emphasize are driven more by economic prospects, state institutions, and timing than by their party's legislative seat share or the nature of their proposals.[14] This may be why early studies found little effect of gubernatorial partisanship on state spending, with some even suggesting an inverse relationship with Republicans spending more.[15]

As the federal government expands, it also provides new incentives (even sometimes requirements) for state government expansion. Federal policies have dramatically increased state responsibilities and constraints on state actions, adding state tasks and reporting requirements.[16] Across 22 policy areas, Congress and the Supreme Court have steadily expanded federal authority over time – especially during the 1930s, 1960s, and 1970s – with no later return to more limited state oversight.[17] They have even more steadily increased the conditionality of federal grants to states – money now comes with a lot more strings.[18] In addition, Congress has continually increased the federal role in state budgets, the responsibilities of governors to submit plans for federal approval, and the requirements for cooperative state–federal enforcement.[19] Congress anticipates state responses and implements expansionary policies with its own goals in mind, delegating or decentralizing decision-making and authority only where it serves national goals.[20] Even in a polarized era, there is significant bipartisan cooperation in implementing federally pushed policies – partisan allies of federal policy opponents, facing local pressures, cannot be counted on to oppose federal initiatives once they reach lower levels of government.[21] Nationwide organizing by state officials can provide opportunities for new state action (such as the joint state action to resolve tobacco industry complaints), but the results usually serve to extend government's scope.[22]

The largest state policy reform movements of recent decades have all been led by federal policy change. Social welfare spending increased dramatically before the 1996 Personal Responsibility and Work Opportunity Act, a large reform and consolidation that instigated a new round of state welfare roll cuts (but was also associated with an increase in state and federal earned income tax credits). Major state education reforms were required under the 2001 No Child Left Behind Act and its extensions, which increased testing, funding, monitoring, and assessment requirements, as well as specialty programs. The largest changes in health policy were driven by the Affordable Care Act, which, alongside a federalization of insurance regulation, led to huge expansions of Medicaid in most states. The largest components of state budgets – health, education, and social welfare – are thus not fully at the discretion of states, even when powers are allegedly devolved. Overall, despite continued efforts to decentralize decision-making, the United States has slowly centralized over the past 200 years, with centralizing spurts during the 1930s and 1960s–1970s that were never reversed, while states have retained fiscal responsibilities with extra federal strings.[23]

Many nationwide trends also leave states without effective policy options. The population is shifting South and West, regardless of Northern states' efforts to stem the tide. Firms invested in the global economy are favoring financial capitals and enlarged enterprises, limiting where they want to invest resources. Policies, such as those designed to revive Rust Belt cities or build export industries, often work against these strong headwinds. Meanwhile, society is diversifying and secularizing, with population growth driven by recent international migrants and religious institutions losing membership nationwide. Conservative desires to resuscitate large and traditional families or small-town religious piety do not suggest obvious policy levers to affect these long-term trends.

At the federal level, conservatives respond to the infeasibility of shrinking government or reversing social change by focusing on policy priorities that are not subject to these difficulties, such as increasing defense spending and cutting taxes without cutting social spending (thereby increasing the deficit). But neither of these policies is available in the states, nearly all of which have balanced budget requirements and where there is no obvious category of spending that conservatives are in agreement on expanding. This means states cannot easily focus on popular Republican policies (such as tax cuts) without also making changes that are substantially less popular (such as cutting education).

State institutional trends also contribute to conservative difficulties. By the time Republicans gained power in the 1990s, state legislatures had undergone a "professionalization revolution" between the 1960s and 1981, becoming more like Congress with developed committee systems, electoral careers, and increased workloads.[24] Nearly every state professionalized dramatically over the twentieth century, increasing legislative time demands and salaries, as well as building centralized legislative institutions.[25] Increasing professionalization led to more complex regulatory policies, more progressive immigration policies, and higher education funding.[26] Professionalization increased government capacity and stability, while courts and federal mandates also increased policymaking requirements.[27] In short, professionalization produced liberal governments of expanding capability.

Other institutional changes also mitigated conservative success. Term limits, even though often implemented by conservatives, raised the costs of legislating while increasing the role of other long-term state actors.[28] State lawmaking institutions remain complex and difficult to navigate, with new legislators facing challenging work adjustments and competing time demands due to constant fundraising and campaigning. Supermajority requirements to raise taxes, another

Republican-led institutional change, initially furthered their goals but became less effective over time, with states finding ways to work around limits to raise new revenue (such as raising and diversifying fees).[29] Tax and expenditure limitations also limit partisan effects on where to allocate spending.[30] Other new rules increasingly earmarked dollars and stabilized existing programs, just as courts became increasingly active in requiring more equitable policies and minimum service standards.[31] Nearly all states have relatively more liberal judges than politicians because the pool of lawyers is so much more liberal than the pool of elected officials.[32] Though Republicans try to appoint the most conservative judges among them, these still tend to lean to the left and limit conservative governance. State executive branches also often divide power between governors and other directly elected officials, such as those overseeing agriculture or education, who tend to protect and seek to enlarge the programs under their direction.

Interest group development also favored status-quo-supporting sectors such as business and teacher associations, hospitals, utility companies, lawyers, insurance companies, and local governments.[33] Where majority parties were strong, these interest groups also tended to be strong. Increasing interest group density in the states has led to less productive legislatures, as incumbent interests become effective at blocking changes that might reduce their resources or influence.[34] Whereas conservative think tanks have influenced public opinion in their states, they have not influenced free-market policies; in contrast, state lobbying groups influence policy directly.[35] The result has been legislatures that limit controversial bills and instead focus on bills required by courts, the federal government, or prior expiring policies.[36] As a result, studies of policy output differences across states tend to incorporate a variety of factors beyond partisanship: policy-specific needs and histories; interest group influence; judicial and executive power; public and elite opinion; political culture; economic context; institutional developments; and electoral competition.[37] The balance of these factors protects against changes in the status quo, limiting conservative policy retrenchment. The policy regimes Republicans inherited were thus difficult to challenge. State expenditures were and remain concentrated in areas that matter to individual lives, such as education, health, transportation, and public safety.[38] By 1980, states had become the major providers of public services, with less direct local or national provision. Despite public services being dependent on them, however, states were caught in the mire of their own dependence on federal dollars.[39] Education spending had steadily increased, with most states equalizing funding across districts, and had become the largest area of spending. Welfare spending had also grown, with big jumps around 1970 and 1990.[40] Major benefits went to veterans, Native Americans, and children, with separate funds for health, foster care, nutrition, housing, services, job training, and energy – all with some federal dollars.[41] Medicaid, jointly administered with the federal government, became the largest state program and is still taking a progressively larger share over time. Regional variation remains in social welfare, labor market, and fiscal policy, failing to match a clear liberal-to-conservative continuum due to few states remaining conservative across economic policy dimensions. Fiscal policy, meanwhile, showed less variation, as states converged on large budgets with similar substantive divisions.[42] By the advent of Republicans' control, state budgets were full of popular programs for sympathetic constituencies.

Republicans also inherited decades of increased regulations and standards regarding education, the environment, health, safety, civil rights, insurance, and disabilities. Occupational licensing was already high, well-developed, and supported by the involved industries. Even areas of Republican innovation such as economic development had already become separate and complicated policy areas, with numerous technically sophisticated tools and byzantine incentive structures, as well as local governments invested in their continuation and expansion.[43] Like spending programs, regulations tend to accumulate and complexify over time. Even requests for regulatory relief tend to be met with more fine-grained regulations, with often-cited periods of deregulation worldwide actually resulting in a more active role for government as prior regulations were redefined.[44] Today, the functional organization and internal networks of US state governments, as revealed by agency websites and links, remain hierarchical and have largely converged. Similarities in Executive branch organization across states are due to their shared economic industries and regions, with ideological similarities playing no role.[45]

The most common measure of the size of governments is public spending as a percentage of the size of the economy. On this basis, federal, state, and local direct spending all rose throughout the twentieth century, but with an especially steep rise from 1945 to the mid-1970s (after which rises stalled).[46] These measures may understate the growth of government for several reasons: (1) the size of the economy (the denominator) includes capital consumption by business along with consumer spending and even includes government spending (the numerator); (2) transfers and tax subsidies are not included, while both have grown as a share of government activity; (3) uncompensated compliance costs not born by the government but reflecting private spending on its policies have also risen; and (4) in using GDP, government spending is evaluated relative to a broadening economy rather than dampened inflation.[47] By 1995, state tax revenues were 36 times as large as in 1954 (with inflation only increasing one-sixth as fast) via increasingly diverse tax types. Moreover, the state share of tax revenues (compared to local and national taxes) had more than doubled.[48]

The many factors that built liberal state governments included growing population size, party competition, and social, religious, and political diversity.[49] By 1990, state policies had come to broadly match the priorities and ideologies of their citizens.[50] Republican gains thereafter did not stem mainly from big changes in the relative conservatism of the states' publics or their policies. Rather, the most dramatic changes have sorted states into parties based on their ideologies – with Republicans coming to power disproportionately in already conservative states.[51] The associated predicament for newly emergent conservatives was most pronounced in the South. Republican gains have been strongest in the region, where state governments had already grown much more slowly than the rest of the nation (despite long being overwhelmingly controlled by Democrats). Southern conservatives thus inherited governments that were already the nation's least expansive (with no big governments to shrink down to other states' levels). The South, though, was only the most pronounced version of a similar story that also played out in the West and the Midwest.

Even where conservative policy reforms were enacted, they were often not in areas large enough to impact social and economic outcomes. Predicted outcomes do not always follow from policies: abortion restrictions may pass without decreasing the abortion rate; right-to-carry laws may expand without affecting gun ownership; new voting requirements may not decrease registration or turnout; right-to-work laws may not reduce unionization; and energy deregulation may not change prices or usage. And yet these kinds of direct mechanisms are the most likely to link policy outputs to important downstream consequences. If the abortion rate is hard to change with stringent abortion restrictions, imagine the difficulty of achieving a more amorphous goal such as increasing entrepreneurship linked to less direct tools such as tax incentives.

Because Republicans more often see policymaking as a directional battle over the role of government in society, they tend to treat policymaking less as choices among a catalog of tools available to address separable specific social problems (as Democrats do) and more as a long-term struggle to refine and protect society while expanding the economy.[52] However, broad outcomes such as economic growth, job availability and quality, subjective well-being, and morality are affected by myriad other factors and interacting circumstances, making them hard to even marginally impact with ideal policies. Once Republican policies face legislative compromises as well as implementation by bureaucracies and local officials (who may not share conservative goals), they are even less likely to have profound effects than in ideal circumstances. Reformulating a state's economy or reversing its social trends is not easily achieved with the kinds of policy tools state legislatures have at their disposal.

Learning from Conservative Difficulties Worldwide

Although some constraints facing Republican parties in American states are specific to their level of government and time period, others are near-universal difficulties facing conservative ideologues and center-right parties worldwide. International and comparative researchers have long wrestled with questions about how governments develop over time, as well as the role of ideology and party power in cross-national policy differences. Comparative perspectives can show both where the American Republican Party's predicament stands out as unique and where it is facing the same difficulties of other conservative parties.

Even among developed, democratic, and capitalist countries, there remains significant variation in social welfare, employment, and economic regulatory policies. A large academic literature studies these differences as examples of the "varieties of capitalism" and "welfare states," usually through typologies of the "worlds of welfare" or "families of nations."[53] Countries developed government intervention in the economy and social service provision at different speeds and with different tools – regardless of whether or not they are best categorized into the ideal types suggested by these analyses, their policies do retain the impact of their developmental trajectories. In these typologies, the United States is uniformly perceived as being among the least intrusive governments, with one of the smallest public welfare regimes. The reasons given include America's early adoption of capitalism and democracy, its diversity and religiosity, its absence of a feudal past, its immigration and frontier life, and the weakness of its left.[54] Critics of American exceptionalism point out that American social spending was higher and came earlier if you include state- and local-level education expenditures, as well as subsidies for employer-provided benefits.[55] Nonetheless, America's relatively light redistributive policies correspond with the Republican Party's resistance to a broader role for government. Across all parties of the right, the Republicans are the world's most consistently conservative party, with right-wing positions (relative to the international average) on redistribution, the role of the state, public spending, and traditional authority.[56]

All countries expanded government's scope dramatically in the twentieth century, but the "golden age" of welfare expansion in the 1960s and 1970s set countries on different paces.[57] Every rich country saw government spending grow in relation to economic growth (measured by GDP) after World War II. Governments then gained share at different speeds from the 1960s to 1990s, with some evidence that citizens voting for parties on the ideological right limited the growth of government to 10 percentage points of GDP, rather than 20 percentage points of GDP in countries voting for left parties.[58] Regardless, all democracies with measurable public spending moved from below 20 percent of GDP in the early twentieth century to above 30 percent of GDP by 1980, with some moving as high as 60 percent of GDP.[59] The effects of particular parties were most evident in nations where one side held power over a long period.[60] Public opinion may help explain these partisan effects on the growth and the persistence of welfare states (because conservative publics unsurprisingly tend to vote for parties on the ideological right), but the effects of public opinion tend to become manifest in broad national differences that remain stable, rather than in changes.[61]

Since 1980, welfare state spending worldwide, while stabilizing, has been largely resilient due to public and institutional support for retaining existing programs. At the same time, the breadth of tasks government spending is meant to address has continued to grow.[62] One review found that both direct public spending and transfer programs have "risen sharply, and almost without interruption, since the early 1950s" with a slowdown in the 1980s and a trend toward less direct spending.[63] Increases in economic inequality have not been stopped by government action, but not for lack of trying: social spending and redistributive transfers are high and growing across democratic governments in response to their continued public support.[64]

Despite differences in the speed of welfare state development (and thus the current level of redistribution and government intervention) across countries, conservatives do not seem able to make a major dent in these programs or policies after they are developed. As political scientist Paul Pierson put it, "almost nowhere have politicians been able to assemble and sustain majority coalitions for a far-reaching contraction of social policy."[65] Studying the most vibrant attempts at retrenchment, Pierson found some differences across programs and nations, with British Tories more successful than US conservatives in the 1980s (especially in housing), but lasting change was quite limited everywhere.[66] How countries fared during the expansionary period of the 1960s and 1970s set the pace for their future policies and public demands, with less room for government ideology to disrupt a country's trajectory.[67] Center-right parties tended to expand transfer payments more often, using them as substitutes for expanded social welfare programs; cutbacks are limited and usually economically driven, reducing the rate of increase rather than the total dollars allocated.[68]

Just as welfare state retrenchment mostly failed, so the deregulation revolution is mostly a myth. Rather, the scope of government regulation grows with the size of the economy.[69] The United States, Europe, and Japan all re-regulated utilities, telecommunications, finance, and transportation after initial deregulatory surges, without decreasing overall levels of regulation. The United States maintains high levels of market freedom, but it is created by concurrent high levels of regulation and government-initiated marketization.[70] Parties of the right did slow increasing environmental regulation, compared to their counterparts on the left, but did not reverse prior regulation.[71]

Even though there is considerable variation in how particular policies map onto left or right ideological categorizations, both studies of party platforms and expert surveys worldwide converge on policies related to taxes, spending, and regulation as being central to the left–right ideological dimension. Globally, moral social issues are less related to this dominant economic dimension of policy.[72] Yet social issues have also been on a global leftward track in rich countries since mid-century. Across several policy areas, researchers have found liberals prefer contemporary policies far more than even the older policies that liberal politicians supported, as civil rights, immigration, and gay rights policies have all moved leftward over time.[73]

Despite this backdrop of increasing worldwide government growth and social change, there is a very large academic literature (concentrated in studies of Europe) about the extent to which party power and ideological conflict determine the levels of policy liberalism across nations. A review of 100 studies that look at changes over time in policy across rich countries found that left and right governments pursued different economic policies until the 1990s, with size and scope of government larger under left governments. After this time, the effects became much less pronounced, with more focus by right parties on privatization and deregulation rather than reducing government spending.[74] Another review of 693 estimates of the effects of parties in government on policy outputs and outcomes worldwide found no clear effects: that the average association was zero.[75] Qualitative coding of 3,000 specific policy changes as liberal or conservative found partisan effects concentrated from the late 1980s to the mid-1990s.[76] Overall, the findings show partisan effects disappearing over time in response to economic change, international competition, and public support for past policies.[77]

Of course, partisan effects on policy could be sector-specific. One study found that, across rich countries, governments from the ideological left spent more on items falling into the "Public Services" category from 1970 to 1997, as well as spending more on education from 1990 to 2006. But parties in government had little influence on many other areas of spending, suggesting limited budgetary effects that may change over time.[78] Another study found that old age, family, and disabilities benefits are higher during left governments, while military expenditure is higher during right governments.[79] However, when outcomes are viewed across many categories, rather than cherry-picked by authors, partisan effects look somewhat weaker: a study that looked at 78 expenditure categories found left governments significantly higher in only eight, which is not much more than would be expected by chance.[80]

Effects of parties tend to be small relative to baseline differences across countries, with partisan effects conditional on other factors. Governing parties respond to impending elections and economic recessions, rather than consistently advance their ideological views.[81] Parties of the left produce more new programs when in office, but governments of the right then often spend even more on these popular programs to maintain public trust.[82] Parties of the right tend to support social insurance programs, perhaps adding market incentives, but generally rely on the value of existing redistributive benefits being eroded rather than direct cuts.[83] The privatization of government functions is more common during right governments, but only in developing countries.[84] Opposition parties on the left tend to constrain governing parties of the right from contracting government, but opposition parties on the right do not constrain those on the left from expanding it.[85] Parties on the right can move countries away from the most interventionist policies toward the US model, but not reverse global trends.[86]

Responses to the recent Great Recession changed only some of these dynamics. European countries enacted far more austerity measures than the United States, but most were restraints on automatic stabilizers (rising program spending resulting from increasing eligibility due to the recession), rather than long-term transformations. Many changes were slow, derivative, or incomplete, with significant reliance on policy drift over active cuts.[87] One study found no general partisan effects across rich countries in the size or composition of fiscal stimulus measures in response to recessions in 1980, 1990, 2001, or 2008.[88] Fiscal consolidations tend to come at the beginning of terms of office, equally often by the left and right, though the right continues cutting more if they succeed.[89] In response to economic crises, left parties also enacted more structural reforms and financial regulations, while right parties did not privatize or deregulate.[90] There is mixed evidence of partisan responses to the latest global recession, but country decision-making was more driven by economic context and budget constraints than by the ideology of the governing party.[91]

Policy drift, or the lack of policymaking in response to changing socio-economic conditions, can have effects that are as important as new policymaking. The classic example is a minimum wage that is not indexed for inflation: it becomes worth less and affects fewer people over time as its value declines due to normal rises in the price level. Similar dynamics could be at play when governments fail to update regulations to match new industries or when the value of (or eligibility for) social programs declines with economic change. Governments that failed to respond to rising inequality with new redistributive initiatives may be considered responsible for its continued rise (the American national government falls into this category in international comparisons). Slowing new liberal policies may thus be considered an important conservative policy trajectory, even without evidence of government contraction. Conservatives can block policy liberalization that some see as necessary to address socio-economic change, though that is not the same as a capacity to actively legislate new policies to contract government's role or achieve conservative goals.

International studies are useful for generating theoretical expectations but are not a foolproof guide to likely findings in American state politics. Even so, it is valuable to consider research on America in an international context, attending to both differences and similarities. There is global evidence of party effects on some policy outcomes, though the findings are often specific to time and place. The overall story, in both the American states and among democracies worldwide, is one of state development largely completed by the 1980s – government grew dramatically in size and scope over the twentieth century, but then slowed without reversing course. Comparative studies also show that decentralization tends to increase overall spending (though with smaller increases for national governments of the right than the left).[92] Thus, American state governments are part of a national political system where state development is to the right of the international ideological spectrum, while also being part of a federal system where they are subject to periodic national expansions in government's role. Both the international record and the state context suggest that conservative parties may be able to slow government expansion and social change, but not reverse it.

The Book's Approach and Evidence

Rather than critique Republicans' values or policy goals, I seek to evaluate conservative policy gains based on their own objectives. I use copious data on American state policy outputs and socio-economic outcomes to track changing policies and their impacts, while integrating qualitative reviews of policymaking across the states and evaluations of major successful Republican policy initiatives. The book takes advantage of astounding data collections by other scholars. Building on several recent large-scale efforts to track policy adoptions and differences across states, my team compiled a dataset of more than 1,500 variables, measured each year for all 50 states (called the Correlates of State Policy). These data enable analyses connecting policy changes to both the partisan and social factors that lead to policy and the socio-economic outcomes often attributed to policy effects. Alongside this quantitative data trove, I analyze qualitative case histories of the states: books, articles, and interviews that cover the political narratives and policy agendas of each state's governor and legislature since the early 1990s. I also compile policy evaluations of major Republican-led policy reforms and track studies of the effects of recent state policy changes. Combined, the book provides a holistic view of the causes and consequences of state policy trends, as well as a first draft of state political and policy history since the 1990s.

Nonetheless, I want to articulate clear boundaries for the analysis. In an ideal world, we would have access to natural experiments where parties randomly won control of state governments, along with randomized controlled trials of each policy that they implemented. This is obviously not possible, so this study is of necessity restricted to observational analysis. That means it typically gives partisan control of government the best opportunity to emerge as seemingly important, even if other factors were associated with both Republicans coming to power and a state's policymaking and socio-economic trajectory. I cannot claim to have causally identified all of the effects of party, nor fully captured the contextual circumstances under which they are likely to reappear. My focus is on policy adoptions and changes in the size and scope of government (as well as their impact) in the 50 states from 1991 to 2018. My quantitative measures of political differences across states, policy outputs, and socio-economic outcomes are mostly standard available metrics. In particular, I extend the many efforts of other scholars measuring the liberalism of state policy. I also rely on interviews with capitol reporters, secondary accounts of each state from political veterans, and prior research to understand the role of the actors in each state and to evaluate the results of specific policy changes. I aim to understand broad trends in policy across states, not to explain the reasons for each choice or to displace the (still-necessary) analyses of each state and each policy issue area. Instead, I summarize the cross-state and cross-issue patterns that collectively appear in their findings. Rather than ignore the select areas where Republican policy gains have been momentous, I study the exceptions closely and compare them to other trends.

I seek to add to and synthesize current findings from a new perspective, rather than overturn existing research. Because Democratic states are advancing new liberal policies at a faster rate, theories suggesting increasing effects of party control on overall state policy liberalism remain accurate. Other studies reporting relationships between the liberalism of public opinion and the liberalism of state policy, often mediated in part by partisanship or conditional on other factors, are also consistent with my analyses. They do not, however, undermine the asymmetry I find in Democratic and Republican successes. My results hold in both descriptive relationships between partisanship and policy, and multivariate models that control for changing opinions and demographics. I also review several issue-specific findings that conditionally relate state opinions and institutional factors to policy change. Where other scholars have already collected relevant evidence, I report and interpret their analyses rather than highlight my original data or analysis for its own sake. Demonstrating that evidence collected for other purposes or in support of alternative hypotheses is consistent with my review should be especially convincing. By evaluating conservative successes and failures from the point of view of those seeking conservative policy, I add critical information to these prior accounts.

The book aims to provide the most comprehensive treatment of state politics and policy over the last 25 years, covering immense political change. It chronicles the period between the low point and (what may be) the high point of Republican rule, creating a timely opportunity to assess the degree and scope of change. I cover state politics – which often fly under the radar – but do so through a national and contemporary lens, attentive to what remains stable as well as what is changing. By integrating quantitative analyses with narrative qualitative accounts, the book strives to be both accessible and rigorous. The hope is to cover important recent political history, but also to contribute to foundational knowledge about political institutions and policy. The results can also help conservatives understand which parts of their agenda are most feasible and why their electoral victories do not always translate into policy victories, while helping liberals identify their structural advantages in state politics and their limits. I also hope that citizens will see why campaign rhetoric does not always match policymaking realities and how the limits of policy change can simultaneously frustrate both Democrats and Republicans.

Plan of the Book

The book looks at the same actors and time period from several different lenses, moving from elections to policymaking to policy results. Chapter 2 tracks 25 years of Republican gains in state legislative and statewide elections, showing that they have produced more conservative state legislators and governors. In an acceleration of normal partisan trends, the two periods of recent Republican gains correspond to the two Democratic presidencies of Bill Clinton (1993–2000) and Barack Obama (2009–2016). The period also coincided with regional Republican consolidation in the South and Plains, along with significant gains in the Midwest. As a result of Democratic geographic sorting into cities, electoral gains were amplified in state legislatures. Republicans were also unusually successful in passing policies designed to reinforce their political rule, such as those defunding political activity by unions and discouraging Democratic voting. Additionally, their control of consecutive redistricting processes was quite effective. Republican members elected over this period were significantly more ideologically conservative than their predecessors, moving their caucuses and chambers to the right. Divided government and divided legislatures declined, giving Republicans control of more states. In 1992, Republicans had full control of only three states; by 2017, that had increased to a hundred-year-high of 26.

Chapter 3 assess the relationship between Republican gains and policy change. The broad trends in state policy outputs do not suggest a successful conservative revolution. Instead, states have expanded government's share of the economy and, even during the Republican ascendancy, have passed more liberal than conservative policies. Using panel and change models of state policy liberalism, new policy adoptions, innovation, and state budgets, I find that Republican gains in the states have prevented some additional liberal policies, but not reversed prior liberal policies, nor advanced many new conservative policies. By the 1990s, states had already set their trajectories for large or small governments, and although Democratic states have increased the scope of government faster than Republican states, none have reversed course. Democratically controlled states have passed additional liberal policy changes more quickly than Republican states, but Republican states have failed to advance much of their own successful policy agenda. As a result, Democratic states are pulling away from Republican states in policy innovation and adoption. However, long-standing features of each state's politics remain distinct. States are now divided between fast-moving Blue states and the rest, with the latter moving slower and failing to produce new governing or economic models. Some Republican policy successes have been significant, but they have mostly been self-reinforcing political wins or attempts to counteract liberalizing federal policy (on economics) and national liberal trends (on social issues). Republican policy gains look more extensive by some measures than others, with changes in the size of government particularly difficult to produce. The broad trends show Republican control has had some important effects without fundamentally re-orienting states.

Chapter 4 moves to reviews of policymaking in more specific issue areas, as well as challenges in specific states. It tracks the substantive areas where Republican policy gains have been most successful, such as abortion restrictions and gun laws, as well as the many areas where non-partisan economic, social, and federal policy trends have made more of a difference nationwide. Republican states have enacted some new policies, such as restrictions on abortion access, right-to-carry laws, charter school increases, and voting identification requirements. Conservative successes, though, are concentrated in salient social issues that lack broad economic impact. Meanwhile, many other liberal policy revolutions have continued unabated, advancing gay rights, drug law liberalization, health access, early childhood education, and business regulation. Other changes, such as declining higher education spending and the rise and fall of prison spending, have responded more to underlying social trends than to partisan control. Still other state policy changes have been directed by the federal government, with conservative states slowing policy liberalization directed from above by an expanding national government. I also content-analyze narrative histories of policymaking across states from 1990 to 2017, as well as interviewing long-time state capitol reporters in most states, focusing on the success and failure of major Republican proposals. The first analysis relies on secondary sources covering gubernatorial administrations and legislative sessions in each state, while the second uses on-the-ground knowledge and local perspective to assess Republican policy results. The stories focus on the dilemmas facing Republican governors in addressing federal policy, electoral incentives, and state economic competition. Newly empowered Republican state governments do win some initial policy victories, but they tend to be less productive in achieving their stated agenda as they age in power. A few Republican states (such as Kansas and North Carolina) have pursued more extensive conservative reformations of state government, but the changes have slowed or reversed after initial bursts of success. Meanwhile, Democratic state legislatures and governors have continued to pass new extensions to the size and role of government, often taking advantage of federal action.

In Chapter 5, I move to policy results, compiling policy evaluations of Republican-led policy changes in state governments since the 1990s. I find only minimal evidence that enacted policies, such as welfare reform and right-to-work, led to the significant social or economic results predicted by proponents or opponents. Reforms often have the intended proximate effects, such as moving welfare benefits to working people or reducing union involvement in politics, but they do not achieve broader results such as increasing business investment or economic growth, or reversing population decline or industrial change. The reforms as implemented also generally lack the broad negative impacts that opponents fear, such as reduced wages or quality of life, in part because their effects are diluted, reversed, or counteracted by private or local actors. Yet Republican policies have had important electoral effects, helping to extend their power. Their institutional advantages are mostly stronger than ever, meaning Republican advances have been a successful political project despite the weak socio-economic results of their implemented policies. I also review claims that Red states or Blue states have better outcomes overall. I find that few broad social or economic results are attributable to Republican policy gains in the states, with no consistent Red state strategy for addressing key policy issues or problems. Socio-economic differences across states are instead mostly attributable to pre-existing and apolitical factors. Important outcomes sometimes attributed to party policy differences, such as income stagnation and inequality, life expectancy and health, innovation and economic vitality, and increasing education levels, are more often the product of broader demographic and economic trends that do not line up well with state partisanship. The supposed outcomes of Red and Blue state strategies are mostly spurious. Even when specific policies such as redistributing the tax burden from income to sales taxes do have real economic effects, the policies and their effects are often not strong or widespread enough to account for key state differences. Rather than trying to improve upon models of how each social indicator differs by state, my focus is on debunking broad claims about the social and economic results of Republican state policies.

Finally, Chapter 6 reviews the implications for American government, two-party competition, and the goals of the conservative movement. Despite taking control of 24 new states and installing more conservative leaders, Republicans have little to show for it in terms of reformulated state governments or sustainable policy results that have real-world implications. However, this does not mean that elections lack consequences or that American governments would not have developed differently if Democrats had remained dominant. Republican states grow at different rates, slow some liberal policy trends and enact some compensating conservative policies with identifiable results. The Republican Party, and the conservatives that have taken control of it, help make American government exceptional in terms of its relative aversion to redistributive policies and active market interventions. This is all part of the Republicans' broadly successful efforts to make the United States exceptional in many international comparisons of policies and social outcomes. But as is the case at the federal level, that influence is achieved mainly by slowing policy liberalization and limiting further economic interventions, rather than realigning the role of government in society. There are successful policy revolutions, such as the growing role of charter schools and the turn away from punitive criminal justice policy, but they tend to advance through partnerships between liberals and conservatives. This means that while citizens, interest groups, and politicians who share conservatism's objectives are likely to remain better off aligning themselves with the Republican Party, the broader conservative effort to sell a restoration of traditional American values, a return to a historically smaller and less interventionist public sector, and a refocus of government away from social welfare and toward security, is mostly an unachievable ideal. Voters can be sold on a broader vision of smaller government and social restoration, but this does not translate to an implementable policy agenda for governments at any level. The

Republican Party, as the world's strongest instantiation of across-the-board conservatism, can avoid some of the compromises of center-right parties elsewhere, but it cannot overcome the inherent barriers to conservative achievement.

This conclusion is not a critique of Republican values. I aim to show that Republican-supported policies have neither the broad positive results they anticipate nor the dismal negative results that Democrats anticipate. As Republicans are unable to pass their wider policy agendas, I am assessing only the impacts of their limited policy gains, rather than the potential social and economic results of their wider objectives. However, the results have implications for political professionals seeking to address social problems and advance policy solutions. Republicans will find more success in pursuing policies that redirect the role of government, rather than seek to contract its size and scope. They can succeed electorally with only modest policy results, but even overwhelming electoral victory does not bring revolutionary policy change. Partisans on both sides will recognize that much of policymaking remains non-partisan and state-specific; even nationwide and previously controversial shifts in policy are often the product of work by both parties following apolitical trends.

The results can also help citizens better evaluate American institutions. Partisan victories and defeats do sometimes produce policy change, but then so do many other factors that tend to either be constant differences across states or nationwide trends. This means we cannot expect a party to counteract state tendencies nor move against national forces in attempting to enact its wholesale agenda. Even when policies do pass, they seek to address problems that have many interacting causes and – even when they do make a difference – they often have limited effects, along with unintended consequences or trade-offs. The enacted policies tend to be compromises as well, having to take account of existing policies and programs, as well as addressing critiques.

Recent Republican efforts to respond to teacher protests by increasing education spending – in the process overturning some of their own prior policy moves – thus does not represent an aberration from an unstoppable conservative trajectory. Instead, it is a reminder of the inherent limits of the conservative agenda in popularity and sustainability, and the particular constraints that Republican state governments face in matching their ideological aspirations to their particular responsibilities in the American federal system. State governments still look a lot like they did in the early 1990s, and while Republicans have left important legacies, they have not realigned their role.

Republican tendencies to overpromise and underdeliver are helpful in understanding why the party's voters more often mistrust government and politicians, including their own party leaders. Though the rise of right-wing populism and the nomination of Donald Trump do represent unique recent twists in the story of American conservatism, they are also reliant on Republicans' long-running tendencies to prefer vague restorative promises over detailed and achievable policy proposals. Like many Republican governors, Trump also drew on the perennial conservative fiction that government can be transformed by heroic individual action, using private sector formulas to make government run (more efficiently) like a business. The stability of government institutions and programs, combined with conservative disinterest in broadening government's role, limits Republicans' feasible policy agendas. That opens the party to regular insurrection from dissatisfied activists and voters, who believe the party has abandoned its principles or lacked strong enough will.

The findings presented here should also help liberals understand the conservative dilemma. The Republican Party represents the American public's long-standing conservative predispositions, which stand out internationally as being particularly skeptical of a grand role for government in organizing society or equalizing resources. Yet the party has advanced to challenge the growth in government's size and scope, as well as the accelerating changes in social mores and order, long after conservative parties anywhere in the world have been able to succeed in counteracting government's liberalizing tendencies. Republican gains in the American states have not proven an exception to this rule. They thus remain a source of disappointment for the conservative movement, even as their successes alarm liberals accustomed to seeing government policy evolve to respond to new social challenges. Though Democrats may see many unsolved problems and resent Republican attempts to counteract their efforts to address them through government action, they should also recognize that, conversely, Republicans see themselves as engaged in a battle over the direction of government and society that they seem continually to lose.

Notes

1 Little (1998).
2 A nice outline of the agenda appears in Lezar (1994), an edited volume of think tankers addressing state policy issues and forwarded by Ronald Reagan.
3 Jost (1996).
4 See Alexander Hertel-Fernandez and Theda Skocpol. 2016. "Democrats are Losing to Republicans at the State Level, and Badly. Here's Why." Vox. Available at: www.vox.com/2016/8/3/12368070/democrats-losing-state-level.
5 The federal story is covered in my recent book, Grossmann and Hopkins (2016).
6 This count includes Nebraska, which officially has non-partisan government but operates with Republican control, and West Virginia, where the governor switched parties to give Republicans full control.
7 Hertel-Fernandez (2018).
8 Higgs (2015) updating Higgs (2004)
9 Pierson (1994), citing economic studies of path dependence and increasing returns.
10 Eriksson and Strimling (2015); Prothero (2017).
11 Jackson et al. (2019); Prothero (2017).
12 Erikson, MacKuen, and Stimson (2002).
13 Kausser and Phillips (2012).
14 Kausser and Phillips (2012).
15 Clingermayer and Wood (1995); Rogers and Rogers (2000).
16 Squire and Moncrief (2015).
17 Kincaid (2019).
18 Kincaid (2019).
19 Zimmerman (2010).
20 McCann (2016).
21 Meyer-Gutbrod (2018).
22 One example is the infusion of resources from the 1998 tobacco settlement. See Harris and Kinney (2003).
23 Kincaid (2019).
24 Squire and Hamm (2005).
25 Squire and Hamm (2005).
26 Squire and Moncrief (2015).
27 Van Horn (2006).
28 Jenkins (2016); Rosenthal (2009). Hertel-Fernandez (2018) argues that conservative institutions have taken advantage of term limits by feeding

young legislators a national agenda. This can be a blessing in passing cookie-cutter legislation, but is also indicative of the lack of local power and resources to understand and restructure long-standing state programs.

29 Lee (2018) shows that supermajority requirements decay in effectiveness by ten years after enactment due to state workarounds.

30 Yu, Jennings, and Butler (2019).

31 Rosenthal (2009).

32 Bonica and Sen (2017).

33 Morehouse and Jewell (2003).

34 Hansen, Carlson, and Gray (2017)

35 Leeson, Ryan, and Williamson (2012).

36 Rosenthal (2009).

37 Gray and Hanson (2004).

38 Morehouse and Jewell (2003).

39 Morehouse and Jewell (2003).

40 Gray and Hanson (2004).

41 Gray and Hanson (2004).

42 Bjorklund (In Press).

43 Gray and Hanson (2004).

44 Alleged deregulation in the United States and Japan in power, telecommunications, finance, transportation, utilities, and broadcasting mostly resulted in expanded government roles, with re-regulation. See Vogel (1998, 2018).

45 Kosack et al. (2018).

46 Gray and Hanson (2004).

47 Higgs (2015).

48 Morehouse and Jewell (2003).

49 Barrilleaux (2006).

50 Erikson, Wright, and McIver (1993).

51 Erikson, Wright, and McIver (2006).

52 Grossmann and Hopkins (2016).

53 Varieties of capitalism is mostly associated with Hall and Soskice (2001) and worlds of welfare with Esping-Andersen (1990). For a review, see Castles and Obinger (2008).

54 Garfinkel, Rainwater, and Smeeding (2010).

55 Garfinkel, Rainwater, and Smeeding (2010).

56 See Grossmann and Hopkins (2016) on the international surveys conducted by Herbert Kitschelt for the Democratic Accountability and Linkages Project.

57 Jensen (2011); Pickering and Rockey (2011).

58 Pickering and Rockey (2011).

59 Tanzi and Schuknecht (2000).

60 Blais, Blake, and Dion (1993) began a large literature on the topic, studying 15 democracies from 1960 to 1987.

61 Brooks and Manza (2006) explore public opinion effects. Breznau (2015) finds that they are mostly a product of long-standing welfare regime differences.

62 Seeleib-Kaiser, Van Dyke, and Roggenkamp (2008).

63 Iversen (2001).

64 Elkjaer and Iversen (2018).

65 Pierson (2001), p. 416.

66 Pierson (1994).

67 Jensen (2011).

68 Pierson (2001).

69 Vogel (2018).

70 Vogel (1998, 2018).

71 Garmann (2014).

72 Benoit and Laver (2007).

73 Broockman and Tyler (2018).

74 Potrafke (2017).

75 The review found more evidence for party effects on the overall size of government than for specific policies, and more success for governing parties after the 1970s. Imbeau, Pétry, and Lamari (2001).

76 Hartmann (2015).

77 Estimated effects of party control, however, are stronger when studies estimate long-term effects of full terms of service, rather than year-to-year variation. Schmitt (2015).

78 Potrafke (2011).

79 Bove, Efthyvoulou, and Navas (2017).

80 Castro and Martins (2017).

81 Herwartz and Theilen (2017).

82 Jensen (2010).

83 Jensen (2014).

84 Roberts and Saeed (2012).

85 Jensen and Seeberg (2015).

86 Jäger (2017).

87 Kersbergen and Vis (2013).

88 Some effects were found in very large welfare states. Raess and Pontusson (2015). Other research found higher post-crisis social spending in left governments recently. Hartmann (2015).

89 Hübscher (2016).

90 Galasso (2014).

91 Studies of unemployment and sickness benefits in recessions also showed more retrenchment from parties of the right. Allan and Scruggs (2004). However, another study found that welfare state retrenchment is actually larger under leftist or centrist governments due to it being politically risky for the right. Armingeon, Guthman, and Weisstanner (2015).

92 Baskaran (2011).

2 THE RISE OF REPUBLICAN RULE

New US House Speaker Newt Gingrich provided the face of the 1994 Republican revolution and national "Tea Party" Senators such as Marco Rubio became synonymous with Republican gains in their comeback revolution in 2010. These twin victories were not only in Congress; they were just as sweeping in American state governments and have had long-lasting effects on the political complexion of the states. In 1994, Republicans gained 10 governorships, 397 state house seats, and 131 state senate seats. Democrats regained some ground between then and 2010, only for Republicans to then win 5 governorships, 564 state house seats, and 134 state senate seats, flipping control of 20 legislative chambers. Both elections represented backlashes against new Democratic presidents – Bill Clinton in 1994 and Barack Obama in 2010 – but their influence on control of state governments was profound. Democrats regained some ground in 2018, just as they had in 2006, but did not come close to their prior levels of state control.

Rather than focusing solely on a few dramatic elections, I examine the period of Republican rise from 1992 to 2017. The stark changes that occurred were not steady or without setbacks, but broadly speaking the story of the period is of a party in widespread ascension, coming in from the state politics wilderness to take total control of major regions. Just as Republicans had long been the minority national party in Congress, so they had also struggled to gain control of state governments. Given the tendency of America's political pendulum is to swing back the other way after one party gains strength, the Republican

Party's ability to withstand backlash and gain increasing control of state governments while moving decidedly rightward is both notable and unprecedented.

From the vantage point of 1992, when Bill Clinton was elected president in the midst of a recession, Republicans did have reasons to expect a resurgence. After all, they had been triumphant in the 1980s, electing a proud conservative president (Ronald Reagan) and then his vice president (George H. W. Bush) as successor. Many foresaw better luck in the Southern states, where despite Clinton's success as governor of a Southern state, voters maintained conservative attitudes alongside their long-running Democratic voting habits in state elections. Even so, the scale of Republican gains over the following quarter-century are still something to behold.

The Reddening of American State Governments

American state governments have gotten a lot redder over the last few decades. An illustrative starting point is to look at how Republicans were placed in 1992 and how far they had come by 2017. Figure 2.1 compares Republican control of state legislatures (house and senate) and governorships in 1992 with control in 2017; with each chamber and the governorship counting for one point on a three-point scale. In 1992, they were reduced to full control in just Utah, South Dakota, and New Hampshire, with sporadic control in other areas. By 2017, they were in full control of most of the South, Midwest, and West, losing ground only on the West Coast. Their biggest gains were in the South – broadly defined to include states such as Texas, Kentucky, and Florida. But they had also achieved a near monopoly in the Midwest (with Illinois an outlier) and the interior West (with Colorado an exception). Even with states that proved relatively even in terms of presidential competition, the map of state governments had grown deeply red.

Comparing two years at the beginning and end of a period, though, can mask trends occurring within it. Figure 2.2 tracks change over time in the average amount of Republican control across states (on a scale of 0 for complete Democratic control to 3 for complete Republican control). Across all states from 1990 to 2017, the average state moved from Republican control of just one out of the house, senate, or governor's office to two out of three. This is the equivalent

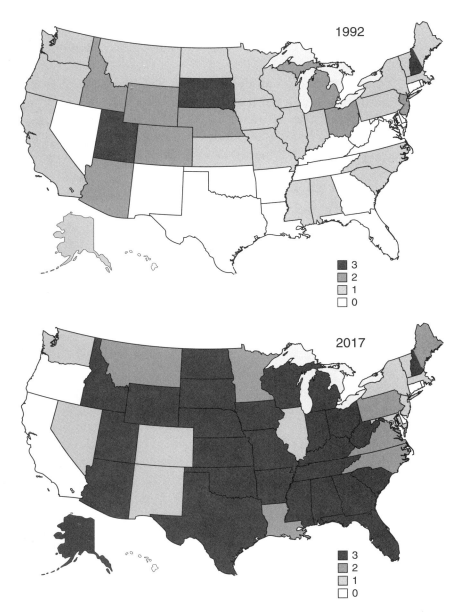

Figure 2.1 Republican control of state legislative chambers and governorships, 1992 and 2017 (Correlates of State Policy Project)

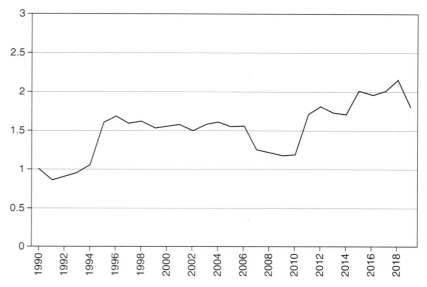

Figure 2.2 Average number of Republican state legislative chambers and governorships per state (originally from Carl Klarner, updated in the Correlates of State Policy Project)

of gaining 50 governorships or 50 state legislative chambers – though of course Republican gains have been concentrated in some states and absent in others.

The gains were also not a linear increase over time. After losing the 1994 elections by large margins and holding steady for eight years, Democrats gained some governorships and state legislative chambers back after the 2006 elections. But Republicans won back their lost ground as well as conquering new territory after the 2010 elections. They then saw another uptick in 2014, Obama's second midterm election. In 2018, despite their 2014 gains being rolled back amid significant national Democratic advances, Republicans managed to hang onto many of their prior gains. Although not always steady, Republican gains have been large over the period, and the ground they have gained will not easily be lost.

These patterns are not just the consequence of Republicans winning chambers by close margins. Rather, they have instead gained ground, on average, within both legislative chambers across states, meaning they have an increased share even in the states where they already held control, as well as becoming more competitive in others.

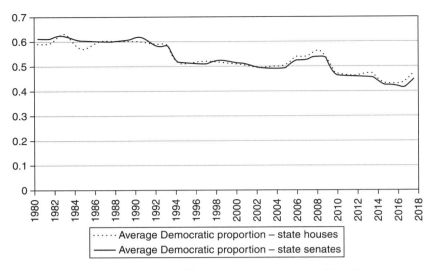

Figure 2.3 Average proportion of house and senate seats held by Democrats over time (originally from Carl Klarner, updated in the Correlates of State Policy Project)

These increased legislative shares can be important beyond just chamber control. Specifically, they make Republican-favored policies easier to pass even in the face of dissension, gubernatorial vetoes harder to sustain, and future Democratic control harder to win back.

Republican advantages in state houses and state senates have followed similar patterns over the last quarter-century. Figure 2.3 reports the average proportion of seats held by Democrats across each state's lower and upper chambers in each year. The correlation across the two chambers is 0.98, with very few years where they do not move in tandem. Since there are few independents or minor party affiliates across American state legislators, the trends are the mirror image of Republican gains. The range runs from just over 0.6 to just over 0.4 in each chamber, suggesting that competition has been close overall (when you average across all states), despite a substantial shift. Democratic losses were pronounced in both chambers after 1994, with gains returning after the 2006 election (especially in state houses) and then receding further since 2010 (before the slight 2018 uptick). State senates show an ever-so-slightly steadier downward Democratic trend, with the same key elections driving change. Trends in the *number* of legislative chambers that Democrats control thus match trends for *degree of control* within each chamber. Over 25 years, Republicans went from controlling, on average, about 40 percent of state house and senate seats to controlling almost 60 percent.

Although headlines usually talk about the total number of state legislative seats won or lost across the country, changes in the proportion of legislative seats held by each party is a better measure because of large variation in chamber size that does not match state populations: some small states such as New Hampshire have huge lower chambers (400 members), while some large states such as Texas have small upper chambers (31). But even the average share across states (the measure used here) weights each state equally – this does not account for variations in population and thus does not show how many individuals are governed by each party. It also masks significant variation across states: Republicans gained veto-proof majorities in some states and lack even a veto threat in others.

The 2018 election did end an era of steady Democratic losses in the states, but even so the party did not come close to regaining their full strength. Democrats gained 252 house seats and 72 senate seats nationwide, gaining 3.9 percent in the average house chamber and 3.4 percent in the average senate chamber. This returned them to about where they stood before the 2014 election, but nowhere near their pre-2010 high. This did not come close to matching Republicans in 2010, when they gained nearly 9 percent in house seat share and 7 percent in senate seat share in the average chamber. Going back further, they gained almost 8 percent (house) and 6 percent (senate) in 1994. Thus, although there is some indication of a swing back in the Democrats' direction, they have failed to regain the substantial ground they lost in the 1990s and 2010s.

Some of these trends can be attributed to the Southern realignment. Although received wisdom connects the racial divisions of the 1960s and 1970s to the move of Southern voters to the Republican Party, at the state level this occurred much later. Generally speaking, it proceeded first in presidential voting, then in congressional voting, and then in state legislative voting, with many Southern-born incumbent Democrats retaining seats in the South despite the regional partisan realignment. State politicians were less tied to the liberalizing image of the national Democratic Party and retained more local reputations. The Republican Party had long failed to even contest many Southern-Democratic-held state legislative seats (either at all or, if so, then with quality candidates). Republican gains in the 1990s, 2000s, and even

2010s were thus partially a product of conservative voters and those bearing high racial resentment finally aligning their state votes with their national Republican voting. This means that Republicans took control disproportionately in already conservative states – that shift is more likely to be permanent. If "the South" is limited purely to the states of the former confederacy, the change in voting patterns does not account for the level of Republican gains. But Republican gains were also disproportionate in border states such as Kentucky, Tennessee, and Missouri, as well as Northern states with larger culturally Southern regions such as Ohio and Indiana.

Two states in the outer South provide useful illustrations of some especially pronounced trends over the period. In Oklahoma, Democrats controlled both chambers of the legislature for all of the twentieth century (except for one brief period of Republican House rule from 1921 to 1922), until Republicans took control of the House in 2005. In 1993, they controlled the Senate 37–11 and the House 68–33. Democrats also controlled the governorship and nearly every executive office for a century – excluding only 19 years – up until 2011. By 2017, though, Republicans controlled all statewide offices and had majorities of 42–6 and 75–26 in the state Senate and House respectively. In the course of just a quarter-century, Democrats had gone from dominant to uncompetitive. National elections had presaged the shift, with Republicans winning every presidential election in the state since 1968 (with 1976 the only close contest and the last four elections decided by margins of more than 30 percentage points). Despite this national Republican shift, Democrats kept winning state executive offices with moderate or conservative candidates and localized campaigns through the 1990s and 2000s, losing everything only in 2010.

Similarly, Democrats had controlled the North Carolina state legislature from Reconstruction to 1994, when they still held majorities of 39–11 in the state Senate and 78–42 in the House. Even today, the state has had only three Republican governors since 1901. Despite Democrats winning back the governorship in 2016, Republicans held majorities of 35–15 in the Senate and 74–46 in the House. Like in other parts of the South, the trends began earlier in national politics, with Nixon and Reagan both winning twin presidential victories and Senator Jesse Helms coming to power on an explicit brand of racial conservative politics. But North Carolina has remained a swing state in presidential elections, with Democrats retaining some White and rural supporters. Without controlling the redistricting process after the 1990 or 2000 census, they could take permanent control only in 2010. By the time Republicans came to power in the state with clear majorities, they consisted of conservatives willing to disrupt state government, as well as governors who saw their role as undoing Democratic institutional strength and their public policy legacy. This has made it far more difficult for North Carolina Democrats to overcome gerrymandering or change electoral rules to increase Democratic voting, especially without a citizen initiative process to pursue reforms.

Republican control of the electoral rules, however, cannot be blamed for all the Democrats' losses. Democrats have also lost popular support over the recent period, with those identifying themselves with the Democratic Party dropping by almost seven percentage points in the average state between 1987 and 2010.[1] Democrats used to have a large group of non-liberal public supporters (not just in the South), but this relative advantage has declined over time as conservatives and moderates moved to the Republican Party and remaining Democrats increased their liberal identification. In 1980s exit polls, the percentage of people who identified as Democrats was 20 points higher than the percentage identifying as liberal, with that advantage declining to 10 points in recent elections. In contrast, there are now slightly more people identifying as conservatives than Republicans. The ever-shrinking swing voter contingent in American elections are disproportionately Democratic-leaning independents who are also conservative-leaning moderates.

Until 2008, Missouri was considered a national bellwether, having voted for the winner of the presidency in every election but one since 1904. The state saw many close gubernatorial and Senate elections as well and Democrats kept winning numerous statewide offices in the 1990s, 2000s, and 2010s. Meanwhile, their legislative trajectory has been clearly downward. In 1992, they held a 23–11 Senate majority and a 98–65 House majority but now Republicans control both by large margins (24–10 and 116–47) and Democrats are not threatening to regain control. That coincided with Missouri Democrats losing support in every area of the state except the major cities of St. Louis and Kansas City and the college town of Columbia. They did not just lose support in the Southern regions. At the federal level, northern Missouri used to be represented by Democrats like Armed Services Chair Ike Skelton and National Rifle Association stalwart Harold Volkmer; once those kinds of culturally conservative Missouri Democrats disappeared, so did the party's more widespread geographic support in the state.

Like Missouri, North Dakota hung onto a Democratic senator with a distinct local reputation until 2018. Although Democrats failed to gain much of a foothold in the state for the majority of the twentieth century, by the late 1980s they controlled the North Dakota Senate, nearly all state executive offices, and both US Senate seats. But by the time Heidi Heitkamp lost in 2018, they were not competitive in state elections, controlling only 9 of 47 Senate seats and 13 of 94 House seats and having lost the last governor's race by nearly 60 percentage points. With that level of uncompetitive support in the state, now concentrated in Native American areas, there is not much hope of a resurgence.

Popular discussion of "Red states" and "Blue states," with the now canonical color-coded maps in television coverage of politics, has focused on increasing geographic polarization over this period. There is certainly evidence that Democrats and Republicans are becoming more concentrated across states and localities, producing fewer areas with narrow partisan divides. There is also an increasing concentration of Democratic strength, both in larger cities within states and in (mostly) East and West Coast states nationally. This concentration, along with Republican control of redistricting processes, has meant that Republicans have built significant advantages in state legislative elections. Republicans can now regularly lose the statewide vote across all legislative candidates while still winning control of both chambers. This is because Democrats are more likely to win a limited number of (typically urban) seats by overwhelming margins, especially in states where Republicans have purposely drawn these overwhelmingly Democratic districts. Since Democrats are now concentrated mainly in large cities, college towns, and (the few remaining) rural areas with high racial minority concentrations, it has become harder to compete across state legislative districts.

Republican gains were well timed to take advantage of redistricting processes. Republicans retained control of many states in time for the post-2000 redistricting period and then (after losing ground in 2006 and 2008) gained substantial ground in the 2010 election, just before the next redistricting process. Increasing mapping capabilities, decreasing court scrutiny, and aggressive Republican majorities all

enabled more effective gerrymanders. This meant Republican legislative chambers were insulated from Democratic shifts in the electorate.
However, some gerrymanders were eventually overturned by courts
and others became less effective later in the decade due to internal
migration and increasing Democratic strength in the suburbs.

Even so, the effects of the redistricting processes were still
pronounced in state legislatures in the 2018 election, despite Democrats
regaining control of the US Congress with a similar share of seats and
national popular votes. For example, Michigan Democrats won the
2018 vote for both the state House and Senate, but, due to Republican
gerrymandering and Democratic concentration in metropolitan areas,
gained only five House seats and six Senate seats (far short of the
majorities that had been predicted by pre-election models). Wisconsin
Democrats, despite winning statewide offices, actually lost ground
in their Senate and won only one seat in their Assembly. Meanwhile,
North Carolina Democrats won 50 percent of the statewide vote but a
mere 24 percent of House seats.

Like 2018 Democratic victories, the 1992–2017 Republican
gains had mostly followed traditional partisan waves, with the
president's party losing seats in midterm elections (especially their
first one). Since the period covers two Democratic presidents and one
Republican president, it naturally includes more Republican gains. In
fact, Democrats may have been particularly unlucky with the timing
of the 2002 midterm election – George W. Bush's first. Since it was
held in the aftermath of the response to the 9/11 terror attacks, the
war in Afghanistan, and the build-up to the (initially popular) Iraq
War, it coincided with very high approval rates for Bush. This may
have deterred Democratic candidates, made the election more about
national security (an issue where Republicans generally have the confidence of the electorate), and deprived the Democrats of the typical
backlash to a new incumbent president's policies and declining popularity. Democrats presumably won some seats in 2006 and 2008 –
when Bush was far less popular – that they would otherwise have won
earlier, but even so the quirk of the 2002 election's timing may still
be responsible for Democrats not having a more fulsome resurgence
under Bush.

Adding to Democratic difficulties, the 1994 and 2010 elections
were historical outliers in the degree to which the party that did not
hold the presidency made gains. Democrats achieved significant policy

moves to the left in the 1993 and 2009 congressional sessions, and these may partly be responsible for the size of the backlash (matched only by 1966, after Lyndon Johnson's Great Society). But they also gained presidential power just as elections were becoming more nationalized, with partisanship and the party's national images more entrenched, split-ticket ballots and independent candidate reputations in decline, and greater similarity in campaign content across the nation.[2] A Democratic state legislator running in the 1978 elections might have avoided too much association with an unpopular president Jimmy Carter, for example, because the public evaluated their local elected officials independently and Republicans did not contest state elections as part of a national anti-Carter message. But by the time Clinton and Obama came to office, nationalized politics were in full swing. This meant the electoral impact of backlashes suffered by these Democratic presidents was particularly pronounced. All Democratic candidates bore the brunt of resentment against unpopular presidents who were judged by swing voters to have moved policy too far leftward and were much more likely to stimulate turnout from upset Republicans than grateful Democrats. Meanwhile, state legislative elections have become increasingly divorced from citizens' views on what is happening in state capitols, and instead more attached to their views of the current president.[3] Even elections for state office are becoming more like national referendums on the party of the president. Voters are less likely to know their state legislator or perceive them as having ideas and accomplishments independent of their party.

Republicans are correct to point out that Democratic losses in the states were particularly stark under Barack Obama, perhaps due to his leftward moves on policy or a cultural backlash based partly on his race. But it may also reflect two oddities of Clinton's presidency rather than anything unique to Obama. First, Clinton won the presidency in 1992 with only 43 percent of the national vote, due to the presence of historically popular third-party candidate Ross Perot. As a result, Clinton did not bring with him any substantial lower level victories in his initial election. Obama, though, won 53 percent of the vote, bringing along both new voters and state legislators and giving the Democrats further to fall during his presidency. Second, Clinton's second midterm took place during the build-up to his impeachment by the House of Representatives – which was quite unpopular with the electorate as Clinton's job performance remained strong, the economy was booming, and the impeachment effort was seen as a partisan exercise with no hope of success. This substantially dampened Democratic losses, with both differential partisan turnout and vote swings against the congressional Republican Party also manifesting in reduced support for state-level Republicans. In contrast, both Bush's and Obama's second midterm were associated with lost seats for the president's party.

Despite the historical contingencies, the patterns over a quarter-century demonstrate substantial Republican gains and limited Democratic resurgence until the presidency of Donald Trump. This includes cyclical partisan swings that were much stronger for Republicans than Democrats, as well as longer-term secular shifts in the broader South that are unlikely to reverse. Finally, Republicans used redistricting to effectively entrench their majorities at a time when they could increasingly concentrate Democrats in a few urban districts. This means Republicans were set up to control the policymaking process in many more states during the 1990s, the 2000s, and the 2010s than they had been in prior eras.

Democratic Prospects and Geographic Polarization

Partisan governance usually leads to a backlash that makes long-term majorities unlikely and creates a political pendulum that swings between left and right. Political scientists Stuart Soroka and Christopher Wlezien have argued convincingly that public opinion moves thermostatically, against the direction of policymaking, as voters see the policies enacted by Republicans as "too cold" and those by Democrats as "too hot" compared to their moderate preferences.[4] Also, a partisan executive usually energizes opposition political participation rather than stimulating further participation by those who first elected them. In fact, historically speaking, majority parties in the states have usually created the grounds for their own destruction: those that narrowly win legislatures actually find their ability to win future elections reduced.[5]

Despite these patterns, Democrats had been unable to win back control of state governments under President Bush or in response to prior Republican gains during the 1990s, 2000s, and 2010s. The perceived unpopularity of President Trump, elected in 2016 with a minority popular vote during an acrimonious campaign, seemed to offer Democrats their first real opportunity to regain state control. Indeed, in the 2018 midterm elections, Democrats did make gains, winning 324 state legislative seats and flipping seven state legislative chambers (including New York Senate, which was controlled by a minority party coalition, and Connecticut Senate, which was previously tied). They also won seven new governor's offices and full control of six new states.

However, Democrats mostly consolidated legislatures that leaned in their direction, winning swing-state gubernatorial elections rather than overturning Republican majorities. Republicans lost full control of only two legislatures (Minnesota and New Hampshire) but gained control of the Alaska House. Taking into account governors' races, this gave them full control of one new state (Alaska) while losing full control of five. They had also gained control of West Virginia in 2018 due to the governor there switching parties. Democratic gains fell well short of what Republican wave elections. Put in historic perspective, since 1900 an average of 12 chambers change hands every two years; given this, Democratic state gains were relatively modest.

The states where Democrats did make the most gains in 2018 were those with some swing voters who still mostly vote Democratic in presidential and congressional elections. This included Colorado (gaining 17 percentage points share in the Senate and 8 in the House), Maine (gaining 11 points in the Senate and 8 in the House), and New Hampshire (17 points in the Senate and 15 in the House). They were prevented from major gains in Red states by a combination of gerrymandering, geographic concentration, and the modest size of the shift from the national vote that occurred in 2016. While battleground states do still swing between the parties, especially in statewide governor's races, there is also increasing polarization that limits the legislative swing. The correlation between the state presidential vote and midterm gubernatorial vote is also going up steadily over time, with fewer counties, districts, or individuals voting for one party nationally and another at the state level.

The few remaining exceptions to this trend did not help Democrats at the state level in 2018. Republican governors Charlie Baker (Massachusetts), Larry Hogan (Maryland), and Phil Scott (Vermont) won easily in deeply Blue states, but Democratic gubernatorial candidates lost in Arizona and Ohio despite strong US Senate performances. Democrat Laura Kelly did defeat Kris Kobach in

Kansas, reflecting a polarizing Republican candidate and a split in the Kansas Republican Party dating to Brownback. Even in their banner year, however, Democrats could not match Republicans' recent state performances under Democratic presidents.

Democrats will have additional chances to make gains, especially if President Trump remains widely unpopular. The 2020 election will be important not only in this respect, but also as the election preceding the next redistricting period (though Democrats may have a hard time matching Republican gains from gerrymandering due to their concentration, while some Democrats are even leading reforms of the process to reduce partisan advantage in states where they are gaining power). Overall, increases in geographic polarization – in the form of Democrats' urbanization – will make it difficult for them to move beyond consolidating gains in Blue states, with control of solidly Red states that used to be competitive or perennially in their column seemingly now out of reach.

Increasingly Conservative Politicians

Republican control of state governments has been rising at the same time as the party has been moving rightward. Given increasing gridlock at the national level, conservative activists, donors, and organizations turned to the states to fulfill their goals. An entrenched federal government run by career politicians, large bureaucracies, and status-quo-supporting interest groups might restrain national action, they reasoned, but the states offered open green fields for fast-paced and coordinated action. New crops of ideologically committed legislators could quickly take over state parties, without succumbing to liberal drift in office. In elections, conservatives succeeded in moving their candidates and officeholders to the right without sacrificing the parties' electoral gains.

The legislators of both parties have been moving apart ideologically, with fewer roll call voting defections to the other side, and since Republicans have been gaining share across the country during the period of polarization, this has meant more state governments run by more conservative politicians. Figure 2.4 reports the cross-state average conservatism of the median member of each Republican caucus in each chamber, with higher numbers indicating higher levels of

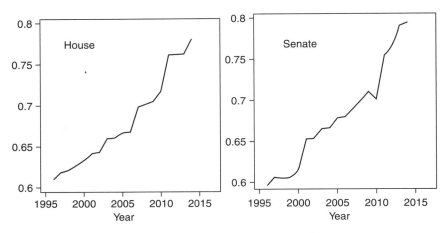

Figure 2.4 State Republican Party median conservatism in house and senate over time (Shor and McCarty, Measuring American Legislatures, american legislatures.com)

conservatism (meaning Republican legislators are voting more often in favor of conservative policies and more often against liberal policies in their chambers). The indicators, from Nolan McCarty and Boris Shor, are based on the same kinds of methods used to assess congressional polarization based on roll call votes. Cross-state comparisons are available because many state legislators end up in Congress, where voting behavior can be tracked and compared to former state legislators from other states. The trends in each state, visible at americanlegislatures. com, vary quite a bit by state, despite rising overall polarization. I asked state legislative reporters to comment on the outputs of these measures for their state, with most confirming that they matched local qualitative perceptions; there were no overt mismatches between data and on-the-ground knowledge.

In the figures, the clear trend is toward steadily increasing conservatism, with Republicans in both chambers moving to the right in both legislative chambers nearly every year from 1996 to 2015. Although these data begin slightly later and end slightly earlier than previous data, a longer time period would likely reflect the same upward sloping line. On the one hand, the trend seems to fit with conventional knowledge of polarization; yet, it is more surprising when one considers that it has occurred as Republicans have been steadily gaining ground in less conservative districts. Usually, parties gaining seats and majority status tend to increase their power share by adding moderate members, while minority parties move to extremes more quickly as they lose swing districts with more moderate voters and only members representing highly partisan voters in safe districts remain. In short, Republicans replaced moderate Democrats with increasingly extreme Republicans, which moved both parties' legislative caucuses to the extreme.

Trends in both chambers again move up in similar fashion, from about 0.6 to nearly 0.8 on the scale, in which 0 is meant to represent the midpoint between liberalism and conservatism. These trends mean there are no longer many Republicans more liberal than even the most conservative of Democrats in their legislative chambers, while there are more Republicans on the party's right wing. Furthermore, Republican legislators at nearly every point in their caucus's distribution – from the most moderate to the most conservative – are substantially to the right of their predecessors just 20 years before. Democrats in the states have been moving leftward at the same time that Republicans have moved rightward, as they have lost control of more chambers and become a shrinking minority. While in Congress Republicans have consistently moved to extremes faster than Democrats, Democrats in state government have been moving away from the center faster than Republicans in many places. This will become important as we evaluate the potential for the minority of Democratic-controlled states to move policy leftward. But, for now, the broad takeaway is that Republicans have shown a surprising ability to become entrenched majority parties in many states, despite a steady rightward march.

As David Hopkins and I have argued in our book *Asymmetric Politics*, Republicans are also the more comfortably nationalized and ideologically driven of the two major parties.[6] They pursue a national agenda of smaller government, unfettered capitalism, less redistribution, traditional values, social restoration, nationalism, and safety through security in every state, rather than adapt their policies to particular state circumstances. Democrats, instead, tend to identify particular problems affecting each of the social groups in their constituencies, and create particular policies attuned to local needs. As a result, compared to Democrats, Republican bills look more similar across states and attend less to unique state characteristics, as revealed in an analysis of text re-use in cross-state bill language.[7] Republicans in the states are also organizing nationally as a party. In doing so, they have broken away from equal participation in non-partisan organizations such as the National Conference of State Legislatures to instead participate more in conservative organizations such as the American Legislative Exchange Council (ALEC).[8] Some object to the non-partisan groups, saying they are dominated by mostly liberal staff, and others just want to meet only with those who share their values. Republican governors are also increasingly attending separate partisan meetings, rather than those of the National Governors' Association, and submitting joint op-eds for national papers with partisans in other states, like those objecting to Obama health and immigration policies.[9]

Most state old-timers in both parties express disdain for contemporary state politics and significant nostalgia for bygone eras of supposedly bipartisan cooperation. In the past, they say, state legislators used to have more bipartisan working groups, used to know each other (and their families and districts) better across the aisle, and used to socialize more without regard to party. Previous generations of state legislators were less diverse than those of today, so some of their perceptions might be chalked up to generational conflict in a changing society. But on balance, the old-timers have a point. Their perceptions reflect real trends in state politics, backed by other data. Indeed, as the parties have sorted themselves into ideologically cohesive coalitions, they have also moved apart socially and strategically. The two parties now have less in common in terms of social background, with gender and racial diversity concentrated among Democrats, and find fewer cross-cutting issues where they can find common ground with the other party. Furthermore, they have established institutions to reinforce partisanship on everything from campaign fundraising to legislative rules to the relative frequency of partisan and non-partisan meetings. In other words, polarization is real and has broader social consequences. Because it came at a time of increasing Republican control of government, the result is that Democrats lost power just as minority parties had less ground for involvement in majority-party policymaking.

Republicans thus came to control more state governments with party caucuses that are more conservative, while not appearing to have paid much of an electoral price for their increasingly extreme opinions (possibly because they have been running against more extreme Democrats). The party has a stronger shared ideological view and more agreement on issue positions than ever before. A straightforward reading of this would suggest that, compared to the Democrats, they should have found it easier to agree on a (conservative) platform, put forward (conservative) policy proposals, and achieve (conservative) policy gains. But it remains to be seen whether they succeeded.

The Electoral Triumph of Conservatism

To review, over a 25-year period, Republicans gained state legislative seats and chambers, as well as governorships, at an unprecedented rate. They increased the number of states they fully controlled by a factor of nearly nine: from a low of only three states to a high of twenty-six. They were able to do so with candidates and officeholders who became increasingly conservative over time, with legislators who would previously have been considered among the most conservative in their caucus now standing merely at the caucus median.

Because the American two-party system is a near monopoly, Democrats faced the opposite electoral fate over the same period – maintaining full control of only six states before 2018 and losing control of chambers in a majority of states. Their legislators have also been polarizing, such that Democratic state house and senate caucuses are now substantially more liberal. But whereas the Republicans' move right was associated with electoral gains, the Democratic move left was associated with losses.

The American party system provides lots of avenues for party resurgence, with the winner of each presidential election immediately the favorite to lose the next midterm election. The electorate tends to react to liberal policy gains by becoming more conservative and to conservative policy gains by becoming more liberal, and this is a pattern that has persisted under presidents Clinton, Bush, Obama, and Trump. The economic cycle is unpredictable, potentially helping or hindering either party depending on timing. All the while, the American public has remained deeply divided, with presidential elections having remained mostly close contests. America's built-in mechanisms for two-party competition and losing-party resurgence make the period from the 1990s to 2017 even more remarkable. During this time, the Republican Party repeatedly gained ground in a near-national upsurge, despite becoming a more consistently conservative party across issues, across states, and across legislators. Such a sustained period of Republican resurgence will be difficult to replicate, and so I now turn to assessing what it won for them in terms of public policy results.

Notes

1 Franko and Witko (2017).
2 Hopkins (2018).
3 See Hopkins (2018) on the national trends in election outcomes and Rogers (2016) on the relative importance of presidential approval and state legislative approval on state legislative voting.
4 Wlezien (1995).
5 Feigenbaum, Fouirnaies, and Hall (2017).
6 See Grossmann and Hopkins (2016); Hopkins (2018).
7 Linder et al. (In Press).
8 Hertel-Fernandez (2018).
9 Jensen (2017).

3 STICKY LIBERAL POLICYMAKING

Sam Brownback, a stalwart conservative Senator, was elected Governor of Kansas in the 2010 Republican wave. He vowed to enact an unprecedented conservative agenda, creating a "real live experiment" to serve as a "Red-state model" for Republicans to tout as a national example. While other Republican politicians moderated their views once in office, Brownback followed through, with the *Washington Post* claiming: "If you want to know what a Tea Party America might look like, there is no place like Kansas."[1] Brownback abolished state agencies, cut spending dramatically, refused federal grants, and dramatically cut taxes. Kansas had been fully Republican-controlled as recently as 2002, and the legislature had remained solidly Republican even during Democratic governorships, so his ascension did not represent a breaking of the dam for held-back legislation. Brownback nonetheless took a "far-right turn," leading the "most conservative legislature ever" for the next few years. The conservative revolution within the party nationally had been applied to the states, and it seemed to be driving full-speed ahead.[2]

By 2017, however, the experiment had essentially ended. Kansas legislators, still overwhelmingly Republican, voted to repeal most of Brownback's major tax cuts in a veto override. They also developed their own, more generous, school funding formula. The prior tax cuts had forced cutbacks to education spending, resulting in well-publicized early school closures and creating a political backlash that led to the defeat of Brownback's legislative allies.[3] Those still around were not in the mood to continue following the governor's lead. Some of Brownback's reforms increasing the restrictiveness of the state's health and social welfare programs survived the backlash, but even so the limits to the conservative revolution were exposed. In 2018, the Republicans again nominated the most conservative candidate they could find for governor, Secretary of State Kris Kobach; but he was defeated by Democrat Laura Kelly in the most notable 2018 Red-state Democratic gubernatorial victory.

Kansas was an outlier, both in the scale of its conservative push and the size of the backlash, but its troubles illustrate the difficulties of translating Republican victories into conservative policy change. Coming to power in already-conservative states, their government-shrinking proposals inevitably involved cuts to core services and federal benefits. Unlike at the federal level, deficit spending could not cover the direct consequences of tax cuts, so citizens sat up and took notice when revenues and funds for schools were reduced. The electoral backlash eventually hit the party, even in deep-red Kansas, but not before the party itself had decided to pursue a different path. How representative is Kansas in understanding the effects of Republican control? I use quantitative assessments of state policy outputs to judge Republican policy gains in this chapter, before turning to qualitative evidence and issue-specific cases in the following chapter.

The Direction of State Policymaking

It is first useful to look at the broad trends over time in state policy to see the degree to which they reflect a conservative turn. Given Republican gains in state governments, some analysts expected (and some politicians and interest groups promised) a fundamental reshaping of the role of government in society. The transnational limits to conservative governance, however, show those outcomes are a tall order. Like elsewhere, the broad trends in the size of state government and the direction of state policymaking do not suggest fundamental retrenchment.

The most common way to assess the size of government is to look at expenditures. Figure 3.1 adopts this approach, tracking state government expenditures over time in three different ways. Because most states have balanced budget requirements, these measures are closely correlated with trends in tax revenues. The top panel looks at average state spending in constant dollars (adjusted for inflation) and

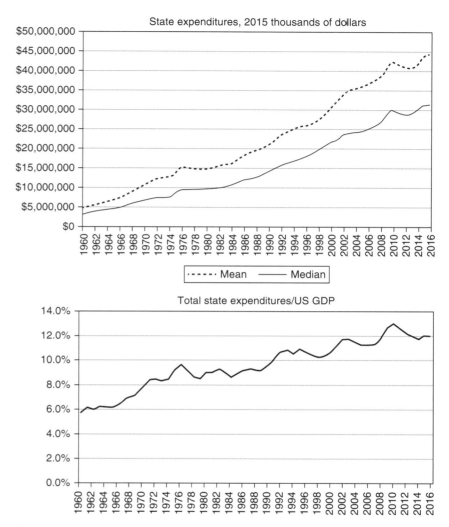

Figure 3.1 State government expenditures over time (US Census Bureau, Annual Survey of State Government Finances)

the median state's spending (also adjusted), while the bottom panel compares state spending (across all states) to the size of the national economy. The dominant trend is toward rising state spending since 1960. In mean and median state spending, there was a flattening in the late 1970s and an acceleration in the 1980s and 1990s, followed by a slowing at the turn of the century (and a bump surrounding the 2009 federal stimulus programs and their expiration). The mean figure has grown apart from the median over time, becoming much higher as state spending has grown more concentrated in larger high-spending states.

Compared to rising economic growth (the denominator in the bottom panel), the upward trend in state spending is less pronounced. The upward movement of the 1960s looks steeper until a temporary bump in the mid-1970s; there are then three rises and falls in the 1990s, the early 2000s, and the late 2000s. Nevertheless, state spending has doubled its share of the economy since 1960. The best case to be made for a retrenchment is that state spending may not be able to continue growing as a share of the economy, with each of the last three rises associated with later falls. But early reports from the National Association of State Budget Officers on 2017 and 2018 state spending suggest a continued rise: it is expected to be up 3.8 percent in 2017 and 4.6 percent in 2018 (compared to inflation of 1.7 percent and 2.5 percent, and GDP growth of 2.3 percent and 3 percent respectively).

There is no visible break in any of the three series as Republicans began to gain control of more states in 1995, though there is more of a downward trend after 2011 (coinciding with both the end of stimulus funding and more Republican state control). This (perhaps unfairly) also reflects changes in federal funding to the states, rather than independent decisions by states to increase spending. Federal funds became a higher share of state spending from 2008 to 2011, but federal and state funds have both been rising fairly steadily over time.[4] Since the 1980s, Medicaid has been the primary driver of state budget growth (accounting for especially large rises in recent years). This is a federal–state joint program that, while benefiting from increasing federal spending, also requires significant state investment. Expenditures have also grown in education, corrections, transportation, and many other areas. Combined, education and health have long accounted for more than half of state spending and continue to do so under increased Republican rule.

That does not imply that there have been no changes in the share of spending going to different programs. Overall, state spending on Medicaid and social welfare programs has crowded out other spending priorities, but within these constraints, Republican states have spent disproportionately on higher education while Democrats have spent more on K-12 education and social welfare.[5] In Chapter 4, I will review further studies demonstrating some partisan effects on these spending decisions. The bigger picture, though, is that state spending

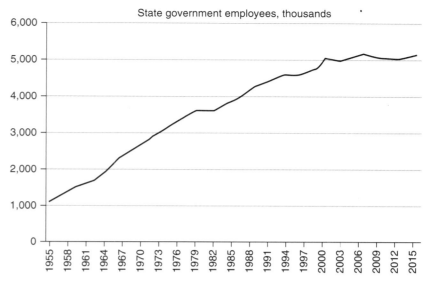

Figure 3.2 Annual state government employment (Bureau of Labor Statistics, annual average of monthly data)

has continued to grow despite a shift toward the party professing support for small government, and that spending is still concentrated in traditionally Democratic-party-owned issues such as education and health.[6]

There has also been no mass privatization or move toward contracting. Figure 3.2 looks at the size of government in another way, tracking the number of state government employees over time. State governments tripled in size by this metric from 1960 to 1992, before the Republican resurgence. Employment kept rising until 2002 but has since been fairly steady at about 5.1 million workers. There is variation across states, of course, but much of it is driven by their demographic and economic circumstances. By contrast, federal government employment has remained in the range of 2.7 million to 3.2 million workers since 1967 – despite a quickly expanding budget, the federal government has increasingly relied on contractors and grantees. Local government employment, which includes lots of teachers reliant on state funding (a majority of local workers are in education), rose from 4.5 million in 1960 to 14 million in 2005 (and has since remained about that level). The state employment trends thus largely match both the trends in the state budget and in local employment, showing a large rise followed by a recent plateau. Unlike the federal government, though, the state and local workforce grew as its responsibilities multiplied. State governments have thus taken on a larger share of both government employment and spending (as well as tax levels) relative to the federal government since the 1970s, though there have not been any further increases in share since 2001.[7] Neither the size of state government nor its primary roles have changed dramatically in the decades since Republicans began making intense gains.

The picture looks somewhat different if we shift to an assessment of individual liberal or conservative policies passed into law by state governments. For this analysis, I rely on data from many scholars, compiled into the Correlates of State Policy dataset.[8] I use two different methods of categorizing 208 specific policies as liberal or conservative. The first is based on the size and scope of state governments: policies expanding state government's scope through spending or regulation are coded as liberal; those that contract the scope of state government are coded as conservative; and those that do not have any effect on state government or have mixed effects with no clear direction are coded as neither. This is the primary distinction used in the literature on federal policymaking.[9] The second categorization relaxes the strict definition to count any policy mostly supported by a liberal political coalition as liberal, and any policy mostly supported by conservatives as conservative. This is closer to conventional usage, but less theoretically defensible as an inherent measure of policy content (because it defines policies' ideology based on who traditionally supports them, rather than what they do, and may thus define whatever is passed under their watch as equivalent to each party's initial agenda).

Figure 3.3 looks at trends over time in net liberal policies passed (liberal minus conservative policies) by these two definitions. In every year, there are substantially more liberal than conservative laws in states based on either definition. The conventional net policy liberalism measure (what I call the "size-of-government measure") increases fairly steadily from 1990 to 2008 and then plateaus. Due to lack of data for a large number of policies after 2010, I assumed no change from the previous year for those policies; that artificially reduces changes in the level of policy liberalism after 2010.[10] The net liberal policies indicator is closely correlated with the average total state expenditures from Figure 3.1 (the correlation is 0.96), even though it measures dichotomous policies rather than spending, and counts every change equally rather than weighting by the size of a program. The alternative measure

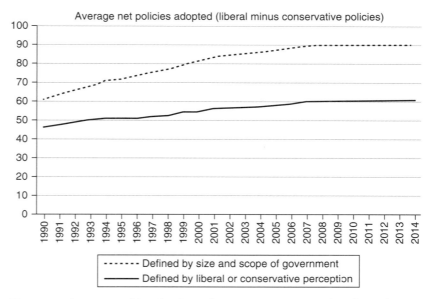

Figure 3.3 Average net liberal policy adoptions over time (analysis by author. Data from the Correlates of State Policy Project. Policies not available for all years are extended from their value in the previous year, which artificially reduces change after 2010)

based on conventional support by liberals or conservatives (what I call the "coalition-based measure") shows a less pronounced rise in policy liberalism from 1990 to 2008, with a slight pause after 1994. It is closely correlated with the size-of-government measure ($r = 0.99$). For both definitions of liberal and conservative policy, I have data on a smaller subset of dichotomous policies for all years since 1960; that shows a longer and steadier upward trend.

Neither measure shows an abrupt conservative shift in the 1990s, though they do suggest some role for Republican gains in 1994 and 2010. As was the case for the state expenditure measures, the mean is generally greater than the median for both measures. The higher mean rate indicates that the most liberal states are raising the average more than the most conservative states are reducing it. Meanwhile, the median state (mostly a Republican state in the more recent time period) has not been passing many liberal or conservative policies and has thus not changed its level of net policy liberalism.

A case can be made that conservative gains in the states have slowed the advance of policy liberalism, especially if the count is not reliant on (relatively rare) contractions in the role of government. For example, increased restrictions in abortion laws, which have been frequent in the last few decades, would be counted as conservative policy changes by the second measure, even though they increase regulation. The international norm that government expands in scope over time makes it difficult to achieve reductions in government spending or contractions in government's role, but even so it may not prevent conservative legislators from passing laws that do not fit on that spectrum. As in Congress, state legislative majorities are much more able to exercise negative agenda control – keeping policies off the agenda and making them less likely to be enacted – than to proactively succeed in passing new policies.[11]

By any measure, state governments have grown dramatically and become more liberal since the 1960s, with recent trends unable to significantly reverse the longer-term ideological direction of state policymaking. These trends provide a starting point for the evaluation of conservative policy success. The huge gains Republicans have made in state elections – as well conservatives' increasing, and firm, hold on the party's legislative majorities – have not easily mapped onto a reversal of prior state policy trends. Instead, the size and scope of state government has continued to grow during a period of growing conservatism in American state legislatures and governorships.

Measuring Party Effects

Given these trends, what policy outputs have increases in Republican control of state governments enabled? Has the Republican Party used its newfound power to successfully move public policy to the right? Have the effects been immediate or built over time? And how does the scale of Republican-brought change compare to these liberal trends in overall policymaking and the stable differences in policy across states?

Traditionally, scholars used fairly crude measures to test the liberalism or conservatism of state policy over time, making it difficult to satisfactorily address these questions. The measures usually showed the ideological position of state policy matching state public opinion, with less direct input from parties. The level of social welfare spending, the stringency of gun regulation, or the rates of income taxation usually matched the conservatism or liberalism of a state's electorate, regardless of the party that was in charge at any given moment. However, several recent analyses take advantage of new data to suggest that party control may now be producing big policy gains in the ideological direction preferred by the winning party.

The most sweeping of these is an impressive data compilation by political scientists Devin Caughey and Christopher Warshaw of specific policies and differences across states, which led them to create new measures of policy liberalism in each state and year, including separate measures for the degree of liberalism or conservatism of state economic and social issue policies. They show that their scales of state policy liberalism correlate with party control and public opinion for both economic and social issues.[12] Although they have collected data on state policy outputs since 1936, they find that party control has little predictive impact before the 1980s. Since then, however, Republican or Democratic control increasingly explains policy liberalism.

Part of today's larger association between state partisanship and policy is due to the increasing ideological sorting of the states by party, especially the move of conservative Southern states to the Republicans, but Caughey and Warshaw also show that recent party control has been associated with aggregate change in policy nationwide. Public opinion in each state predicts a state's policy liberalism directly, independent of its smaller effects on party control of state government, meaning that policymakers respond to public opinion regardless of the party in power. Kansas Republicans moved policy leftward as the public reacted to Brownback's policies, for example, while also losing a governor's race that may lead to further liberal policy change.

Interestingly, public opinion on social issues has been trending leftward over time – and state policy has been following it in that direction – even during periods of increasing Republican control. Policy opinion on economic issues has been more balanced and less subject to large shifts. Even though Caughey and Warshaw resuscitate the idea that party control changes state policy, they find that party control does not explain most state policy differences. Instead, there remain enormous state-level differences that are not explained by partisan change or public opinion. The scholars sought to find as many conservative and liberal policy indicators as possible over the period being studied, but they avoided broad measures such as total government spending as well as traditional analyses based on policy diffusion (the fast or slow adoption of policies that most states eventually adopt). Their measures track the relative liberalism or conservatism of each state in each time period, but (by design) their analyses minimize broader moves across all states in a liberal or conservative direction.[13] This means they are geared toward explaining what policy moves can be explained by party control rather than constant state-level differences or nationwide changes over time.

Rather than combine all policies, political scientist Jacob Grumbach provides more fine-grained measures of policy output differences in states across 16 issue areas. Grumbach finds that Democratic-controlled states have been moving leftward on the environment, guns, health care, immigration, gay rights, labor, and taxes, while Republican states have been moving rightward on abortion, guns, and labor issues.[14] Those findings show policy polarization has been increasing since 2000 (Republican and Democratic states are increasingly adopting different policies), but not primarily due to rightward movement in Republican states. Rather, the contrary is true. Only on the issue of abortion are the Republicans solely responsible for the parties' moving apart (on all the other polarizing issues, Democratic states are moving leftward). Grumbach finds some issue areas with little polarization, including, surprisingly, campaign finance, civil rights, criminal justice, and education. Among these unpolarized issue areas, only education has seen a rightward move overall – primarily due to the expansion of charter schools and school choice programs (coded as conservative by the measure). In the other less-polarized issue areas, policy continues to move in a liberal direction over time.

Overall, seven out of sixteen issue areas have seen leftward moves since 2000, with two showing rightward moves, and the others mixed. Grumbach's analysis, based on scales counting the number of liberal and conservative policies in each state (and placing continuously variable policies like tax rates on the same scale), enables more change over time shared across states than the Caughey and Warshaw measures. Grumbach's overall scales showed policy liberalism rising until 2001, when it plateaued. However, both broad measures hid some important issue-level variation that Grumbach's issue area analyses uncover.

Instead of reviewing all policy results, political scientist Alexander Hertel-Fernandez focuses on the specific policies advanced by the conservative movement.[15] Hertel-Fernandez argues that a right-wing "troika" made up of (1) a network of conservative think tanks (operating independently but known as the State Policy Network), (2) the Koch brothers' grassroots network Americans for Prosperity, and (3) the American Legislative Exchange Council (ALEC, an organization of conservative state legislators) together transformed state policy. The most convincing evidence is for ALEC's effects, where Hertel-Fernandez uses plagiarism detection software to compare the text of introduced and adopted bills with an archive of ALEC model bills. This has enabled him to see when legislators (or their staff) lifted legislative language directly from the group's archive of suggested bills. Copies or derivations of ALEC bills made up an increasing share of introduced and adopted legislation during the 1990s, peaking at over 1 percent of passed bills. By contrast, approximately 18 percent of state laws originate from state bureaucracies.[16]

ALEC copied bills were most common in Republican-controlled states and more commonly introduced by Republican legislators (though Democrats and Democratic-controlled states also passed ALEC bills). Although several of the most commonly passed bills were token resolutions targeted at the federal government (such as a resolution on Taiwan or against Obama administration policy), others were significant policy changes: education reform including charter school expansion, vouchers, and teacher accountability measures; health reform including medical liability limits, high-risk pools, and long-term care insurance deregulation; and 529 college savings accounts. In addition to promoting ALEC model bills, the troika was especially effective in promoting anti-union laws, slowing Medicaid expansion, and pre-empting liberal laws (such as environmental regulations) being put forward by local governments through superseding state legislation. The Hertel-Fernandez approach identifies this conservative agenda, reviewing their successes regardless of party control of government. Their most significant victories, though, occurred in states that had recently elevated Republicans to full control.

These studies indicate that party control of state government has had rising importance on policy outputs in recent decades, while a few examples show successful conservative proposals passed across many legislatures. However, this may not mean that Republican-controlled states have led policy innovation during the period. Knowing how much to credit to the party requires a close look at how policy impact is measured, how its relationship to party control is assessed, and how party-driven changes compare to baseline differences in state policymaking across states and time.

Predicting the Passage of Liberal and Conservative Policies

To begin the analysis, I first return to the simplest way I assessed policy outputs: counting the number of liberal and conservative policies passed by state governments.[17] The initial measure is again based on the size and scope of state government, with liberal policies defined as expanding state government's scope and conservative policies defined as contracting it. This provides a reference for thinking about conservative efforts to roll back the state, the primary domain in which the parties historically battled but also the one in which conservatives have been unsuccessful internationally.

Using this definition, Figure 3.4 illustrates the results of models predicting net liberal laws in each state-year (liberal minus conservative laws) from 1991 to 2014. With the help of my research assistant Zuhaib Mahmood, I use several different models, each designed to assess the effect of Republican chamber and governor control; the key variable takes a value of 0 if Republicans control neither the state house or senate or governorship of a state, 1 if they control any one of those three, 2 if they control any two of those three, and 3 if they have complete control of the policymaking process.[18] The top left figure reports the results of a panel model predicting net liberal policies with Republican Party control, with only state and year fixed effects.[19] This means, like prior models, it assesses differences based on party control that are not explained by consistent state differences or changes across all states in the same year. In the Kansas example, this model would attribute to the Republicans policy change resulting from Brownback replacing a Democratic governor but would not give them credit for Kansas's overall conservative tilt or the 2010 election's tendency to produce relatively conservative moves even in Democratic states.

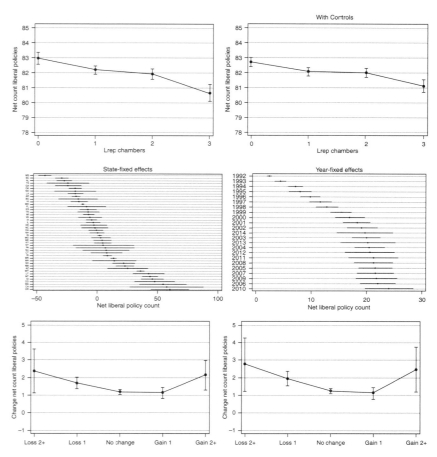

Figure 3.4 Predicting net counts of policies expanding minus contracting scope of state governments (data compiled from Correlates of State Policy Project; top left illustrates results of panel model without controls, top right and middle from panel model with controls; bottom left from change model without controls, and bottom right from change model with controls. The dependent variable is government expanding policies minus government contracting policies. The main independent variable is Republican control of state houses, senates, and governorships)

The top right figure illustrates the results of the same model but with added control variables: the log of Gross State Product (GSP), the log of state population, the economic liberalism of the state's mass public, and the social liberalism of the state's mass public, along with a factor variable for each region. The logic of this model is that some things correlated with changes in state party control of government (trends concurrent with Republican or Democratic gains like state population or economic growth but not actually caused by the parties) might actually be responsible for leftward- or rightward-moving policy changes. If the state gets richer, increases in population, or has a change in public opinion, it may lead to policy changes regardless of who is in power. The middle two panels report additional results for the model with these added control variables: the modeled state fixed effects and year fixed effects. The state fixed effects are arbitrarily compared against Arkansas, so the specific numbers are less important than the distance between states. The year fixed effects are compared against the first year (1991), so they give a sense of how much change there has been since the early 1990s.

The results demonstrate significant but limited effects from Republican control. There is evidence that full Republican control leads to two fewer net liberal policies than full Democratic control. Note that the baseline level of net liberal policies is between 80 and 83, however, with the range of change attributable to party control low. Regardless of partisanship, most states have many more policies that are liberal rather than conservative. The graph of year fixed effects shows an increasing number of liberal policies over time (20 more on average in 2014 compared to the baseline year of 1991), meaning that states have tended to incrementally adopt liberal policies over the period (at least until 2010). Even with regional controls, there is also substantial state-level variation in fixed effects. That means individual states still have disproportionate levels of liberalism or conservatism, independent of their partisanship, public opinion, or region. State- and year-level variation is also substantially greater than variation due to partisan control. The range due to stable state differences is nearly 100 net liberal policies, and the range due to differences across time is 24 net liberal policies. Even assuming Republican states could reverse liberalizing trends over time, the model suggests it would take a half-century of Republican control to move Oregon to Alabama's level of policy liberalism.

The bottom two panels in Figure 3.4 represent the results of models of *change*, rather than levels, of net liberal policies. Change in net liberal policies is predicted alongside change in the level of Republican control: from losing two out of three chambers and governorships to gaining two out of three chambers and governorships.[20] The bottom left figure represents the results of the change model without controls. The bottom right includes the same control variables as those used in the panel modes, but I shift all of them to represent changes (change in log GDP, change in log population, change in public economic and social liberalism). This means that the model is assessing whether Kansas made changes in the year after Republicans gained the governor's office, rather than assessing how conservative they were over the full period of Republican versus Democratic governors. Both results from the change models show small relationships, with both large Democratic and large Republican gains associated with more policy liberalism. If the estimates are taken at face value, the model actually projects more liberalism after major Republican gains and losses. Any effect of Republican gains on reduced liberal policymaking visible in the top panels thus does not appear to be driven by instant changes in policy-making following dramatic election victories. There is more evidence that liberal gains in Democratic states could be immediate.

Net Party-Preferred Policies

These small or non-significant effects may be driven, in part, by the definition of liberal and conservative policies. In Figure 3.5, I present analyses of net liberal policies defined more broadly to include all Democratic-preferred policies minus all Republican-preferred policies. This means that policies are not judged on their ideological content but are instead assessed purely on the political coalition that usually supports them. The cost is that there is some danger of reverse caus-ality, where policies are judged as conservative because Republicans supported them rather than due to their inherent content. Democrats have come to be positioned in favor of both liberalization of drug laws and increasing regulation of tobacco smoking, for example, even though they seem to logically conflict. The benefit is that there are other policies such as exchanging business taxes for sales taxes that do not affect the overall size of government but clearly redirect the burden of costs away from Republican electoral constituencies.

For clarity, Figure 3.5 focuses on illustrating the model with controls, along with year fixed effects (although I ran all of the same models as for the previous measure). With this measure, there is a similar relationship, with more Republican control leading to two or three fewer net liberal policies. Across the range of Republican con-trol, however, net liberal policies move from about +57 to +54. The

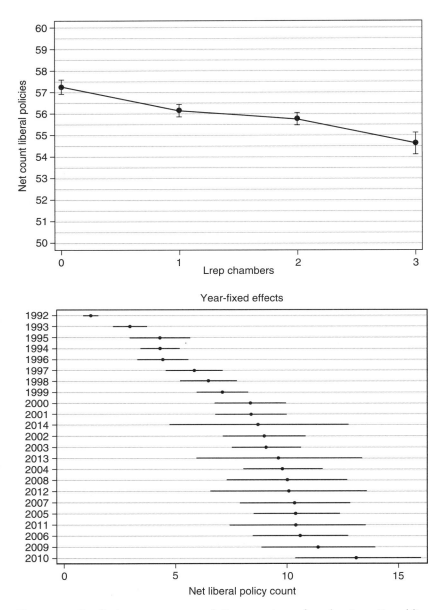

Figure 3.5 Predicting net counts of Democratic-preferred minus Republican-preferred policies (data compiled from Correlates of State Policy Project. The top panel illustrates results of a panel model with controls. The bottom panel illustrates year fixed effects for the model. The dependent variable is Democratic-preferred policies minus Republican-preferred policies. The main independent variable is Republican control of state houses, senates, and governorships)

broader range of policies defined as liberal or conservative leads to larger estimated state fixed effects, with a range of nearly 110 net liberal policies between the most conservative and most liberal states. The year fixed effects (pictured) again show an increasing number of net liberal policies from 1991 to 2006, but now show more volatility afterward, with leftward moves in 2009 and 2010 followed by a rightward move across states from 2011 to 2014. Recall that changes after 2010 are limited by assumed stability on policies with missing data, which likely affects these results. The range of policy differences due to full Democratic or Republican control (two or three net liberal policies) is again lower than the range attributable to change over time (13 net liberal policies) and far lower than the range due to stable state differences.

Models of change from year to year again show increased Republican control having no immediate conservative effect on policymaking. Combined with the substantial state fixed effects, this suggests that the relationships we observe come from long-term differences across states associated with typical patterns of partisanship, rather than a party's ability to reshape state governments in the short term. Kansas immediately after Brownback was an outlier in terms of the size of its conservative shift (most newly Republican states do not immediately shift rightward); Kansas may be more typical in its smaller rightward shift under sustained Republican versus Democratic governors. I also separately analyzed how many liberal policies and how many conservative policies each state had passed; these models mostly show fewer liberal policies passed under Republican control but also show slightly more frequent conservative policies.

A new analysis of policy diffusion helps flesh out the dynamics of these patterns of liberal and conservative policymaking. Frederick Boehmke and colleagues tracked any policy that had diffused across states since the 1930s. They found that 35–40 percent of new state policies were liberal in each decade; while conservative policies accounted for only about 5 percent of new policies in the early decades they tracked, slowly increasing to 30 percent of new policies by 2000 (other policies not covered by these percentages were neither clearly liberal nor conservative).[21] Confirming other analyses, most state policies considered and adopted are liberal. Rather than attribute these policies to Democratic successes, researchers usually consider them as policies that spread and are adopted due to states noting what other states are doing. Furthermore, Boehmke et al. find that whereas liberal and moderate policy diffused through similar networks of states (such as by neighboring states successfully copying one another's policies), conservative policies spread through Republican-specific networks (less often based on shared state geography). This lends credence to a recent analysis by Andrew Karch and colleagues, arguing that "the tendency to limit diffusion research to widely adopted policies ... leads scholars to systematically overestimate the impact of geographic diffusion pressures and policy attributes"[22] over internal political factors. Since most widely adopted policies are liberal, the upshot is that liberal policies are considered a natural outcome of states learning from one another, whereas conservative aberrations are attributed to Republican political success.

Though simple counts of conservative and liberal policies provide a useful starting point for analyses of party control effects, they also raise a number of concerns. First, they weight all policy changes equally, even though some are clearly more important than others: they treat the legalization of gay marriage as equivalent to deregulation of nursing, for example. Second, they rely on dichotomous and specific policy adoptions rather than continuous measures that reflect overall policy. Rather than looking at tax rates, for example, they only look at the presence of a state income or sales tax. Third, they are highly dependent on the lists of policy changes that scholars are able to collect. These lists have unknown biases and might potentially focus more on liberal policy changes as indicators of policymaking success. Liberals could theoretically pass four new social programs, for example, that are later consolidated and reduced by one conservative policy. Relative counts of liberal and conservative policies are useful and directly interpretable, but they are better understood in comparison with analyses of broader measures.

Predicting Broader Measures of State Policymaking

To assess party effects on the size and scope of state government, the most common measures used in international studies assess government expenditures as a share of the economy. Figure 3.6 presents my analyses of state government spending as a share of gross state product from 1991 to 2010. Since nearly all states have balanced budget amendments, this measure is highly correlated with total state tax

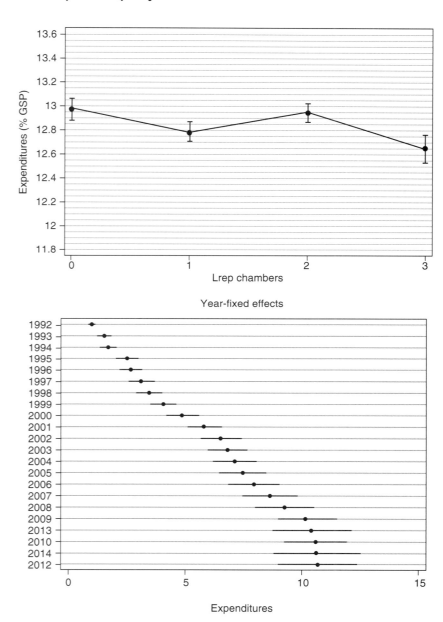

Figure 3.6 Predicting state government expenditures as a percentage of state economy (data compiled from Correlates of State Policy Project. The top panel illustrates results of a panel model with controls. The bottom panel illustrates year fixed effects for the model. The dependent variable is state government expenditures as a percentage of the size of state economies. The main independent variable is Republican control of state houses, senates, and governorships)

revenue as a share of the size of the economy. Even so, the expenditure model includes some spending that states have been able to accomplish through borrowing or workarounds, as well as the acceptance of federal funds and even services funded by user fees. I thus also analyzed the tax measure and found equivalent results. Figure 3.6 illustrates the results for the panel model of expenditures with controls, along the year fixed effects below.[23]

The models for government spending show a slightly different pattern than those for the policy counts. Rather than a continuous effect across levels of Republican control (as in Figures 3.4 and 3.5), these results demonstrate no strong difference except between states where Republicans control both chambers and the governorship of a state and those where Democrats control all three.[24] With full control, Republican states spend a bit less, though the move is from approximately 13 percent of GSP to 12.7 percent of GSP – we are therefore looking at relatively small differences in the size of state government. In comparison, state fixed effects range more than 20 percentage points from the most conservative to most liberal state. Many Western states have much smaller governments, and many Eastern states have much larger governments. Rather than shifting dramatically in response to party control, these variations in size of government between states have been built up over decades.

Year fixed effects again show growth over time (compared to the 1991 baseline), with spending as a share of the economy rising more than 10 percentage points from 1991 to 2010 and then stabilizing. As most state economies grew considerably over time during this period, this suggests that not only are state governments keeping up with their economic growth, but they are actually exceeding it. This also means they are growing well beyond the rate of inflation, which was substantially lower than economic growth over this period.

Models predicting change in the size of government, which require effects to materialize within a year of electoral gains, again show the increasing Republican control is associated with either no change in the size of government or an insignificant increase in state spending. Recall that this measure is nearly perfectly correlated with tax collections, meaning that Republican claims to substantially lower taxes (at least immediately) do not appear to be systematically supported. Instead, the evidence indicates that the governmental share of a state's economy is persistently lower in some states compared to others. That said, state governments subject to full Republican control over a long period do take up slightly lower shares of their state's economy.

Policy Liberalism

I also replicate models of the continuous measure of policy liberalism used by Caughey and Warshaw.[25] Recall that this scale minimizes broad liberal or conservative shifts over time and is designed as a relative measure, meaning that there is no baseline level of liberalism. Figure 3.7 illustrates the results of the panel model assessing policy liberalism with controls, with state-level fixed effects below. The results are far stronger and more consistent. Democratic-controlled states produce substantially more liberal policy than Republican-controlled states, with the greatest disparities between unified Democratic and unified Republican states. Policy liberalism moves from approximately +0.2 to −0.17. These models suggest real changes in policy when one party has a trifecta (controlling the house, senate, and the governorship) and smaller changes resulting from intermediary control.

As Caughey and Warshaw report, party control still exerts relatively little influence compared to underlying variation across states and time. The estimated state fixed effects range a total of four full points on the scale, suggesting that stable, long-term differences in policy liberalism are an order of magnitude greater than those associated with state party control. Overall, Southern states and the Dakotas are more conservative, while Western and Eastern states are more liberal. Year fixed effects show lower variation, with policy liberalism generally in decline since the 1990s. The over-time variation is purposely constrained by the model due to its attempt to discount broad changes across all states in each policy's level of acceptability.[26] Models of changes in policy liberalism attributable to changes in party control again show that new Republican victories do not immediately shift a state's policy liberalism. In contrast, there is some evidence that increases in Democratic control do lead to an immediate uptick in policy liberalism.

Reconsidering State Policy Liberalism

The original model from Caughey and Warshaw includes a relative measure of policy liberalism that combines 148 policies enacted

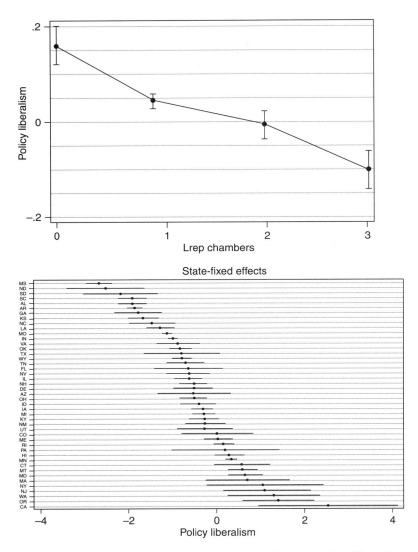

Figure 3.7 Predicting underlying dimension of state policy liberalism (data compiled from Correlates of State Policy Project. The top panel illustrates results of a panel model with controls. The bottom panel illustrates state fixed effects for the model. The dependent variable is policy liberalism, treated as a continuous variable by Caughey and Warshaw (2016). The main independent variable is Republican control of state houses, senates, and governorships)

between 1936 and 2014. Most policies (approximately four in five) are categorical (such as whether states have an income tax), but they do include some continuous measures (such as states' tax rates). They specifically selected salient policy outputs like social welfare spending and Affirmative Action, rather than institutions (such as the presence of an agency) by reviewing interest group statements, political histories, and party platforms. In doing so, they found that policy liberalism increased from 1930s to 1970s and then plateaued. Most states remained relatively stable as they became liberal.[27] As with prior models, they found states in the South to be collectively a conservative outlier across time periods. With their measure, part of common trends across states toward liberalism and declining conservatism are attributed to the relative difficulty of passing each policy. Relaxing the assumption shows liberalism rising substantially more prior to 1990, as all states ended policies such as banning interracial marriage.

Caughey and Warshaw first compared their measure with ideological placements of legislators. They found that while the relationship between legislator liberalism and policy liberalism was relatively flat at the conservative end of the spectrum, it was strong at the liberal end and grew over time. This implies that replacing conservative legislators with ones who were even more conservative did not have as much of an effect as liberal legislators moving leftward, or liberal incumbents being replaced by even more liberal newcomers. That is presumably because more conservative legislators still succeed mainly in stopping liberal legislation, whereas more liberal legislators enable the passage of new government expansions. They also found that the most liberal legislatures were distinguished in their type of spending, most likely through more redistributive policies like those providing health coverage to poor children or services for those with disabilities.[28]

Caughey and Warshaw (now with Yiqing Xu) later reviewed the impact of party control of government on their measure of policy liberalism. In doing so, they found that electing more Democrats led to more liberal policies, but that the effect had doubled in magnitude after 1980.[29] Even so, the effect was still relatively modest compared to enormous differences in (relatively stable) policy liberalism across states. By their estimate, the potential effect of having a Democratic governor was less than one-twentieth of the standard deviation of cross-state differences, corresponding to a one-point increase in a state's percentage of liberal policies. This is an important and likely visible effect, but not one that matches the differences in campaign rhetoric of most debates between gubernatorial candidates. When New Jersey Governor Chris Christie faced Democrat Barbara Bruno in a 2013 debate, for example, he made the typical Republican attack: "To pay for all of her extravagant promises, Senator Buono will raise taxes," while Bruno said of Christie: "He's consistently on the side of the wealthy, and he's turned his back on the working poor and the middle class."[30] Debates often suggest these fundamental and across-the-board differences in policy.

Yet states do not typically flip from Christie's preferences to Bruno's. As the authors of the analysis point out, "many decades of Republican governors and legislatures would be required to make the policies of Massachusetts as conservative as those of Mississippi." Even in that unlikely scenario, Republicans in Massachusetts would be less conservative than those in the South, limiting the effects. Moreover, their actions would have a higher likelihood of causing an electoral backlash, making stable Republican partisan control after conservative policymaking unlikely. Even if somehow the stars aligned in such a manner, conservatives would not be able to undo the state's long history of policy liberalism, only prevent its growth.[31] Policy effects of party control are not even close to the differences in estimated ideal points (the level of liberalism or conservatism that their legislative voting record suggests represents their true policy preferences) between the two parties. Indeed, the effects of party control are estimated as constituting a mere 1 percent of that difference.[32] The parties vote like they are on very different sides of most issues, but do not follow through with enacting policies that achieve that level of difference when they are in office.

Caughey et al. use both panel models like those deployed here and a regression discontinuity estimate (designed to uncover causal effects based on close election outcomes), finding similar effects (with the discontinuity estimates slightly larger). Their evidence reflects differences due to party control based on causal impact (electing Democrats over Republicans was what made the difference), rather than unmeasured factors related to it (because a Republican governor winning or losing by a few percentage points likely reflects mostly random factors, rather than the systematic factors leading to uncompetitive elections on one side or the other). The new analysis explains that until the end of the twentieth century, Democratic governors were actually associated with more conservative policies, and that the effects of legislative control had ebbed and flowed – clear effects were evident only in recent years. Seat share within legislative chambers had little independent effect beyond overall control, suggesting that the policy impact came almost entirely from having legislative majorities.[33]

Caughey and Warshaw followed up this research by incorporating public opinion and dividing the analysis between social liberalism and economic liberalism to disaggregate the two orientations.[34] They found that the liberalism of state public opinion predicts changes in state policy liberalism, but that the relationship is three times as strong on social issues. According to them, economic issues like taxes give states less discretion compared to social issues like gun control, which are more easily understood and can be combined with symbolic appeals to voters based on fundamental rights or morality.[35] However, partisan control of government mediates only a minority of state policymakers' responsiveness to public opinion – more liberal public opinion does not need to be mediated by Democratic victory to have an impact on policy. Shifts in public opinion directly impact incumbents of both parties even if it does not change election outcomes, and that cross-party public responsiveness has also increased over time. That helps to explain the pattern in Kansas, where public aversion to education cuts led to Democratic electoral victories and some Republican legislative moves back to moderation.

The effects Caughey and Warshaw find are slow and persistent: it takes more than a decade of stable opinion for even a half of the long-run effects of public opinion to be realized. Responsiveness to public opinion has been increasing since 1972 and was effectively zero before that time.[36] The effects of public opinion on party control are not large[37] and are mediated by mass partisanship; public liberalism makes state governments more Democratic only because it is associated with increasing Democratic party identification.[38] Public opinion thus has impacted state policy mainly on social, rather than economic issues, and only partially based on partisan electoral outcomes.

Political scientist Jacob Grumbach recently criticized the Caughey and Warshaw measure as understating polarization because of its limited issue coverage, its limitation of change over time, and its misidentifying liberal or conservative orientations of particular policies.[39] According to Grumbach, because laws on social welfare and racial discrimination differentiate states most, their adoption makes the most difference in determining a state's level of policy liberalism each year. This reasonably separates states by ideological bent but perhaps does not address the breadth of their policymaking. Grumbach also shows that Caughey and Warshaw's estimates for abortion, licensing, and regulatory policies do not consistently match conventional understandings of liberalism (for example, nurse licensing counts as the fifth most conservative policy in the dataset and some alcohol regulations change ideological direction).

Grumbach's alternative category of measures substantively codes policies in specific issue areas, as well as their importance, and also enables analyses of differences between measuring liberalism in absolute terms (how high are tax rates) and relative terms (are taxes higher or lower than other times or places). He shows substantially more polarization across all his measures, with absolute indices (matching those based on the number of liberal or conservative policies passed) showing an approximate doubling of average state liberalism since 1970. In these models, the effects of Republican control have increased since 2000, with fully Republican states increasingly moving against the direction of the average state. When states' ideological positions are measured in relative terms, the effect of Democratic control is larger than Republican control. But when policy is measured in absolute terms (with increasing average liberalism over time), Republican control also has a large effect. Republicans, in other words, help slow absolute policy trends moving in a liberal direction. The number of regulations might be rising overall, for example, but with Republican states increasingly having lower levels.

Grumbach argues that the Caughey and Warshaw measure understates polarizing tendencies in the states by failing to incorporate substantive knowledge of policy. His breakdown of the policies used in the prior measure and which of them play the largest role in determining how liberal or conservative states are scored is instructive. Grumbach shows that few specific policies among all those considered actually cause states to be scored substantially more conservative, with some no longer relevant due to nationwide liberal moves (such as school segregation and bans on interracial marriage) and most of the others covering social issues such as abortion, guns, and immigration. The policy liberalism measure is thus incorporating mostly liberal policies to expand government alongside a mix of liberal and conservative policies about social issues (especially discrimination) but differentiating states more based on the latter.

Another measure of policy liberalism by political scientists Jason Sorens and Fait Muedini found that most states clustered in the slightly conservative section of the scale, with a lot more differentiation on the liberal side than the conservative side.[40] They found that differentiation across states was mostly driven by social issue differences in areas such as abortion, driving regulation, and the environment. They argue that their policy liberalism measure, which re-analyzes policies in each term to see if their liberal or conservative connotations have changed, better reflects party-preferred policy moves. Even so, their findings are quite consistent with those for other absolute measures, showing more liberal than conservative policies and a greater liberal advance on social issues.

The ideological measures of state legislative parties developed by McCarty and Shor add an important wrinkle. They show that any public opinion effects on policy may already be baked into cross-state differences in legislative parties. The ideology of the median legislator roughly matches state public opinion due to parties shifting with the relative conservatism of a state's public. As a result, the most conservative Democratic parties across all states end up (ideologically) not too far from the most liberal Republican parties.[41] This means that partisan electoral victories may have less impact than they would have if very liberal or very conservative parties replaced one another when states changed hands. The Kansas Democrats who won in 2018 were more conservative than their counterparts in California; likewise, the Republicans who defeated Democrats in Oklahoma were also replacing conservatives with conservatives. That helps to explain the limited results of party control on policy.

The revolution in measures of state policy and ideological trends has thus brought important conclusions and shown real partisan effects, but they still show that states rarely move from conservative to liberal or vice versa. When this does happen, it usually only does so incrementally and when accompanied by large changes in public opinion and state partisanship. When states move, they tend not to overturn the prior policy regime but to drift in a different ideological direction over time. Rather than overturn these conclusions, the models in this chapter demonstrate that an aggregate measure of policy liberalism can still move in tandem with party control of government while evidence also points to liberalizing trends across all states. Republicans cannot override the build-up of decades of policy liberalism. It is also easier for parties to adapt social issue policies to match changes in public moods rather than restructure the scope of government. A party can quickly change gun regulations but cannot rapidly restructure health care.

Reconciling Views of State Policymaking

What can we say about the effects of Republican control of state government on state policy after this review? The variation in results illustrates the lack of correspondence between theories of strong Republican impact and the actual effects of Republican control. Any analysis taken on its own might lead to a strong conclusion for or against party effects, even when other models do not support the same definitive conclusion. Here, I sought to define what had and had not changed in response to partisan control, rather than to definitively show that change has been massive or minimal.[42]

The results support some clear conclusions. First, citizens should not expect immediate changes from shifts in state party control. None of the models of change show that Republican control immediately leads to more conservative policies. Many of the results suggested that party control exerts a long-term rather than short-term influence. Second, Republican-associated policy changes do not seem to have strong effects on the size and scope of state government. Neither the counts of expanding minus contracting policies, nor the measure of state expenditures as a share of the state economy, showed dramatic or consistent effects. The size and scope of state government seems harder to shift than other policies associated with Democratic or Republican governance. Third, the effects of party control are generally quite a bit smaller than stable differences over time and across states. Differences between Red and Blue states today may codify long-standing regional or state-specific distinctions rather than be illustrative of clear partisan effects. Fourth, measures that allow variation over time or direct counts of liberal or conservative policies confirm that most new policymaking is liberal, and states tend to grow in their liberal policy adoptions over time (even during a conservative era).

Nonetheless, I do not want to discount the effects of Republican control of state governments from these quantitative models. They suggest that Republicans do reduce the number of liberal policies passed, especially when they move from no control to full control of state governments. The broadest measure of policy liberalism does show clear effects of party control. Although they take a long time to develop, state policy differences reflect the partisan character of governments. Partisan elections now matter and have predictable results. This matches the qualitative story I will tell next: there are real examples of Republican-initiated policy gains and other examples of liberal policies stymied by Republicans, but there are also inherent constraints on Republicans' broader government-reshaping agenda.

My findings thus help to reconcile prior findings. Like Caughey and Warshaw, I find that party control in the contemporary era is associated with differences in state policy, but that the remaining range of policy differences across states is far greater than the portion attributable to party control. Like Grumbach, I find that Republican states have had different policy outputs than Democratic states, but that the patterns are not consistent across different manifestations of liberalism and conservatism. Democratic states have maintained their leftward trajectories while Republican states have moved slower in either direction.

Republicans are able to slow or stop the spread of policy liberalism in the states, especially regarding policies unrelated to the broad size and scope of state government. However, they are less able to shift the fundamental character of state policy, adjust the role of government in a state's economy, or move formerly liberal states such as those in the Midwest to match the long-standing conservatism of other states such as those in the South. Partisan control of state government in the contemporary era is impactful but it does not follow that the Republican revolution has succeeded in achieving conservative objectives. Instead, it mostly demonstrates the constraints that Republicans face in forestalling the liberal march of policy, even when Republicans control state government. The next chapter reveals how these Republican efforts played out in specific issue and state contexts.

Notes

1 Annie Gowen. 2011. "In Kansas, Gov. Sam Brownback puts tea party tenets into action with sharp cuts." *Washington Post*. Available at: www .washingtonpost.com/politics/in-kansas-gov-sam-brownback-puts-tea-party-tenets-into-action-with-sharp-cuts/2011/11/02/gIQAkbnOAP_story .html?utm_term=.47c45f59df42.

2 Personal interview with state political reporter.

3 Franko and Witko (2017).

4 See the annual "State Expenditure Report" from the National Association of State Budget Officers at nasbo.org.

5 Adolph, Breunig, and Koski (In Press).

6 Egan (2013).

7 Grumbach (2018a).

8 Jordan and Grossmann (2018), with substantial data from Boehmke et al. (2018) and Caughey and Warshaw (2016). I discuss several of the measures in more detail in Chapter 3.

9 Erikson, MacKuen, and Stimson (2002); Grossmann (2014).

10 Part of the plateau is thus a measurement artifact due to incomplete data. Analyses of the full data up to 2010 do not show any major differences.

11 Crosson (2019).

12 Caughey and Warshaw (2016, 2018).

13 By using time-variant difficulty parameters, it suppresses average change over time. See Grumbach (2018b).

14 Grumbach (2018a).

15 Hertel-Fernandez (2018). My analysis is based on a draft produced for a book conference in 2017.

16 Kroeger (2018) finds this average across ten states with relevant data. These bills often expand the scope of agency power.

17 The database is a product of work by myself, Marty Jordan, and several other research assistants to find and link together data on state policy and its potential causes and effects. It relies on substantial work by many other scholars; we simply compiled their work into one large dataset. Together, it covers a large number of state policies. Our analyses of dichotomous policy adoption primarily rely on work by Caughey and Warshaw as well as work by Frederick J. Boehmke, Mark Brockway, Bruce Desmarais, Jeffrey J. Harden, Scott LaCombe, Fridolin Linder, and Hanna Wallach as part of the State Policy Innovation and Diffusion Database (Boehmke et al. 2018).

18 Nebraska, as a unicameral non-partisan legislature, is not included.

19 But following prior practice, we also include a dummy variable for the South. This baseline follows Caughey and Warshaw (2016).

20 There are a few instances of three chambers and governorships lost or gained, but we combine them with the two change cases to avoid assessing a few outliers (models measured from −3 to +3 do now show major differences).

21 Boehmke et al. (2018).

22 Karch et al. (2016).

23 I again ran models of change as well, but do not picture their results. All models, extensions, and robustness checks are available on my website.

24 Models do not show a statistically significant effect resulting from level of party control when that control is assessed as a single continuous variable.

25 This measure scales both categorical and continuous policies over a period of decades on the same underlying spectrum. Although Caughey and Warshaw also separate their underlying policy measures to produce independent measures of economic and social issue policy liberalism, I find similar effects for each output (matching their analyses). Here I present results for the combined measure.

26 With different methodological choices, the measure would show significantly more over-time variation but less consistency in the ideological direction of policies. Grumbach (2018a); Sorens, Muedini, and Ruger (2008).

27 Caughey and Warshaw (2016).

28 Caughey and Warshaw (2016), with personal correspondence. They compared their measure with one assessing which states prioritize public goods such as parks over distributive policies like welfare, showing policy liberalism to be negatively correlated with that measure (conservative states spent relatively more on public goods such as security and parks compared to distributing benefits to particular constituencies). The relationship was only strong on the liberal end of the spectrum. The comparison was with a measure developed by Jacoby and Schneider.

29 Caughey, Xu, and Warshaw (2017).

30 See Associated Press. "Buono, Christie Hurl Barbs in Final Gubernatorial Debate." October 15, 2013. Available at: https://newyork.cbslocal.com/2013/10/15/buono-christie-to-face-off-in-final-gubernatorial-debate/.

31 Caughey, Xu, and Warshaw (2017).

32 Caughey, Xu, and Warshaw (2017).

33 Caughey, Xu, and Warshaw (2017).

34 Caughey and Warshaw (2018).

35 Caughey and Warshaw (2018).

36 Caughey and Warshaw (2018).

37 A one standard deviation increase in the public's social liberalism increases Democratic control by 5 percent of the distance from full Republican to full Democratic control; an equivalent increase in economic liberalism increases party control by only 2 percent of that distance.

38 Caughey and Warshaw (2018).

39 Grumbach (2018c).
40 Sorens, Muedini, and Ruger (2008).
41 Shor and McCarty (2011).
42 For those that want to see the full range of outcomes, I have archived the many models and robustness checks we ran with slight variations, along with all the underlying data, on my website. The results presented in this chapter are representative of the broader findings.

4 CONSERVATIVE DILEMMAS IN ACTION

From 2012 to 2017, states collectively increased general appropriations funding for pre-kindergarten education by 47 percent, with ten states moving toward near-universal provision and only six states declining to fund pre-kindergarten programs.[1] States use everything from lotteries to tobacco settlements to fund the programs, which enroll 33 percent of US four-year-olds – more than double the number enrolled in federal programs. One third of gubernatorial State of the State addresses in 2018 specifically highlighted their state's pre-kindergarten programs, including new initiatives from Republican governors in states such as Mississippi, New Mexico, Alabama, and New Hampshire.[2] Twenty-nine out of 36 winning gubernatorial candidates in the 2018 elections embraced early childhood education, including newly elected Republicans in Ohio, Arkansas, and Idaho.[3] The programs are expensive and, once established, tend to grow in both in the number of children enrolled and the cost per student. Although this represents a classic welfare state expansion that is closely tied to liberal goals in national politics, the steady increase in programs and funding since 1995 (when Georgia initiated the current wave by universalizing eligibility) has been nationwide and largely bipartisan.

That history differs markedly from recent trends in gun control, where conservative Republican states have been swiftly deregulating firearms, in contrast to Democratic states, which have increased controls.[4] The gun sale boom and increased National Rifle Association (NRA) advocacy greeting the Obama presidency led to the enactment of 292 state laws increasing gun access accompanied by 205 new state gun control laws in the same period. From open and concealed carry to "stand your ground" laws to reduced waiting periods when purchasing guns, conservative states rolled back their already light gun regulations. Meanwhile, liberal states increased gun regulation, often following mass shootings. But even in this polarizing case, there were a few signs that the tide might be turning. After Parkland high school student protests, Florida modestly increased its gun controls; in the 2018 elections, groups in favor of gun control (for the first time) dramatically outspent the NRA.

Beyond the broad patterns reviewed in the previous chapter, issue- and state-specific determinants remain influential in state policymaking. They help to explain why liberal trends can continue nationally in some areas, such as early childhood education, while polarizing policy trends remain rampant in others, such as gun control. At any given time, state policymaking is collectively moving leftward on some issues, rightward on others, and in opposite directions by partisanship in still other areas. The patterns are not a random walk, with policy equally likely to drift in either direction. Instead, there are more persistent problems translating conservative policy goals into action that are apparent in assessments of individual states and specific issue histories.

I seek to track the areas where Republican policy gains have been most evident, as well as the issues where national trends were clearer. Republican-led policies were most common in social issues such as guns and abortion, while liberal policy gains continued in other social areas (such as gay rights) as well as on most economic issues. Other state policy changes have been consequences of federal policy or non-partisan social trends. Along with compiling and assessing quantitative research, I rely on a qualitative content analysis of policymaking in individual states, as well as interviews with state capitol reporters, to understand the determinants of Republican proposals' successes and failures. These local narratives address the need by Republican governors to balance budgets while responding to public needs and statewide opinions. Some of the most extensive conservative reformations achieved by Republicans have even been overturned after they have proven to have problematic and visible consequences. Democratic states have meanwhile continued to expand their agendas, often taking advantage of federal action. Both the broad patterns and the specific stories are important for understanding how partisan politics changes state policy.

Broad Studies of Policy Outputs

Quantitative political science and policy research has not ignored issue-area differences. Instead, there has been considerable attention paid to party effects on disparate policies in the states. One promising review looked at 32 different policy outputs and outcomes from 1941 to 2002. It used a regression discontinuity design to help uncover causal estimates of the effect of Republican versus Democratic governors after winning in close elections. Recall that this design looks for large differences in policy between bare Democratic winners and bare Republican winners to minimize the possibility that the association between governor partisanship and policy is the product of other differences between states that tend to vote Republican and those that tend to vote Democratic (the logic is that if a governor wins by one percentage point instead of losing by one percentage point, it does not signal lots of differences in background factors but can isolate the effect of the governor's victory). The review found no differences across nearly all of the measures, including those covering taxes, welfare, government employment, and revenue. One difference was higher minimum wages in states with Democratic governors, though some outcomes are liable to look statistically significant simply by chance when looking at so many at once.[5]

Other regression discontinuity studies find more differentiated effects.[6] Democratic governors, for example, are associated with states dedicating more resources to high-minority districts, even though overall effects on spending statewide are weak.[7] For example, Michigan Democratic governors may send more money to Detroit without increasing funding overall. Democratic governors also dedicate a higher share of state expenditures to hospitals and education, but with no overall effect because Republican governors spend more elsewhere.[8] Another study found that health care expenditures do not differ by party, but prescription drug costs do show partisan differences.[9] A broader study looked at the size of government, tax structure, and labor market regulation in the states from 1993 to 2009, finding that conservative Republican governors have been more active in deregulating labor markets, despite limited effects on taxes and the overall size of government.[10]

Other studies using traditional analyses of over-time changes within states have also found party-policy relationships that are specific to particular issue subcategories, with some applying only to legislative (rather than gubernatorial) partisanship. One analysis found that there was no relationship between economic freedom measures and full party control of state legislatures, but there were some tax effects for Republican legislatures.[11] In another, Democrats tended to spend more on redistributive programs, with Republicans spending more on developmental projects.[12] Another found that welfare reforms came with many types of work options emphasized by different states, including training, job search assistance, and child care; welfare generosity was greater in states with stronger political parties, rather than simply more liberal states.[13] Partisan effects might also depend on more complicated relationships between parties and interest groups. On gay rights policies, party control of government mattered only in religiously diverse states.[14] On education policy, for example, strong teachers' unions decrease performance-related pay policies, but the effect is especially strong in Republican states. Partisanship effects on charter schools and vouchers tend to depend on education group mobilization. Policy determinants may also change over time as more states adopt innovations: charter school adoption grew from 10 to 40 states from 1995 to 2003, with voucher adoption moving up more slowly to 10 states; performance-related pay came about much later.[15] Recall the evidence from Jacob Grumbach, who found that states had moved collectively rightward only in education, with Republican states also moving rightward on abortion, guns, and immigration, and all states moving leftward or remaining the same on most other issue areas.

Partisan Agendas and Achievements

Like quantitative models of state partisanship, qualitative reviews find varied effects that can depend on issue-specific ideas and interests, as well as state-specific or national trends. With the help of my research assistants Emily Jenkins and Iris Robare, I content-analyzed 18 book-length histories of policymaking across 15 states.[16] In total, we reviewed 163 books on state politics but chose these 18 as most closely matching our criteria: they were non-partisan, long-form narrative descriptions of legislatures and governors within particular states, covering as much of the era from the 1990s to today as possible. From these books, we sought to identify the most important legislative or gubernatorial policy proposals in each time period and draw from the authors' narrative descriptions of the politics surrounding them. We analyzed 92 total author explanations for the success or failure of particular proposals since the 1990s across the 15 states. For every proposal, we coded whether it was enacted into law; its primary issue area; whether the issue at stake had important implications for the state (according to the author); whether the debate was primarily along partisan lines; whether it was led by Republicans; and the factors judged important in its passage or failure. The procedure matches that used in my previous book on the history of federal policy change.[17]

Across the major policy proposals we analyzed, 77 percent were enacted into law. This is a much higher percentage than for all bills introduced in legislatures; but the passage rate is similar to those from federal analyses based on presidential proposals or major bills discussed in *Congressional Quarterly*. The authors were likely analyzing only those proposals that had been major policy initiatives and stood a chance of becoming law.

Figure 4.1 reports the issues covered in policy proposals reviewed in these books. The most common proposals concerned taxes, education, and health care (together compromising more than half of the proposals). These are all big-ticket items related to the state budget, and when combined with the next two categories (social welfare and the budget overall), it suggests that more than two-thirds of major policy proposals since the 1990s was related to the overall size and scope of government. Some education or health proposals also incorporated social issues, such as those related to charter schools or abortion, but they were usually small parts of much broader proposals. The qualitative literature thus suggests that, although much of the easy-to-count action in the states is in social issue domains, the most important debates each year often concern the overall budget and where to allocate resources.

Figure 4.2 reviews the factors mentioned in the success or failure of these proposals. According to the state policymaking histories, partisanship was the most common factor in driving policy success or failure – though no single element was judged important in a majority

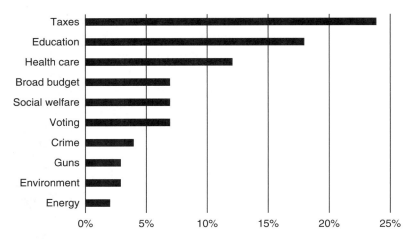

Figure 4.1 Primary issue areas of state policy proposals (analysis from author, based on 92 proposals across 15 states)

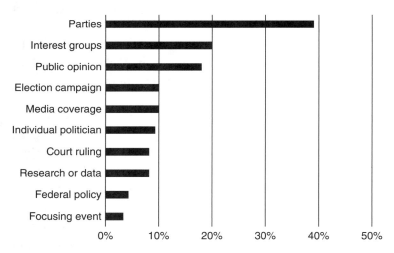

Figure 4.2 Author mentions of explanations for policy success or failure (analysis from author, based on 92 proposals across 15 states)

of cases. Other key factors included interest group pressure and public opinion, though many authors told multi-causal stories, some of which included interactions between a number of factors. The partisan stories more often concerned cooperation between legislative leaders and the governor (as well as support from associated interest groups), rather than campaign victories leading directly to policy change. Elections and media coverage were each judged relevant in only one in ten cases.

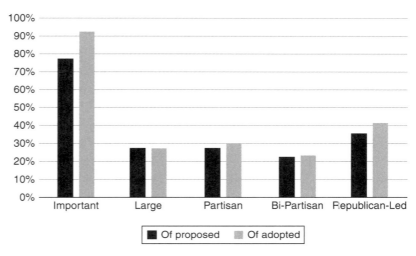

Figure 4.3 Characteristics of proposals and policies adopted (analysis from author, based on 92 proposals across 15 states)

Individual entrepreneurship by politicians, usually the governor, was mentioned in several cases, as were court rulings or new research or data on the size of problems. Federal frameworks or funding threats played a role in a few cases, but (despite the focus on policy diffusion in the state politics literature) no policy histories credited the copying of other states' policies as a factor. Major focusing events such as oil spills were also rare. Compared to my prior analysis of federal policy change, state political history authors see less influence coming from individual politicians, interest groups, and research, with equivalent influence coming from public opinion, media coverage, and courts.[18]

Figure 4.3 compares the characteristics of proposals and enacted policies. Most proposals were considered important to the state (at least in the view of the books' authors) and important proposals were more likely to be enacted into law. However, some proposals were considered more symbolic than important, and only a minority of these proposals passed. Just 27 percent of the proposals featured debates that the author identified as one party facing off against the other (others were multi-dimensional or bipartisan). Bipartisanship can be helpful, but rather than a sign of near-universal political support it can sometimes be an indicator that a governor or legislative leader does not have their own party caucus on their side. Only 26 percent of the proposals were clearly identified as being led by a Republican governor or legislative leader, which is somewhat surprising in an era of increased Republican control. But the Republican-led proposals were more likely to pass, often because the Democratic proposals came from Democratic governors during a period of divided government. The books suggested that Republican proposals often pass in revised form, often with some Democratic support.

Qualitative histories provide a chronology of events that acknowledge compromises politicians made along the way to success or failure. There were several stories of multiple attempts to address revenue shortfalls, education funding inequities, health coverage, sentencing reforms, and energy production. The products of these compromises were not usually characterized as liberal or conservative (by state historians), but often as extensions of previous efforts modified to appease various politicians and interest groups. Although the objectives of each governor and legislative session differed, the policy histories did not portray each set of politicians as having the power to set their own agenda regardless of circumstances. Instead, many issues were pushed onto the agenda by budgetary constraints or by the expiration or unworkability of previous policies. Looming large in all of this was the need to balance the state's budget, which was usually threatened more by economic circumstances and unforeseen policy results than by the plans of party leaders. State political histories thus see sustained policymaking challenges. Republicans have found no way to avoid the typical fiscal focus of state policymaking, limited by inevitable budget constraints.

The View from State Capitols

My interviews with state capitol reporters confirmed many of the above dynamics, illuminating the mechanisms by which Republicans propose policy change and respond to the constraints of their state institutions. I sought in particular to speak with long-time reporters who could comment on the last few decades (though this was not always possible). While concentrating mainly on states that had seen Republican gains, I also interviewed reporters in states that had maintained Republican or Democratic control, and even a few that had seen Democratic gains. I refer to reporters only by the state in which they work, as I promised anonymity to ensure openness.

The overall impression was that Republicans were less pro-lific than Democrats and more likely to run out of new policy prior-ities. They came to power mostly in already-conservative states, they were constrained by courts and executives, they squabbled over the largest changes, and they were forced to respond to events and rev-enue shortfalls. They did have success more in national efforts to move social issue policy rightward through cookie-cutter legislation, but they ran up against large roadblocks when trying to reduce the size of state government.

Conservative states are rarely motivated to quickly pursue a lot of new legislative action. "We are a state that doesn't like fast change," an Indiana reporter informed me, before adding: "We prefer to wait for others to act and don't mind if we're late." "Steady as she goes is what [the governor] would probably say his legacy is ... he's more of a manager than a leader," a Utah reporter told me, before commenting of the previous governor: "he was in office for so long, it would seem like he would have more of a legacy." "There was no great cry for [education reform] and nothing that stands out in health care," a South Dakota reporter said, "lawmakers have shown interest in [social welfare restrictions] but they don't pass ... they keep gov-ernment lean but are not willing to strike out for big new programs or changes." He continued: "there's an attitude of 'who cares what other states are doing'; it's more insular, and people are happy to go their own way." In South Carolina, "there's an annual feeling of what have we been talking about and why haven't we gotten anything done ... we say 'you guys are about to go home, why haven't you sent the governor anything to sign?'" Alabama recently had a "do nothing session ... they didn't really pass anything of real note," even letting a Democratic priority be the central bill of the session. According to the Alabama reporter: "The governor hasn't rolled out any major plans. She hasn't come out and held a press conference and introduced a major effort on anything. Her whole platform was 'steady the ship of state.'" The legislature seems to concur with that approach: "They work on a few things a year, work on them slowly, and see what happens." I did not encounter this attitude at all in Democratic states. Nationwide perceptions of active conservative policymaking may be skewed by the most high-profile efforts in states like North Carolina or Michigan or those led by colorful governors in states like Wisconsin and Kansas.

Part of the explanation for limited agendas elsewhere is that Republicans came to power in states that were already conservative. Southern states have seen the largest changes in partisanship, but already had right-leaning policies under Democrats. According to locals, this has meant less potential for change. As a Georgia reporter told me: "There hasn't been a monumental change. The Democrats who had been in charge were conservative. In some cases, like criminal justice, conservative government has led to less conservative policies." The Democrats in control previously were "in some cases in the legislature, even the same people who switched to the other party." Republicans also maintained power in already conservative states outside the South, where there was also less work to do. "You won't even hear fiscal conservatives saying cut sales taxes because that's all we have," said a South Dakota reporter, "they just say not to raise it, while increasing user fees." Utah, which has maintained Republican control throughout the period, saw some conservative moves such as significant tax cuts but also a move toward reduced social conservative influence.

Republicans often had a lot to learn before being able to act effectively in the states where they gained control. "Democrats had all this institutional knowledge," a Georgia reporter told me. "Republicans had to catch up. That put the brakes on lots of conservative legislation." South Carolina Governor Mark Sanford "came in with a cheapskate reputation trying to control the budget, but it was contentious with the legislature because lawmakers had been there a long time and liked their process." Reversing legislator-friendly traditions of district-favoring appropriations and budget priorities is an uphill battle.

Republican majorities also often feel like calling it a day after a round of success. "The majority came with an agenda, mostly achieved it, and ran out of new things to do," an Indiana reporter told me, while a North Carolina reporter claimed: "The legislature was not very ambitious last time; they figured they had already done most of what they wanted."

There were also significant constraints. Many high-profile Republican initiatives were caught up in the courts. "It's government by litigation, a lot of things have gone to court," a North Carolina reporter said, citing gay marriage, transgender bathroom bans, and other social issues. Immigration and health care laws were "mostly undone by the courts" in Arizona. Abortion laws were shot down by courts in Oklahoma. Courts also drove new legislation, such as prison reform in Alabama and increased social worker spending in Michigan and Oklahoma. After courts limited Alabama's restrictive immigrant work legislation, a reporter said, "it hasn't really come back up." After passing hardline immigration legislation, Georgia also softened it due to a backlash.

Other initiatives are foreclosed by direct democracy. Georgia voters rejected the governor's plan for a state takeover of failing schools. Ohio tried to pursue anti-collective-bargaining initiatives, but labor unions put it on the ballot and reversed it easily, "chastening the governor" and limiting further anti-union pushes. "No one wants another Senate Bill 5 [the union legislation]," an Ohio reporter said. Voters foiled abortion ban attempts in South Dakota. A Florida reporter sees "a growing use of ballot initiatives to get around a legislature that won't do things," citing increased education funding.

Sometimes internal Republican conflict jeopardizes action. "Even where the governor and legislature are controlled by Republicans, they never seem to agree – no matter the issue," said a South Carolina reporter. "That is why very little gets done around here, even like other places where there is a party split." A North Carolina reporter said: "It's herding cats in the Republican caucus, a lot more [ideological and regional] factions than in the Democrats." They added that fights regularly broke out between Republican-aligned business interests and social issue activists. In Kansas, a more moderate legislative leadership constrained some backbench right-wing action. In Kentucky, meanwhile, a more moderate Senate constrained the House. The same was true in Oklahoma, with a reporter saying that "bills that grab headlines when they come out of the House tend to wither when they get to the Senate." A Florida reporter told me that attempts to privatize several state services had been "thwarted by moderates in the Senate." Bills also often get stuck in the South Carolina Senate, where the chamber leaders wait out the end of the session. Beyond chamber disputes, other Republican divides include urban and suburban versus rural (Oklahoma), major metropolitan versus outlying areas (Utah), social versus economic conservatives (South Carolina), and south versus north versus middle (Alabama). In Utah, the Mormon Church also drives action, rightward in most areas but also toward more liberal immigration and criminal justice laws.

Governors also sometimes lose their ideological stridency once they take office. Kentucky Governor Matt Bevin "lost his Tea Party reputation" once he had to deal with state budget politics. Arizona Governor Doug Ducey tried to "shift the tone" by minimizing discussion of the divisive social issue debates that the prior governor, Jan Brewer, had engaged in; that included Ducey's liberalization of gay rights and his active avoidance of the immigration issue. In Florida, Republican Governor Charlie Crist came in as a moderate who reached out to unions and later became a Democrat. His successor Rick Scott "has an ideology that changed every election year. He came in as a Tea Party Guy, now running as a moderate, almost the opposite of where he started." Three Republican Utah governors in a row, according to a local reporter, "tried to lead from the middle compared to the legislature. It is the standard dynamic of becoming more moderate when you come into office versus trying to appeal to party activists to be nominated."

Governors are often forced to address good government concerns: in Georgia, "The Governor wanted warm relations, but the legislature wanted more tax cuts. The Governor also had to worry about jeopardizing the bond ratings." In Michigan, Governor Rick Snyder tried to address public employee legacy costs and had to bail out the city and school district in Detroit. He went along with union-targeting laws such as right-to-work but slowed some tax cuts and vetoed some social legislation. In Ohio, a reporter told me "either the Republican Party left John Kasich or he left it. He was able to get Medicaid expansion approved and they went along with it, but then they parted ways."

Some states did experience major conservative success, but it did not always last. In North Carolina, "they tried a lot and accomplished almost everything," though some gains were overturned by courts. In Kansas, Sam Brownback was "the most conservative governor ever, pushing the supply side experiment further" but it was a "massive debacle they're slowly unwinding … Now there's no desire to return to the Brownback drama." Kentucky passed a lot of legislation within the first week of having full legislative control – while much of it remained in force, later sessions were devoted to the persistent budget problems that resulted.

Some experiments end in scandal. Ohio pursued "school choice enthusiastically," a reporter said. Their voucher program remained small, but charters grew vigorously until a scandal with an online charter school exposed financial waste and apparently corrupt ties with charter school operators. Several other governors over the period were caught up in major political corruption scandals, which often reduced their agenda to being purely about self-defense. Democratic governors Rod Blagojevich, Edwin Edwards, and Don Siegelman, as well as Republican governors John Rowland and George Ryan, were convicted of corruption. On the Republican side, Governor Robert Bentley resigned in disgrace, Bob Taft was ordered to apologize to Ohio, Fife Symington was convicted of extortion, and Guy Hunt was placed on probation. Meanwhile, Democrat Jim Guy Tucker was convicted of fraud. A Republican legislative affair scandal and attempted cover up also diverted the Michigan legislature.

Events also sometimes force change. Florida Republicans enacted gun control following the Parkland shooting. In South Carolina, "our entire last session was almost all devoted to a nuclear project, where the provider cancelled, and the state still has to pay." In Alabama, the BP oil spill response was central, with the monetary settlement associated with the spill then resulting in years of controversies over how to spend the money. The "tug of war over a new pot of money," a reporter said, meant parochial concerns drove legislative negotiations more than conservative priorities.

Some Republican governments are remembered for issue-specific successes, often tied to the agenda of ALEC, the American Legislative Exchange Council. Michigan and Kentucky pursued right-to-work and prevailing wage laws supported by the group. "We've had some tort reform to minimize lawsuits, with groups like ALEC calling the shots," said a Utah reporter. In South Carolina, "one set of bills on abortion come up in each session; there's always something." In Florida, meanwhile, "The biggest change is education, testing in everything, closing the gaps, and large vouchers." The reporter added that Governor Jeb Bush's efforts presaged the federal No Child Left Behind changes. Bush brought most of the change, the reporter said, despite being considered more moderate in today's Republican Party: "There has been a lot of change that stuck; the workers compensation program slashed benefits." Some states, though, missed out on conservative action. Charter schools and vouchers were not a high-profile issue in Kansas, South Dakota, or Oklahoma. Union reforms were mostly absent in the low-union South and West. Gun laws were not changed as much in Oklahoma, partially due to vetoes. Overall, the areas of success tended to rely on national campaigns with straightforward and pre-baked legislative solutions, suggesting that conservative efforts to build cross-state institutions to push policy change were successful in spreading legislation but failed to increase Republicans' local capacities to find conservative solutions to specific state challenges.

Often, it seemed to local observers that Republican rhetoric about smaller government did not lead to real proposals to limit the size and scope of government. In Alabama, a reporter says, "nothing of note has occurred" on the size of government, even though it is mentioned in campaigns. In Connecticut, Republicans focus on "taxes and budgets and the economy only and nothing else," though they rarely have much control. Budget problems driven by economic circumstances dominated discussions in many states, regardless of partisanship. Pension crises were difficult to deal with in Kentucky and Connecticut, where both parties' governors made deals with public employee unions that they later tried to limit as they consumed so much of the budget. In Oklahoma, "the legislature has been single-focused on the budget, everything else goes to the wayside … It's more to do with the actual economic situation than who is in power." Some states fail to solve their perennial problems. In Georgia, "Education allotment has long been a problem and never fully funded by either party." Despite child welfare being viewed as a big bipartisan problem in Florida and South Carolina, they have not agreed on a comprehensive fix. Other states, such as Utah and Florida, have positive economic and population trends that enable increased spending without policy change. Spending has also risen faster under Republicans in North Carolina, despite tax cuts – but because of economic gains, a reporter said, they did not have to choose.

On taxes, many successes involved trading consumption tax increases for income tax cuts, sometimes enacted over several years, such as those in Kansas, Kentucky, and Oklahoma.

A Florida reporter said the state "cut corporate and income taxes and shifted the burden to the locals, but it was never a high revenue state under the Democrats, never flush." Utah cut taxes overall but increased gas taxes. South Carolina is moving in the same direction but has not yet agreed on any overhaul, despite many gubernatorial proposals. Other states cut and shifted the tax burden, regardless of who was in charge and based more on the state of the economy: "Ohio has been a tax cutting state," a reporter told me, "[Democratic Governor Ted] Strickland delayed a tax cut for one year but went along. [Republican Governor John] Kasich has not gotten his full way, but income taxes are declining while sales taxes increase. They're spending the surplus on tax cuts. Strickland didn't have that [option] because the roof fell in economically, so spending actually grew more slowly under him."

Criminal justice reform was largely bipartisan, despite this seeming to go against traditional Republican "tough on crime" rhetoric. An Oklahoma reporter old me, "I'd get in trouble if I call it liberal, but [Republicans] did turn away from their previous position" on sentencing and drug laws. That is what Governor Mary Fallin "will be remembered for." Georgia also followed Texas, the leader in conservative moves against imprisonment, with reforms "pitched as conservative but moving left. It was Governor Deal's signature policy achievement." In South Carolina, a prison riot focused attention but, after lots of debate, no legislation went forward.

Other common bipartisan efforts (in Oklahoma and Michigan, for example) included court-driven reforms to child welfare agencies (usually involving more caseworkers), and reforms to mental health services (usually involving increased expenditure). When large federal dollars are at stake, they are pursued jointly by Republicans and Democrats in South Dakota, where everyone loves wind power and mining projects. Education program expansions are often started by Democrats but later embraced by Republicans. In Georgia, there was a big expansion of pre-kindergarten and college scholarships which everyone touts, and no one says they will cut. In Alabama, the state's prior pre-kindergarten programs are held up by both parties, since it is seen as the one area where the state does not rank near the bottom.

Several reporters, including those in North Carolina, Kentucky, Arizona, and Oklahoma, mentioned that the 2018 teacher protests, or threats of walkouts, had changed Republican governance dramatically. In Kentucky, "The Republicans were more liberal this session due to threats from the teachers, where they have direct local interests at stake." In Arizona, "the debates changed dramatically in response to the teacher protests, Red for Ed." Citing a new budget debate and education funding, the reporter told me: "this year will probably go down as a marked shift." The teacher protests also accelerated leftward trends in other states, such as Oklahoma: "They raised taxes last year. It was building but the teacher walkout was the catalyst ... Budget shortfalls redirected the policy agenda [to tax increases] along with the teachers." South Dakota also boosted teacher salaries via tax increases, after a compromise with new online sales taxes. The successful pushback against spending cuts (that even motivated tax increases) constitutes a fundamental constraint on conservative policymaking and highlights an important distinction with federal policy. Whereas US Congressional Republicans can cut taxes and increase defense spending without affecting public services (due to deficit spending), that option is not usually open in the states: budgetary trade-offs are real and immediately noticed by constituents.

How do these reports compare to those in states that have been moving toward Democrats? Colorado experienced "a big surge to the left starting about 14 years ago, led by the four horsemen [a group of liberal legislators and funders]. They were well-funded and focused on social issues." But change was still limited: "There was lots of gridlock. Spending formulas are based on population and not easily shifted. The Democrats were pro-business and wanted economic development too." Despite this, they were able to pass gun control, social welfare expansions, and environmental policies. California, according to a reporter, has become the most liberal state on gun control, abortion, climate change, and immigration. Fiscal matters, though, are somewhat different; Governor Jerry Brown is "not as profligate as free spending lawmakers but did get the voters to increase taxes." Pre-kindergarten and early childhood programs have also grown, but the state has resisted a single-payer health care system despite liberal lawmaker interest. Connecticut moved leftward, raising the minimum wage several times, eliminating the death penalty, enacting criminal justice reform, passing sick leave, bailing out the City of Hartford, expanding Medicaid, endorsing gay rights, enacting strict gun control, and raising income taxes across the board. But the state's public employee liabilities mean that there is no budget available for new programs. Governors from both parties later tried to reduce the unionized workforce, but with limited success; in response, both parties have cut aid to localities.

Democratic governors' legacies tended to involve creating institutions, such as building the community college system, new scholarship programs, or revising mental health administration. Democratic governors in Florida were remembered for education reform and bringing in tobacco settlement funds. Even when revenue is tight, as in California, governors pursue large-scale items such as high-speed rail, water infrastructure, and energy regulation. Some Republican governors also want to get in on the legacy-creating by building new institutions or enhancing university systems.

Overall, my conversations with state legislative reporters were consistent with the cross-state quantitative analyses and the qualitative state-specific histories. Democrats are more motivated to pursue new programs and policies than Republicans, with Republican governments often mixing conservative priorities with maintenance of liberal programs. Non-partisan factors – such as budget constraints, economic gains or losses, disasters and events, or even social protests – affect policy across states. The most strident conservative moves in the states are often short-lived and liable to be partially reversed. Liberalizing state trends, such as criminal justice reform, mental health changes, gay rights laws, or education expansion, sometimes propagate regardless of who is in power. Republican policy gains are not uniform: some states pursue more hot button social issues while others focus on tax reforms or anti-unionization efforts. Democrats tend to have larger across-the-board agendas, though they still face significant budget constraints in many states.

The interviews also helped clarify some of the mechanisms behind conservative constraints. First, Republicans inherited more states that were already conservative, which meant they had slower-moving legislative cultures and entrenched but limited budgets. Second, conservative campaign messages often get transformed once legislators – and especially governors – move to real policymaking. Responsibility for balancing budgets, overseeing state employees, and responding to court challenges, interest groups, and voters tend to promote moves toward less policy transformation (in particular, curtailing the elimination of programs or policies) and more compromises. Third, although states respond to national trends in conservative and liberal legislation, everyday policymaking revolves around relatively stable tax and budget structures, where there is little room for maneuver. States often have few real tools available to transform fiscal policy, with the conservative options becoming less enticing once real cuts are on the table. Unlike in the federal government, both parties have to respond to real-world changes in revenue flows or unexpected expenditures. If tax revenues fall, cuts have to be made or new taxes added. Cuts to education, health, or transportation spending become quickly visible and unpopular.

The Fall of Wisconsin?

No state has generated more attention for its recent move rightward than Wisconsin. As journalist Dan Kaufman writes in his book *The Fall of Wisconsin*, the concentrated publicity is a product of both the state's long legacy of progressivism, which included its prior enshrinement of the University of Wisconsin's role in policymaking in the form of the "Wisconsin idea," and the dramatic and widely covered union-led capitol protests and recall attempts targeting Scott Walker.[19]

Wisconsin has indeed moved rightward on policy relative to neighboring states such as Minnesota; it was a primary site for the increasing influence of the Koch brothers' network and ALEC.[20] The state's conservative trajectory has also taken on national significance. In *The Politics of Resentment*, political scientist Katherine Cramer explained Walker's rise as a product of rural resentment, leading many commentators to see Walker as a prototype for the later rise of Donald Trump (which was not coincidentally based on wins in upper-Midwest states, including Wisconsin).[21]

However, the usual interpretation – that Republicans massively overstepped their state's public to make the state a conservative policy bastion – is not quite right. Figure 4.4 illustrates changes over time in Wisconsin economic policy and public opinion on economic issues.[22] Wisconsin was controlled by Republicans for most of the twentieth century,[23] and the progressive build-up in the size and scope of Wisconsin government mostly occurred under Republicans. Wisconsin has long had very liberal economic policies (relative to other states), even with a public that has average views. It remained among the ten most liberal states from 1949 to 1996, even though its public held economic policy opinions a bit more conservative than those of the average state. Economic policy has moved rightward since 1990 in Wisconsin, along with public opinion. Like other states, the public has become strikingly more socially liberal – while policy has remained more stable. But Wisconsin is still well to the left of the average state on social issue and economic policy, remaining the fourteenth most liberal state on economics. In other words, Wisconsin built a liberal government despite

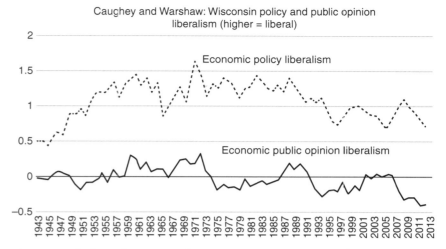

Figure 4.4 Ideological positions of Wisconsin economic policy and economic public opinion (the ideological position of the Wisconsin public and Wisconsin policy over time on economic policy issues. Data from Caughey and Warshaw (2016))

Republican control and a moderate public, giving later Republicans room to move policy rightward. The state's progressive tradition was mostly an elite-led consensus that conservatives have tried to undo, not a set of policies built by public consensus. Public-sector collective bargaining is a useful example in this regard: although not a product of voter demands, its adoption fueled a rise in unionization that benefited Democrats electorally; its dissolution should likewise be expected to benefit Republicans without becoming the top voter concern.[24]

Under Walker's leadership, Republicans reduced collective bargaining rights for public employees (except the police and fire sectors); enacted a right-to-work law and additional constraints on union organizing; enabled energy projects despite environmental risks; enacted voter identification requirements; successfully gerrymandered state legislative districts; and limited funding and governing independence for state universities. These are impressive achievements from a conservative point of view: that is among the most conservative records of recent states. Due to typical voter backlashes to major policy change, it may have been enough to contribute to Walker's 2018 loss. At the same time, these policies do not quite constitute across-the-board conservative retrenchment. They did not bring Wisconsin anywhere near conservative states like those in the South. They brought a liberal state more in line with its moderate public.

A Closer Look at Specific Policy Areas

Like studies of specific states, analyses of particular issue areas are also instructive. To provide a closer study of the particular dynamics at play and help match the more specific agenda items identified as Republican successes in prior work, I (along with my research assistant Babs Hough) studied four policy areas where Republicans were able to make change: abortion, charter schools, taxes, and unions. I located 21 studies of the specific determinants of state policy change in these areas to assess how partisanship interacted with other factors to produce policy change, the size of the partisan effects, and the commonly achieved policy ends.[25] One benefit of these studies is that they are designed to assess all the factors relevant to these policy outcomes, rather than simply track the effects of partisanship. This enables comparisons of influence across different determinants.

Abortion politics is an interesting case of both continuity and dramatic change. On the one hand, abortion has been legal in every state since 1972 – states do not have the power to change its legality and face court scrutiny on attempts to make abortion more difficult to secure. On the other hand, this is perhaps the clearest case where laws have changed following Republican partisanship of states, with many proposals by pro-life groups enacted into law. Policies such as parental or spousal consent requirements, information and counseling requirements, pregnancy term conditions, clinic access and security regulations, and surgical health requirements have all made progress in the states. Data on the restrictiveness of abortion laws is easy to come by, with surprising consensus across researchers and even pro-choice and pro-life groups. Four of the six studies I reviewed found an effect of state partisanship, with Democratic states passing less restrictive abortion laws. The effect of partisanship was weaker than expected in some cases, however, with factors such as public opinion, grassroots activism, constitutional history, initiative and referendum procedures, and Catholic population also mattering. Researchers found less capacity for majority parties to move policy against public opinion in a state; rather, states were increasingly matching policy with prior public opinion on abortion.

Charter school policies provide another useful example of state policy sorting by partisanship. Originally, charters were neither more encouraged nor plentiful in conservative states (and were promoted nationally by Bill Clinton and other Democrats), but the issue became increasingly partisan over the course of the 1990s and 2000s. This leads to conflicting studies on the impact of majority parties. When researchers look for which states were consistent innovators in this area, they find more historical continuity and less partisan influence. However, when they look at changes in whether charters are allowed, as well as the number allowed since the 1990s, they find stronger partisan effects. Two of the six studies I reviewed found an effect of state partisanship (divergence of findings was partially driven by different measurement of charter policy). Only one study found that gubernatorial partisanship affected the extent or nature of charter school policy. Nevertheless, Republican states have lately been expanding charters more often. Factors such as state diversity, urban population, regional diffusion, and school quality were also found to be important in some studies. Private school vouchers were the more conservative-driven policy; once freed to offer them by the courts, five states did so for many poor students, another six did for students with disabilities, and a few more offered them for students without local public schools (but vouchers cover less than 1 percent of students in voucher states).[26]

Tax policy studies find a more consistent pattern in policy preferences, with Democrats favoring a tax code that is more progressive, but party preferences do not always generate different results. Three of the six studies I reviewed found little direct impact of partisan control of state government, though there was some evidence that unified Republican control had an impact. There was little evidence of diffusion in tax policy, but factors such as union membership, population age distribution, common industries, and economic performance did matter in some cases. Due to constitutional provisions and path dependence, state reliance on property, sales, and income taxes is relatively stable (as is, in some cases, the allowed progressivity of income taxes). States often move together in response to opportunities for taxation that arise; in the wake of the US Supreme Court's 2018 decision in *South Dakota* v. *Wayfair*, nearly all states are now rushing to tax online sales. In this quintessential Republican-owned policy issue area, despite there being some evidence of success (including high-profile cases of major changes), the ability to make traditionally liberal states more like traditionally conservative states on tax policy is quite constrained.

State policies designed to reduce unionization (especially in the public sector) and union benefits have been a central aim of conservative think tanks, the network associated with the Koch brothers, and ALEC. It is not difficult to understand why: unions are among the biggest supporters of Democrats while also serving as symbols of liberal policy. Most of the issue-specific research, however, has focused on the extent to which these policy changes were an outcome of prior union strength in the states. Three broad studies of state labor legislation did find some partisan effects on right-to-work law adoption, increasing retirement ages for public employees, and collective bargaining restrictions. When it comes to union benefits, however, studies find that unions have actually been more influential in preventing benefit cuts in Republican states.[27] In union-related policies, Republicans have led high-profile moves – such as Scott Walker's efforts to eliminate collective bargaining for some public-sector workers. Seven states enacted right-to-work laws during the period, though three were under Democratic or mixed party control. These salient changes have been accompanied by less change in other areas like pensions and health benefits, with those changes often driven more by continuing nationwide declines in private sector unionization and rising public sector legacy costs than by partisanship. Republicans' efforts have been targeted primarily at teachers' unions, especially where they donate more to Democratic candidates, and have largely avoided targeting public safety unions.[28]

Republicans have thus had some limited success in changing policies related to abortion, charter schools, taxes, and unions. But again, matching the broader evidence across all policy areas, they have not been able to push traditionally liberal states into becoming overtly conservative. In other areas, such as right-to-work legislation and taxes, they have pursued large-scale changes limited to a smaller number of states. In all cases, partisanship ranks among several influential factors, including some that are issue-specific and others that are widespread (such as a dependence on public opinion or economic circumstances).

The ALEC Agenda

Many of these policy areas were part of the concerted effort by ALEC – in league with conservative think tanks, grassroots organizations, and industry partners – to move state policy in a conservative direction. It is thus worth examining ALEC's agenda and success in detail. The history of ALEC suggests it was designed to counteract perceived imbalances, where Democratic interest groups previously had closer access to (and more influence on) state policymakers.[29] ALEC initially tried to gain adherents in both parties and even its Republican members were initially no more conservative than the broader Republican Party. Since the 1970s, it has increasingly encompassed the most conservative legislators in the Republican caucus of each state and evolved its policy aims from a focus on social issues to a broader conservative agenda from taxes to health care.[30]

In addition to the issue areas I review above, several other ALEC priorities have been the subject of research. ALEC has led a push for tort reform legislation, which has been widely successful, at least in terms of bill introductions: 23 states introduced bills capping lawsuit damages, 34 targeted punitive damages specifically, and 38 tried to set a maximum liability.[31] As in union policy, the goal was in part political: by forcing trial lawyers to defend their existing legal remedies, they were prevented from spending more widely in support of Democratic politicians and causes. But conservatives were also successful in dramatically limiting torts in some states, such as Texas and Utah. The group was especially influential in medical liability reform.

ALEC came to public attention after the Trayvon Martin shooting, when advocacy groups uncovered how the organization had successfully laid the groundwork for "castle doctrine" and "stand your ground" laws justifying firearm use on self-defense grounds. Twenty-three states, mostly conservative and Republican-controlled, have passed strong forms of these laws, though many liberal states have long incorporated similar principles in their broader self-defense statutes. These new laws, usually pursued with the support of the NRA as well as ALEC, have been influential, but they have not been as broadly enacted as extensions of right-to-carry laws.

ALEC's most widely copied bill is a package of seven education proposals aimed at creating charter schools, providing private school vouchers, evaluating teachers, reducing union constraints, and encouraging private contracting. This reflects the broader education reform agenda of recent years – though ALEC and conservative legislators should get some credit for pushing it forward, it has also gained steam from billionaire (mostly Democratic) philanthropists such as Eli Broad and Bill Gates.[32] With the exception of vouchers, these proposals sit comfortably within the education reform agendas of three consecutive

US presidents: Bill Clinton, George W. Bush, and Barack Obama. Much of the successful legislation increasing competition in state education was, in fact, passed in the wake of Obama's "Race to the Top" initiative, in which the federal government awarded states points in a competition for federal grants based on whether they aligned their policies with reform goals.[33] Once policy adoptions led by Obama's initiative are accounted for, party control of the governor or legislature no longer had any significant influence on whether these education reforms were adopted. State charter school policies also converged somewhat across states after adoption, as policymakers listened to proponents and opponents of the initial policies and reacted to policy results.[34] Expanding choice in education is, in one sense, one of the conservative movement's most successful policy trajectories. On the other hand, it has often involved increased public-school funding and succeeded through sustained federal inducement and Democratic support.

Higher education funding has been declining over time as a share of state budgets, though not primarily due to conservative organizing or Republican efforts. One determinant of higher education funding is decidedly parochial: in cases where more state legislators used to attend their states' public institutions, state funding for public higher education rises (and even the share of particular campus alums is associated with funding for those specific campuses).[35] Partisan effects actually show slightly more Republican support for higher education, especially relative to K-12 funding.[36] Republican politicians also made a few high-profile proposals for state interference in faculty tenure and academic policy, but most fizzled rather than transform campus.

ALEC has also been active in asking states to pass pre-emption laws to overrule potential local liberal actions such as bans on plastic grocery bags. But the effort has had only mixed success. The pre-emption attempts arose as conservatives were losing more local policymaking battles in large cities; many statutes that had been passed were later successfully challenged in courts (who often sided with local governments) or stymied by local refusals to comply.[37] ALEC did succeed in diffusing state legislative bills against municipalities declaring themselves "sanctuary cities," where local police would not help enforce federal immigration law.[38] However, these laws followed liberalizing immigration policy by local governments and are also being battled in the courts.

Other immigration policymaking has been mixed. One study comparing integrative (supportive) and punitive state immigration policies found they were not arranged along a single left–right continuum, and that cross-state relationships often differed from the variables causing within-state changes in immigration law.[39] A majority of studies have found no partisan effects on particular immigration statutes, with some pointing in different partisan directions even within the punitive and integrative categories. Overall, though, there was an association between the number of restrictive policies and Republican partisanship. Most of the action has been responsive to federal administrative action under Obama and Trump, but many states are counteracting federal policy.[40]

In both immigration and health policy, the trends have been toward sorting Democratic and Republican states into the policy direction more closely aligned with statewide public opinion. Earlier mismatches between public opinion and state policy on immigration and health have dissipated as the issues have become more salient, taking on more central places in state agendas.[41]

Changing Political Rules to Favor Republicans

ALEC has also supported Republican efforts to reform political institutions to benefit the party. The spread of voter identification laws, especially those requiring photo identification, has been especially pronounced. Requesting identification of some kind had previously been adopted by several states on a bipartisan basis. However, after a 2005 federal commission recommended new strictures, Georgia and Indiana moved toward photographic requirements (not requests), starting a trend among Republican states. They were followed by strict photo requirements in Kansas, Mississippi, Tennessee, Wisconsin, Virginia, and North Dakota. Several other states had their requirements overturned or delayed by courts. Democrats often opposed the new initiatives, arguing that they disenfranchised racial minorities, and Republican states were far more likely to enact strict identification requirements.[42] The partisan pattern of enactment and expected electoral benefit was clear, but the public remained largely supportive of new identification requirements.

Republicans have also not been shy about using other powers to enhance their political position. They made good use of redistricting opportunities in 2000 and 2010, becoming more aggressive in packing Democrats into a few urban districts, thus ensuring Republican representation within state legislatures would be proportionately much higher than their share of the statewide vote. Democrats tried similar tactics (in states such as Maryland) and it remains possible that better mapping technology will in the future enable all parties to use redistricting to their pronounced benefit. However, the pattern of Democratic voters, politicians, and groups pursuing non-partisan redistricting reforms and court scrutiny of partisan redistricting suggests that Republicans favor more aggressive gerrymandering than Democrats.

There has also been a partisan difference in registration laws, with Republicans favoring earlier deadlines and Democrats favoring automated or Election-Day registration. In addition, Democrats want more in-person early voting as well as no-excuse-needed absentee voting, while Republicans prefer in-person Election-Day voting. The alignment is again rather easy to connect to partisan interests, with Democrats seeming to benefit from higher rates of voting among less reliable Election-Day voters. Since Republicans have been more likely to favor easing military voting opportunities, they seem to be restricting other voting opportunities in the hopes of limiting the Democratic vote share (some openly admit that goal). This should be counted as another area of Republican political success, especially after courts have significantly constrained voting rights challenges against new voting restrictions. However, the overall trend since the 1990s is toward dramatic increases in early voting and expanded registration opportunities, so Republicans may merely be slowing liberalization of voting rules rather than making voting harder over time. With 38 states now offering early voting, the number of people taking up the opportunity more than doubled between 2004 and 2016.[43]

Other efforts to change electoral rules have not yielded results. Several Republican states considered changing their distribution of Electoral College votes to benefit Republican presidential candidates, but all states other than (long excepted) Nebraska and Maine still allocate their votes to the winner of the state popular vote. Michigan had considered several plans to allocate some votes by congressional district or by a complicated statewide formula, but demurred just before the 2016 election, when the state unexpectedly went Republican – meaning that the laws (if enacted) would have actually benefited Democrats that year. Meanwhile, several mostly Democratic states have signed on to a state compact allocating their presidential votes to the winner of the national popular vote (rather than their state's winner), on the condition that enough states join the compact to comprise a majority of national electoral votes. These efforts are both worth watching in future elections but have yet to amount to real changes in practice.

Republicans are also now more willing to use aggressive "constitutional hardball" tactics to change governing institutions to benefit themselves. After three recent elections where they lost the governorship (North Carolina in 2016, and Wisconsin and Michigan in 2018), Republican state legislatures considered many rule changes (and enacted some) to reduce the power of the incoming Democratic governor relative to the legislature, such as changes in appointment powers and legal rights. Some also sought to aggressively limit the power of new Democratic state attorney generals or secretaries of state. The efforts were most extensive in Wisconsin, where Governor Walker signed bills transferring rulemaking and appointment powers from the governor to the legislature. These moves suggest that Republicans are quite willing to openly pursue changes in state law that enhance their power. Democratic states, by contrast, do not seem to be frequently adopting similar changes. Republican legislators likely expect to maintain long-term legislative control despite losing statewide, believing their seat to vote share advantage is systematic and impermeable to elections. They also seem to expect there to be no bipartisan achievements with new Democratic governors, meaning their actions are not jeopardizing future compromises they see as important.

Like Republicans in Congress, state legislative parties may believe that asymmetric hardball is in their interests, because executives will take the blame for any dysfunction that result from divided government. The focus on creating institutional blocks to Democratic actions, however, also suggests that Republican legislatures ran out of substantive policy agenda items they wanted to pass before they lost full control of government. Regardless, Republicans seem better able to unite behind political rules changes designed to benefit the party compared to broader substantive policy.

Liberal Trends in State Policy

Even during a period of Republican resurgence, liberals have been making substantial policy gains. Perhaps most surprising to previous generations is the recent speed of liberalization on state gay rights laws. Before the US Supreme Court legalized gay marriage nationwide, states went through a cycle: first, many banned gay marriage in the wake of Hawaii legalizing it in 1993, culminating in 11 voter-approved bans in the 2004 election; then states dramatically reversed course, with 33 legalizing gay marriage (in legislatures, courts, and ballot initiatives) between 2009 and 2014 preceding national legalization. Although states still differ on other gay rights policies, there has also been a dramatic nationwide expansion in sexual orientation anti-discrimination laws.

Many states have also begun passing environmental policies that are more restrictive than federal laws, including efforts to fight climate change. Republican states have largely not been innovators in environmental policy, but they have succeeded in blocking new liberal initiatives even when they only control one legislative chamber.[44] Renewable energy promotion has been more bipartisan. Thirty-eight states adopted a renewable portfolio standard or renewable energy goal, with every state adopting at least one policy aimed at encouraging clean energy production.[45] Liberal states, however, adopted more stringent requirements.

Drug law liberalization has also proceeded quickly. Marijuana is now legal for recreational use in 9 states and legal for medical use in another 22 states. States such as California and Arizona have also reduced penalties for other drug crimes. Public opinion suggests no imminent reversal of these trends, with increasing support for legalization. Reduced or eliminated penalties for these non-violent offenses have been part of a broader (and surprisingly bipartisan) trend in criminal justice.

Criminal Justice Reform

In their recent book, *Prison Break*, political scientists David Dagan and Steven Teles explore one of the most interesting liberalizing trends in American state politics since the 1990s: the move toward a less punitive criminal justice policy.[46] The oddest part of the story is that liberal foundations targeted conservative states and worked through conservative institutions such as ALEC, the Koch brothers' network, and the Federalist Society in order to successfully make their case for reform. The logic was that victory in a state like Texas with the support of conservative groups would inoculate the movement from charges it was weak on crime. The new conservative policy entrepreneurs argued that reformers had the true small government approach. Despite Trump being elected partially on "law and order" rhetoric, there has been no Republican return to tough-on-crime policies. Innovative reforming states such as Oklahoma, Georgia, and Texas are continuing without interruption along their path, despite the visible evidence that many Republican voters support the old approach. Even the federal government has now joined the states in bipartisan criminal justice reform.

After a multi-decade and national push toward longer sentences, treating juveniles as adults, and generally locking up criminals and throwing away the key, the recent pattern has been that states have liberalized policy.[47] The initial trend toward tougher policy had also been broadly favored: by the public, by politicians appealing to racism, and even by African-Americans seeking to police their communities.[48] The death penalty was also widely employed across states, but its use was associated with religious fundamentalism and crime rates rather than state partisanship.[49] The United States remains overwhelmingly punitive, leading to mass incarceration rates that dwarf those of other democratic countries. Even so, the trend has started to reverse. More prisons are closing and fewer are opening, while many states are overturning long sentences for non-violent crime as well as experimenting with accelerated release programs. The result is that incarceration is finally in decline.[50] Republican legislators are even pushing to end the death penalty in six states, while another ten states have banned or suspended it. One related counter-trend has been toward the privatization of prison services, which has been on an upswing as Republicans have taken control of state capitols.

This makes for an interesting case when interpreting the political effects of policy trends. On the one hand, Republican elected officials, donors, and interest groups were involved in promoting a somewhat successful policy transition. On the other, a long-time priority of conservatives (tough-on-crime policies) that had previously been extraordinarily successful reversed course just as Republicans took power in the states. Republicans were "successful" in adopting liberal priorities that go against their past views. In this respect, the policy history looks more like a successful strategy by liberal foundations and interest groups seeking to take on the hardest cases first. What is more, Democratic states are following the same trends and may start to be even more aggressive.

Economic Populism

At the same time as Republicans have been making gains in the states, economic inequality has been rising along with its visibility. Liberals have been seeking more concrete state action to combat inequality and are seeing some results. In *The New Economic Populism*, political scientists William Franko and Christopher Witko find that liberals are making significant under-the-radar progress, sometimes due to Democratic control and sometimes due to other factors.[51] Republicans in Democratic states (such as Charlie Baker) have supported minimum wage increases and equal pay laws.[52] The minimum wage is increasing even in many conservative states, especially those threatened by the ballot initiative; workers saw 2019 increases in 20 states. The Earned Income Tax Credit (EITC) is also increasing, especially in states with growing public awareness of inequality, but has been adopted more in states with the most liberal governments. State tax progressivity has been associated with union membership, public liberalism, and state policy liberalism.

Liberal think tanks such as those affiliated with the Economic Policy Institute and Center on Budget and Policy Priorities were quite effective at advocating for EITCs and other economic policies even in Red states, often with the support of Republican moderates and business groups.[53] In many ways, though, the failure of Republican states to swiftly enact new economic policies in response to rising inequality is a significant effect of partisan control of government. The decisions to expand Medicaid, the scale of minimum wage increases, and the mandated benefit levels of family and sick leave policies, all represent areas that moved leftward in the states overall but moved far less quickly in Republican states. To Democrats, these were straightforward responses to rising social risks, with failure to act often equivalent to legislating increases in inequality.

The Liberal Agenda Ahead

In the 2018 elections, Democrats took full control of several additional states with a broad agenda of potential lawmaking in mind. Many liberal activists claim to have learned from Republican organizing at the state level, seeing their prior focus on national government as myopic and ineffective. What are they likely to achieve? New Jersey Democrats, who took control in 2017 based on their off-year gubernatorial election, may provide a useful early indicator. In their initial term, they enacted Planned Parenthood funding, equal pay and sick leave laws, automatic voter registration, renewable energy and climate regulation, and gun restrictions, but were unable to reach agreement on broader tax and budget reforms. This agenda reflects a pattern: Democratic-controlled states are more reactive than Republican ones to national politics, pushing liberal policies more aggressively when Republicans have control of national government (particularly in Western and Northeastern states).[54]

Democrats are also seeking to use newfound powers to expand voting and reverse Republican-benefiting restrictions.[55] Six states implemented automatic voter registration in 2018 and more have introduced new measures in 2019. Online registration is now available in 38 states. Several states are looking at restoring voting rights to ex-felons, after 2018 voters approved that measure in Florida. In 2019, New York immediately enacted a new ten-day early voting period and other states are exploring expansions of early or mail voting.

Given historical trends, the effort so far looks ambitious but not revolutionary. California Governor Gavin Newsom has proposed six months of paid parental leave. Left-wing think tanks and activists, especially those oriented around the 2016 presidential campaign of Bernie Sanders, have recently proposed broader policies such as universally free college education and state-provided health care. These efforts have so far met with limited success, with single-payer state health efforts failing in Vermont and California, and education reforms having focused on more limited expansions of need-based aid and community college. Even so, newly elected liberal legislators, especially in now fully controlled Democratic states such as Colorado, New York, and Washington, seem intent on expanding the policy agenda and the scope of policy proposals. Nothing has been taken off the prior agenda, but more has been added. As liberals fight the Trump administration, they have also moved battles on issues like climate change to the states, expecting Democratic-controlled governments to both resist federal change and to unilaterally address the problems without federal help. After Trump pulled out of the Paris Climate Agreement, for example, 16 states formed an alliance and committed themselves to following through on the Agreement. Democratic states, if liberal activists get their way, will become sites of go-it-alone policymaking – replacing federal action under Trump.

Assessing Policy Revolutions

Although the broad scope of American state government was mostly settled by the time Republicans rose to power in the last quarter-century, the states have still been active in changing policy. Some state policymaking trends (new right-to-work laws, tort reforms, and private school voucher programs) clearly reflect Republican influence, while others (education reforms emphasizing charter schools and teacher accountability schemes) reflect both conservative movement success and aligned factors such as interest group pressure and federal policy. Other policymaking trends, though, seem to point in a liberal direction. This is despite such policy – for example, criminal justice reform and expanded state-provided early childhood education – often being enacted with Republican support. Still other trends show liberal advance despite some Republican opposition, such as marijuana legalization and increasing gay rights.

According to close watchers of individual state politics, including the authors of state political histories and state capitol reporters, many of these policy trends are not those at the top of policymakers' agendas. Instead, policymaking revolves around the usual, broader fights over state budgets and spending priorities. In these battles, the size of government and the sources of revenues can only be modified at the edges to reflect conservative preferences. The main priorities of government remain similar, with rising costs in education and health care hard to contain even by committed conservative governments intent on cutting taxes.

Republican governments often grab headlines by changing rules to penalize Democratic voters or by refusing seemingly good deals to expand services offered by the federal government. These efforts are real and important (and often designed to electorally benefit Republicans), but they should be put in context of the full panoply of state policy action and the liberal and conservative trends in policymaking. Party control of government does matter for state policy outputs, but Republicans in the states have not found a way to circumvent the typical conservative dilemma of matching expansive electoral campaigns for social restoration and limited government with the more mundane tasks and constraints of governing.

Their policy achievements should not be discounted, even if they were limited to symbolic gains and failed to make much of a difference to state social and economic trends. However, I next turn to evaluating the policies that *did* pass and their intended and unintended impacts on social and economic outcomes. After all, the policymakers who enacted these new laws did so to alter their states' trajectories. While they did succeed in some important governing endeavors, this does not necessarily imply it was enough to move the needle on states' broader outcomes.

Notes

1 Education Commission of the States. "How States Fund Pre-K." Available at: www.ecs.org/wp-content/uploads/How_States_Fund_Pre-K.pdf.
2 First Five Years Fund. "Governors Focus on Early Childhood Education in State of the State Addresses." Available at: www.ffyf.org/governors-focus-early-childhood-education-state-state-addresses/.
3 *The Economist.* "Republicans and Democrats are Taking Early Education More Seriously." January 24, 2019.
4 Reich and Barth (2017).
5 Leigh (2008).
6 Regression-discontinuity studies have come under fire for some assumptions that may not hold up in close races for the US House of Representatives (if closely winning and losing candidates spend vastly different sums or mostly come from the same party in each year, we might erroneously attribute something to party that is actually the product of campaign finance or a reflection of good Republican or Democratic years), but gubernatorial elections may not be subject to the same concerns. Caughey and Sekhon (2011).
7 Hill and Jones (2017).
8 Beland and Oloomi (2017).
9 Joshi (2015).
10 Bjørnskov and Potrafke (2013).
11 Mariani (2019).
12 Yu, Jennings, and Butler (2019).
13 Morehouse and Jewell (2003).
14 Mariani (2019).
15 Finger (2018).
16 Blair and Barth (2005); Boyer and Ratledge (2009); Conant (2006); Cronin and Loevy (1993, 2012); Hardy, Dohm, and Leuthold (1995); Jilson (2015); Lyons, Scheb, and Star (2001); Masugi and Janiskee (2011); Miller (1994); Nowlan (2010); Parry and Wang (2009); Schneier and Murtaugh

(2009); Stewart (2016); Thomas and Savatgy (2016); Weatherby and Stapilus (2011).

17 Grossmann (2014).

18 For a comparison with federal policy history, see chapter 5 of Grossmann (2014).

19 Kaufman (2018).

20 See Hertel-Fernandez (2018) on the role of the Koch network and ALEC and Grumbach (2018b) on the state's trajectory.

21 Cramer (2016). The book was cited throughout the mainstream media in the wake of Trump's election as one of the primary Trump explainers.

22 From Caughey and Warshaw (2016). Updated but not-yet-public data show additional rightward movement by Wisconsin since 2013.

23 Wisconsin did have a Democratic-controlled Assembly from 1971 to 1994 as well as 2009 to 2010; a Democratic-controlled Senate from 1975 to 1993 as well as ten of the years since then; and a Democratic governor from 2003 to 2010 (as well as in the 1970s and mid-1980s).

24 Anzia and Moe (2016).

25 The abortion studies were: Arceneaux (2002); Caldarone, Canes-Wrone, and Clark (2009); Kastellec (2018); Kreitzer (2015); Norrander and Wilcox (1999). The charter school studies were: Alberty (2014); Clinton and Richardson (2019); Hartney and Flavin (2011); Renzulli and Roscigno (2005); Wong and Langevin (2007); Wong and Shen (2002). The tax studies were: Bjørnskov and Potrafke (2013); Chernick (2005); Dennis, Moore, and Somerville (2007); Jacobs and Helms (2001); Leigh (2008); Reed (2006). The union studies were Jacobs (2017); Thom (2017); Wade (2015).

26 Sutton and King (2013). For current laws, see National Conference of State Legislatures. "School Voucher Laws." Available at: www.ncsl.org/research/education/voucher-law-comparison.aspx.

27 DiSalvo and Kucik (2018).

28 Wade (2018).

29 Hertel-Fernandez (2018).

30 Hertel-Fernandez (2018).

31 Hertel-Fernandez (2018).

32 Reckhow (2012).

33 Howell and Magazinnik (2017).

34 Holyoke and Brown (2019).

35 Chatterji, Kim, and McDevitt (2018).

36 Adolph, Breunig, and Koski (In Press).

37 Riverstone-Newell (2017).

38 Collingwood, El-Khatib, and O'Brien (In Press).

39 Reich (In Press).

40 Reich (2018).
41 Hare and Monogan (In Press).
42 Biggers and Hammer (2017).
43 US Election Assistance Commission. "EAVS Deep Dive: Early, Absentee, and Mail Voting." Available at: www.eac.gov/documents/2017/10/17/eavs-deep-dive-early-absentee-and-mail-voting-data-statutory-overview/.
44 Bromley-Trujillo and Poe (In Press).
45 Hoffer (2018).
46 Dagan and Teles (2016).
47 Enns (2016).
48 Enns (2016); Forman Jr. (2017); Alexander (2010).
49 Amidon (2018).
50 See Bureau of Justice Statistics. "Correctional Populations in the United States, 2016." Available at: www.bjs.gov/content/pub/pdf/cpus16.pdf.
51 Franko and Witko (2017).
52 Franko and Witko (2017).
53 Hertel-Fernandez (2018).
54 Miras and Rouse (2018).
55 National Conference of State Legislatures. "The Canvass." Available at: www.ncsl.org/research/elections-and-campaigns/the-canvass-january-2019.aspx.

5 THE MOSTLY MISSING RESULTS OF REPUBLICAN POLICIES

Businessman Paul Chabot moved from California to Texas in 2017 to escape the "ultra-far-left ideology" and "liberal laws" he saw as destroying the state. Not only that, he intends on creating a stampede, and has even founded a new real estate company, "Conservative Move," to help imperiled Blue state residents start over in Red states.[1] Chabot probably shared Senator Ted Cruz's alarm when liberals saw, in Cruz's 2018 Senate opponent Beto O'Rourke, an opportunity to move even Texas leftward. "They want us to be just like California," Cruz warned of O'Rourke's suspicious out-of-state supporters, "right down to tofu and silicon and dyed hair."

Most people avoid completely uprooting their lives in response to state political trends, but bemoaning California's fall to liberalism is a common conservative refrain. Likewise, plenty of Red state residents may consider seeking comfort in a Blue metropolis elsewhere. But are political trends and the policy differences they produce actually responsible for the condition and trajectory of states? Is Sacramento really driving the long-term social and economic transformation of California? Is Texas policy truly responsible for the state's energy-dependent economy? After all, it cannot be that hard to find tofu or dyed hair in Austin, and I would hazard a guess that Dell has plenty of silicon.

In this chapter, I review the consequences of state policy changes, drawing on specific policy evaluations and broader studies. A sober analysis does not give state legislation anything close to such a level of credit or blame. Broad social or economic results cannot easily be linked to Republican policy gains in the states. Republicans have not pursued any consistent policy menu for achieving their aims and we lack evidence that their policies have large effects. Instead, pre-existing and apolitical factors – such as population and economic resources – produce more socio-economic differences across states. Although important outcomes are sometimes linked to party policy differences, they are usually secondary to demographic and economic trends. The outcomes of Red and Blue state strategies might not be those feared by Chabot and Cruz.

Scholars and analysts have pursued quite a few evaluations of Republican-led policy changes in state governments. None of them, though, contain much evidence that enacted policies had the significant social or economic results sometimes predicted by policy proponents or opponents. Policies such as welfare reform and right-to-work were important, but in most cases combined with a multitude of other factors to make small imprints in ongoing trends. Reforms do have some of the intended effects, such as reducing welfare rolls. However, that is a far cry from achieving the broader results promised in electoral campaigns, such as increasing business investment and economic growth, or reversing population decline and industrial decay. Most of the policy changes also lack the broad negative impacts opponents fear – such as reduced wages or quality of life – because their effects can be diluted, reversed, or counteracted by other policies or averted by those affected. Though Republican policies have helped extend their power, and some policies have had real economic consequences, the impacts do not add up to significant differences across states.

Republicans have few, if any, widespread, real-world policy results to show for their state gains. Despite having limited socio-economic impacts, Republican advances have constituted a successful political project, with policies implemented that perpetuate their rule and a long-term shift achieved in the South that Democrats will not easily be able to overturn. But the states where they gained, such as those in the Midwest, hardly became Texas overnight. The reality is that their problems could not easily be solved with approaches transportable from Texas. New policies came with trade-offs, usually because resources were transferred from one constituency to another, but there were no magic bullets available to solve intractable social problems or reverse state economic positions. And, of course, many national trends – even the increased diversity in cuisine so feared by Cruz – affected all states without any help needed from policy.

Do Red States Create Different Social and Economic Outcomes?

The goal of public policy is – or should be – to achieve real impact, rather than simply accumulate political victories. Republican policies are traditionally justified on the grounds that they will create economic growth and prosperity, reward hard work, and sustain social stability and family life. Democrats, while also caring about those concerns, often emphasize solving pressing hardships such as ill health and poverty, or rectifying inequalities and spreading economic and social gains throughout society. We should not expect incremental state policy changes to produce immediate gains in all these areas, but it is fair to ask if policies have impacts beyond political gains for one side or the other.

In public debate, conflicts over Democratic and Republican successes and failures often take the form of comparing Red states to Blue states. The usual evidence is based on simple associations: states controlled by Democrats are better or worse off (or improving or declining more) than states controlled by Republicans.[2] To take some recent examples, a CNBC analysis claims Red states are better at creating jobs and increasing incomes, while a CBS analysis finds employment prospects are better in Blue states.[3]

Sometimes the schadenfreude takes the form of unexpected associations, supposedly proving hypocrisy: one analysis, for example, finds that Red states are better at reducing inequality because "not-in-my-backyard" housing restrictions mean only rich people can afford to live in Blue states. Another analysis, meanwhile, finds that Blue states produce better family life, while Red states stimulate divorce, child marriage, and adultery.[4] Pretty much anyone can pick a metric, produce a ranking, and write a blog post.

These public arguments are sometimes embarrassingly weak, even when pursued by academics. Economist Tyler Cowen, for example, sought to refute an unsourced Paul Krugman claim of Democratic superiority with a link to an article from *The Blaze* website which claimed Republican states are "better run" (based on the top five and bottom five states in a data compilation by another website called

"24/7 Wall St."). This represents pretty minimal evidence with which to back up such broad claims. In fact, there is little evidence that such business climate indicators match objective measures of state economic conditions and outcomes.[5] Cowen and Krugman can each pick an economic indicator that is stronger in the states pursuing their preferred approach, but that is not a good evaluation process.

In 2016, political scientists Jacob Hacker and Paul Pierson wrote a *New York Times* op-ed arguing that "The Path to Prosperity is Blue."[6] In it, they outlined a series of measures, arguing that Blue states have better life expectancy, higher median income, higher educational attainment, and higher patent innovation. Their comparisons were based on presidential voting patterns, rather than state policy results, but the implication was that the Red state model is a failure. However, nearly all these broad comparisons fail to look at change over time in response to partisan control of government. The associations they include also fail to control for the myriad other factors that distinguish California from Texas, or Massachusetts from Mississippi. As with all such comparisons, one inevitably ends up cherry-picking outcomes that make one's partisan side look better. For example, Democrats can pick educational attainment while Republicans pick business confidence.

Sometimes claims of state superiority focus on more reasonable and closer-to-home comparisons. In the Midwest, Democrats in conservative states tend to look enviously at Minnesota, while Republicans in liberal states look to Indiana. Democrats claim that by pursuing more progressive taxation, more education funding, and more urban investment, Minnesota has shown the path out of Rust Belt decay. Republicans retort that Indiana, by limiting union power and business regulation, has shown the true way forward. While these comparisons do sometimes provoke useful reflections on each state's policies (which turn out to not be quite as ideologically consistent as advertised), they also ignore the vast economic, cultural, and demographic differences across states.

Claims of Red or Blue superiority can also be premature. Witness Sam Brownback's claims that Kansas would provide a Red state model for the nation, only for most of his tax cuts to be overturned by his own party within five years of adoption. Specific studies of the most ambitious Republican tax changes in Kansas and Wisconsin show they did not, in fact, spur state economies relative to surrounding or similar states.[7] But the problem is broader: with economic dips in Minnesota or Indiana, prior championing may be made to appear foolish, even if fluctuations are to be expected and unlikely to be driven by policy. Short-term policy results may also not last, even when policies are consistently pursued, and policies may follow social or economic changes rather than cause them. Rust-Belt state economic decline, for example, may cause more spending on welfare programs, rather than that spending causing economic suffering.

Some academic research does take a more systematic look at potential outcomes of policy, but it tends to mix measures of actual policies (like tax rates) with measures of their effects (like inequality). It often takes into consideration only a few outcomes at a time and uses only one measure of state partisanship (such as the party of the governor). The results of these analyses have been less clear than their broad national counterparts. Despite high-profile findings of better economic performance under Democratic presidents, with more widespread and equal gains, the state-level literature does not reach a firm conclusion advantaging either party on economic performance.[8] The president has many more tools to affect the economy than governors.

Compared to federal estimates of party economic effects, which often show broadly better economic outcomes under Democratic presidents, 150 estimates of the effects of state partisanship on economic outcomes show mostly conditional or category-specific effects. Many of the studies also lack clear explanations of policy mechanisms for the relationships they do uncover.[9] One study found that the share of income going to the top 1 percent was unrelated to party control in state government, even though Democratic control of federal government did reduce this share.[10] If federal and state policies are trending in opposite directions (as party electoral trends do in presidential versus midterm years), this might also counteract economic effects. One study found economic growth was higher under Democratic presidents and also when more states had Democratic governors and legislatures; but (since having Democratic presidents led to more Republican control of states) state contributions actually attenuated the national economic performance gap between Democratic and Republican presidents from 1949 to 2017.[11]

A systematic review of all studies on the effects of state government partisanship showed parties in government have been associated with a multitude of policy outputs (such as environmental regulations and food stamp restrictions), as well as a variety of different outcomes resulting from them, such as pollution or hunger.[12] The review, which compared 115 studies, found 72 different assessed relationships between party control and socio-economic outcomes (46 of which were found to be significant relationships). These studies show partisan effects on a variety of economic outcomes, though they tend to be highly specific. For example, studies found partisan-based differences in relative hours worked by blacks and whites, and the employment rate of immigrants. Some of these findings make sense: from 1977 to 2008, for example, Democratic governors increased black working hours and reduced earnings gaps, perhaps through more active labor policy and more widely distributed benefits.[13] It is, though, a highly specific outcome that may have been specially selected to show partisan influence.

Policy effects of partisan governance may also result from anticipatory practice, rather than policy change. One study found that the election of Republican governors led to substantial reductions in state credit spreads, as investors expected less spending and lower taxes.[14] Another found that environmental agencies send fewer warning letters and notices of violation to polluters under Republican governors, with actual pollution enforcement actions reduced by Republican legislatures.[15] These studies provide better causal inference than a series of one-time op-eds in public debate, but still run the risk of highlighting a few significant relationships amplified by publication bias (the tendency for the published research record not to include insignificant or null findings, as they are unlikely to be submitted and less likely to be accepted).

Socio-Economic Impacts of Republican Policy Changes

There are voluminous research literatures on the effects of public policy that are less concerned with their political origins. To focus more directly on Republican-initiated policy effects, I reviewed (with the help of research assistant Jonathan Spiegler) 53 studies of recently passed Republican-supported policies in five categories: right-to-work laws, welfare reform, reduced gun restrictions, increased abortion restrictions, and tax cuts. The goal was to draw from the literature on policy effects, rather than partisan impact. Table 5.1 summarizes the results of our review.

Table 5.1 *Policy evaluations of Republican-initiated state policy changes*

Proximate outcomes

	Right-to-work	Welfare reform	Gun access	Abortion restriction	Income tax cuts
Clear link		Welfare rolls, recipient jobs, and poverty	Gun suicides	Clinic closure, abortion travel	Income growth
Mixed, conflicted, or minimal	Unionization, worker injuries	Income	Child gun injuries, gun homicides, gun hospitalizations	Abortions, timing, contraception	
No link					Employment

Broader outcomes

	Right-to-work	Welfare reform	Gun access	Abortion restriction	Income tax cuts
Clear link	Democratic vote, self-employment				
Mixed, conflicted, or minimal	Wages, manufacturing, employment, firm growth, inequality, business	Poverty rate, college, labor supply	Robbery, assaults, crime	Child death, injuries	Firm growth, economic growth
No link	Home ownership	Marriage, fertility, food consumption	Non-firearm homicides		

I have split the table into two sections, one covering proximate outcomes and the other covering broader outcomes of these four policies. Proximate outcomes are those that could be expected to change via the direct effects of the policy, without requiring a lot of other accompanying changes in behavior or institutions. Broader outcomes are those that require indirect policy effects and are often pursued by many interacting policies. For example, income tax cuts could be expected to change recipient incomes as a proximate outcome but would face a more complex path to affecting a broader outcome like job creation. Across issue areas, there were clear links to many, but not all, proximate outcomes. Studies of broader outcomes, however, usually found minimal or conditional effects, with far more studies with conflicting findings. Even studies of proximate outcomes led to some unclear relationships, often with trade-offs involving both benefits and costs.

Twelve studies of right-to-work laws mostly found significant effects, but there were inconsistencies in the findings.[16] One study pointed to lower manufacturing wages and increased construction deaths as a result of these laws, but no economic impact during recessions or effects on employment. Others found increases in private sector employment and faster growth in firms. Still others found no effect on employment, firm growth, or wages. There were no strong effects on inequality overall, though there were some changes in group differences by race and gender. While some studies revealed effects on unionization rates (a slight acceleration of decline), others found none.[17] One, though, found a significant and impactful decline in union political activity. The studies are limited by the small number of states that have changed right-to-work laws, the long period preceding recent moves when few changes occurred, and the decreased unionization preceding recent adoptions. Overall, however, the picture is of real but modest economic effects.

The 1990s saw a concentration of state welfare reforms – a response to federal welfare reform. Though not exclusive to Republican states, there were some differences in punitiveness and in distributional focus that (to some extent) matched state partisanship. I looked at eight studies of state welfare reform differences.[18] There was more of a consensus in this literature: welfare reform did decrease the number of people on cash assistance, but also left the non-working population poorer. Broader effects on labor supply, income, and fertility were tested but not found. National studies found that changes in other policies (such as the EITC) amplified both the positive effects for new workers and the negative effects for non-workers.[19] States with stricter welfare time limits increased single-mothers' employment rates and perhaps even the likelihood of them getting married.[20] The fact that federal welfare reform had an overall effect that differed by degree across states, however, does not necessarily mean that individual state differences were as impactful. The story here is that workers consistently benefited relative to non-workers, with some amplification based on policy severity.

The review of 14 studies on state gun policy found effects that were relatively consistent but minor.[21] Stricter background checks may reduce suicide and violent crime, while preventing child access reduces injuries. Laws restricting guns from those with restraining orders and criminal records (and effective checks to find these restricted population members before gun purchases) may reduce gun homicide and suicide. But no studies found significant effects on mass shootings or family violence. The evidence for the impacts of age requirements, waiting periods, assault weapons bans, and concealed-carry laws is more limited and conflicting. Overall, suicide effects were easier to show than homicide effects. Broader studies do show that greater restrictions bring decreases in injuries and gun deaths. Several studies differentiated among types of concealed-carry laws but again found limited or conflicting results. Even where new laws restricting access to guns reduced gun violence, it did not necessarily follow that new laws enabling gun access would increase gun violence. Instead, there were two negatively correlated but separable policymaking tracks: toward increasing gun availability and increasing gun control; each had studies of its effects, but they did not always run along the same continuum. There was more, but still limited, evidence of gun control effects, compared to the minimal evidence that gun availability laws made a significant difference in crime or health outcomes.

I also reviewed ten studies on the impact of abortion restrictions.[22] There was some evidence that parental notification or mandated counseling, but not enforced delays, can reduce abortion rates. Strict abortion laws can also cause clinics to close, though this does not necessarily affect the overall abortion rate, with more people simply traveling to neighboring states. Some studies found small increases in contraception use. Several studies assumed that abortion rates would decline with legal restrictiveness, but this relationship was surprisingly difficult to demonstrate. Abortion rates were already lower in the states that adopted new abortion restrictions, so associations might be more indicative of the social acceptability of abortion rather than the effectiveness of more restrictive laws.

I reviewed four studies on the impact of changes in state income taxes.[23] They agreed that total income taxes paid reduce individual income growth, with some potential effects of income tax cuts on the growth of firms and overall economic growth, but the magnitudes were generally small. There were no significant effects on employment, so the benefits arising from income tax cuts seem to go directly to those who pay lower rates. Separate literatures on sales tax increases and income tax progressivity (reviewed in the next section) sometimes showed more significant distributional impacts, with the relative tax burden on different classes associated with income inequality.

Other Issue-Specific Outcomes

I less systematically reviewed research on other policy changes that differed across Democratic and Republican states. Declines in and reforms of corporate tax have also been evident, though not restricted to Republican states. Many states reduced their corporate income or capital taxes, eliminated estate taxes, or tried to limit the negative effects of federal tax reform on their citizens or the state budget (for example, by changing how deductions are calculated).[24] Overall, there is evidence that though corporate tax rate reductions can increase job creation, the effects tend to dissipate quickly.[25] Benefits may go mostly to firm owners, but are also partially distributed to workers and landowners.[26] Cutting state corporate tax rates also leads to increases in income inequality as top earners shift their income to capital (shifting it from personal to business, but sometimes just as an accounting fiction to limit taxes), which in turn increases state investment.[27] Corporate tax cuts can thus be seen as both a shift in resources and a successful stimulus policy, but not one that generates broader-scale changes in state economies. Unfortunately, nearly all states are also still pursuing project-specific corporate tax incentives, despite abundant evidence that they do not provide the economic outcomes touted. In most cases, businesses would have made the same location decisions without the incentives, but incentive packages are still growing far more lavish as they enable credit claiming by politicians.[28]

State regulatory policies may also have a large role in state economies. Aggressive occupational licensing for everything from hairstyling to massage, in particular, potentially increases wages in the affected industries, while substantially reducing competition and increasing prices and inequality.[29] Yet some research finds that actual occupational licensing differences by profession across states do not demonstrate these effects.[30] Although there was an effort, supported by Republican states and the Obama administration, to reduce barriers to occupational entry, it did not result in widespread changes. Instead, Republican states tend to overpromise and underdeliver on business regulation, with efforts concentrated in preventing new environmental and consumer regulations. This can have some effects, like reducing costs for business at the risk of increasing environmental damage, but not at a scale sufficient to put states on different economic paths.

However, economic policies may combine to influence inequality. One study found that spending on unemployment and cash welfare benefits as well as higher corporate taxes reduced income inequality, while high property taxes decreased income across the board.[31] Yet these effects were entirely in the long run, with few short-term impacts, and may have relied on policies that went against liberal citizen ideology in a state (which was associated with increased inequality). Another study found that taxing the wealthy more and the poor less reduced inequality, even before accounting directly for income after taxes and transfers.[32] It also found that labor market policies such as right-to-work and a lower minimum wage increased inequality.

There is a voluminous literature on minimum wages, with more recent studies showing greater opportunities for increasing minimum rates that do not at the same time threaten much lower employment.[33] Recent state minimum wage changes are often much smaller than those tested in the literature, though some liberal states are pursuing eventual moves toward $12 or $15 per hour, which is well above the national wage. However, several Republican-run states have also increased minimum wages in response to initiative threats, so the differences in increase size across states is limited.

An even larger research literature on educational changes, including charter schools, vouchers, and teacher evaluation requirements as well as education finance reforms, assesses effects on student performance, graduation rate, or college success. The charter school literature has been the most contentious, with effects pointing in different directions and selectively deployed by advocates.[34] Though charter schools have been growing quickly, only about 6 percent of US students are enrolled in them,[35] with the rate only slightly higher in Republican states. Voucher studies have also been contentious, with some finding broad effects like improvements in test scores and future academic performance and others questioning them.[36] But even in states with voucher programs, few students receive them.[37]

The effects of most education policies pursued by states are generally small, but there is evidence that school spending and its distribution matter for educational outcomes.[38] Since many states have been trying similar reforms recently (such as personalized learning, charter schools, and teacher accountability systems), there is less consensus on the relationship between new state policies and outcomes. In education, Democrats and Republicans can rely on some studies showing that their preferred changes can directly help some categories of students. In the major outcomes, though, there is considerable continuity, with the same states regularly at the top and bottom of educational rankings.[39]

At the same time, Republicans have been weakening teacher collective bargaining rights in some states. Strong teacher union bargaining is related to high state education spending, but it is another case of a deceptive association: the high spending precedes union rights rather than follows them.[40] Even education spending may not be associated with broader outcomes: a study of self-reported quality of life and subjective well-being found it was not associated with state education spending or redistribution, but was instead most associated with spending on public goods like parks.[41] This spending is usually negatively associated with policy liberalism and is relatively higher in Republican states.[42]

Another major recent policy influence resulting from Republican control was the decision by 14 states not to expand Medicaid under the Affordable Care Act (and others' successful slowing of the process). The research has largely been favorable to Medicaid expansion, showing that it has increased coverage, access to care, and the economic standing of recipients.[43] What is not as apparent is whether Medicaid expansion has improved broad health outcomes. Even if Medicaid has encouraged appropriate treatment, has it been enough to alter rates of disease or symptoms of ill health? Though some studies have shown early benefits, conservatives point to important earlier studies of the Oregon Medicaid experiment, which randomly added beneficiaries and showed mostly economic, rather than health, improvements. It may be too early to tell whether the expansion meaningfully prevented early death, but there is limited evidence so far.[44] Medicaid does change outcomes such as insurance rates, though that is not the same as demonstrating effects on underlying health – where the literature has been far more conflicted.[45] It has increased access to opioid treatments, which may eventually prevent deaths. Medicaid also has downstream political effects, with beneficiaries of more-generous state policies more likely to vote.[46]

Republican-led state health policy innovations have been minimal and not had extensive effects. Policies pooling the population with high health risks generally failed to cover those who were uninsured and had pre-existing medical conditions, and these efforts were made largely obsolete by the Affordable Care Act.[47] Long-term care insurance, which was incentivized and regulated under some state legislation, covers about eight million Americans, but this is mostly unrelated to these state policies. Many states, Red and Blue, increased their health insurance requirements prior to the Affordable Care Act, such as requiring coverage to include autism or mental health issues. They had the predictable consequence of increasing the usage of services that insurance policies cover but spreading the costs of the increased usage across policy holders (increasing prices).[48] Many of these insurance mandates were later superseded by federal requirements.

Some Republican-led tort reforms may have had important effects. Major auto liability rules changes potentially affect auto insurance costs (though without changing insurance take-up).[49] Medical malpractice reforms may have reduced costs for doctors or consumers, but did not substantially change medical practice or reduce defensive treatment.[50] Tort reform may also have negatively affected medical innovation by reducing doctors' need to eradicate errors (for example, by making it harder to justify upgrading surgical instruments).[51] There is thus a case to be made that tort reforms moved resources from law firms to doctors and insurance companies, but (as usual) broader changes are more difficult to demonstrate.

Effects of Less Ideological Policy Trends

There is evidence that policies pursued by most states regardless of partisanship may have had important socio-economic consequences. Early childhood education, for example, has received lots of research support aimed at improving later life outcomes, though the level of improvement is closely tied to the quality of teachers and the resources available in the program. There has also been controversy about whether scaling up the best efforts statewide can succeed.[52] Criminal justice reforms may have measurable benefits for offenders (such as less time in prison and higher employment), with less clear implications for wider social outcomes (such as reduced crime).[53] Much of the benefit of incarceration seems tied to the direct removal of crime-prone populations from the public, rather than any successful deterrence. The recidivism rates of those released from prison remain high, though this is in part because of an increase in monitoring and the increased risk of probation violations.

There has also been a significant nationwide decline in support for state-funded public higher education, though a few oil-rich Republican states have gone against the grain in increasing spending to build their university systems. These declines in public support have had the predictable consequence of increasing fees and tuition costs, which directly impact students. Universities also claim broader public benefits, but it is easier to demonstrate the historical relationship between strong higher education systems and socio-economic success (for example, by raising state education levels and patent innovation) than it is to show that recent modest differences in state support levels make any significant difference to outcomes. Michigan, North Carolina, and California have decided to move state resources away from higher education, for example, but the universities in those states are stable institutions that retain strong reputations built up over decades that are unlikely to change due to cuts. College savings plans (offered by all but two states and incentivized by more than 30) have provided direct benefits to those who enroll, but such benefits have been concentrated among the highest-income earners.[54]

There may be a general association between the evidence underpinning policy changes and the bipartisanship of the coalition for passage as well as the number of states that pass it. If an issue becomes politicized (such as charter schools), chances are that there is conflicting research regarding the effectiveness of the most widely used policy tools. In contrast, widely adopted policies (such as early childhood education) tend to have more research support. This could be a sign of the politicization of research, however, rather than proof that consensus solutions are the most likely to produce positive results. That said, it is striking that Republican governments have mostly been on firmer research grounds when they have followed Democratic trends rather than when striking out on their own.

This policy-specific review of policy evaluation studies demonstrates that even the most successful Republican policy achievements may not be met with wide social and economic impacts. The strongest evidence seems to be for new programs (mostly initiated by Democrats) that expand access to government services (such as Medicaid expansion), especially regarding their direct impact on beneficiaries. Republican effects, meanwhile, are mostly due to government *not* enacting a policy or enacting one less extensive than those in Democratic states. Although significant, this does not demonstrate key conservative outcomes from the Republican revolution in the states, just that "Democrat-light" policies may have weaker effects.

Even straightforward hypothesized relationships, such as the ability of abortion and gun restrictiveness to impact the number of abortions and guns, turn out to be more difficult to show (with weaker relationships) than expected. Where there are clear outcomes, they are often mixed: welfare reforms increased employment among a subset of former recipients while making others less well-off. All of these influences take place within the context of national policy trends: for example, all states enacted welfare reform of some kind, and all states must retain legal abortion and the right to bear arms. National trends thus make overwhelming impacts resulting from state policy differences less likely. Without discounting the effects found for numerous policies and the potential impacts of many state programs, the evidence does not add up to a sea-change driven by partisan policy priorities.

Redistributing Tax Burdens and Increasing Inequality

The best case for Republican impact may be distributional. In *Taxing the Poor*, sociologists Katherine Newman and Rourke O'Brien find that conservative states have been redistributing their tax burdens away from property and income taxes, and toward sales taxes that fall disproportionately on poorer residents.[55] However, they place particular emphasis on the long-running tradition of Southern states' reliance on these kinds of taxes, pointing to their racial history from the Civil War onwards. In response to the threat of less-tax-averse voters after black enfranchisement (and long before the California tax revolt), Southern states also helped spread property tax limitation amendments, which further shifted relative tax burdens from property to sales taxes (with higher burdens for the poor). Democratic governors such as Bill Clinton tried (but failed) to redirect the Southern tax burden to higher-income earners. The high tax burdens on the poor are also associated with reduced social spending, creating a double route to potential detriment.

Newman and O'Brien find that shifting the tax burden to the poor increases their mortality, along with several indicators of health (such as obesity) and poverty that predict mortality. The estimated effects are substantial: for example, 13.5 deaths per 100,000 people per year due to the South's greater taxation of the poor. However, Newman and O'Brien say these estimates match those measuring the effects of financial resources on other communities, for example those measured from large community resource inflows from casinos on Native American lands (increasingly taxing the poor, they claim, may have similar magnitudes of impact to the effects of those efforts to increase the resources of the poor). Although the authors frame their investigation as a study of the effects of taxing the poor and reducing their benefits, the national trends I reviewed in Chapter 3 suggest that overall state social spending doubled during the decades they investigated (1980–2008). As they acknowledge, Northeastern states were shifting the tax burden *away* from the poor over the same period – thus the results of one region relative to another also reflect how much liberal states enacting policies that may have increased the life expectancy of the poor. Newman and O'Brien do show clear partisan effects on an outcome – death rates – that could hardly be more important, but much of the story is due to Republican states doing less than Democratic states, rather than enacting new policies that have resulted in more deaths for the poor (though without property tax limitations, Republican states might rely on less regressive taxation).

Overall, state government liberalism is associated with reduced economic inequality, but has no effect on the share of income going to the top 1 percent of the income distribution and little effect on the top 10 percent.[56] The effect seems to come from efforts by liberal states to help the poor and middle class through social programs (and perhaps reduced relative taxation). To the extent that Democrats succeed in maintaining higher levels of unionization, this could also reduce inequality – both within the labor market and via increased taxes and transfers.[57] Additionally, Democratic governments at the state level seek to reduce unemployment more than Republican governments, but face resource and policymaking constraints the federal government does not. This means they only succeed in reducing unemployment when economic growth is already high, whereas they prove no better or worse than Republican states when facing poor economies.[58] These Democratic governments were also often working against Republican congresses and presidents, but still succeeded in altering the upward distribution of income.[59] In other words, while economic inequality has been rising nationwide Democratic efforts in the most liberal states may have partially offset these tendencies.

Evidence-Based Policy

As research on public policy has professionalized and proliferated, state governments have not been ignoring the evidence. While many politicians continue to selectively consume and deploy evidence to support their existing policy views, state administrators and political leaders are seeking to ground their efforts in more systematic evidence. Led by foundations such as the William T. Grant Foundation, the Laura and John Arnold Foundation, the John D. and Catherine T. MacArthur Foundation, and the Pew Charitable Trusts, a movement for evidence-based policy has caught on in some states and agencies. Federal law and some state efforts have institutionalized the use of evidence in evaluating programs and policies, especially in areas such as the environment, health, and education. Data-sharing partnerships between government agencies and researchers have also enabled better investigations and inferences on the effects of policy, including quasi-experimental investigations where participation comes randomly from arbitrary cut-offs or participation lotteries.

However, the movement toward evidence-based policy has not been uniform across the country. The Pew Charitable Trusts rated all states based on whether they had sought to: (1) define appropriate evidence; (2) inventory their programs; (3) compare costs and benefits; (4) report outcomes in their budgets; (5) target funds to the highest-scoring programs; and (6) require evidence-based action in state laws.[60] Their goal was to help states focus "limited resources on public services and programs that have been shown to produce positive results ... [to]

improve the outcomes of services funded by taxpayer dollars." They assessed progress in four issue areas with relatively straightforward outcome metrics: behavioral health, child welfare, criminal justice, and juvenile justice. As a result of this, they rated five states as leading the effort: Washington, Utah, Minnesota, Connecticut, and Oregon. An additional 11 states were rated in the next highest category: New Mexico, Colorado, Kansas, Missouri, Tennessee, Mississippi, Florida, Ohio, Pennsylvania, New York, and Vermont. That suggests a modest tilt toward Democratic states, especially in the leading category, but no monopoly. Such efforts could easily be used to justify cutting programs or assessing conservative policy approaches, so there is nothing necessitating a link between evidence-based policy and a liberal agenda, especially since criminal justice policy constituted half of their assessment.

Even so, given that evidence-based policy is overwhelmingly used to assess government interventions in society and the economy, it tends to provide estimates of the relative cost-effectiveness of policies that expand the scope of government. The Pew Charitable Trusts has compiled several different policy research rating systems into a "Results First Clearinghouse" designed for state policymakers. It lists 2,893 policies and programs, rating them into categories based on accumulated research evidence as "highest-rated," "second-highest rated," "mixed effects," "no effects," "negative effects," and "insufficient evidence." Using their database, I rated each policy and program as liberal, conservative, or neither based on the same distinctions used in prior chapters: that is, both the traditional definition of expanding or contracting the size or scope of government and the more lenient definition based on the political coalition that is usually most supportive of them. Table 5.2 reports the results.

Many more programs are conventionally liberal than conservative in that they entail new government actions or programs and have traditionally had more support from Democratic activists and interests than their Republican counterparts. By the scope-of-government categorization, 27 percent of policies and programs are liberal and only 1 percent are conservative (with 72 percent not coded as either). By the coalitional politics criterion, 25 percent of policies are liberal and 3 percent are conservative (with 72 percent mixed or not easily categorized). Some of those in the neutral category did not include enough information to code, but my relatively generous coding scheme also included programs such as school curricula, psychological

Table 5.2 *Evidence assessments of policies and programs by ideological perspective*

	Liberal (gov. expanding)	Conservative (gov. contracting)	No change in gov. scope	Liberal supported	Conservative supported	No clear slant
Highest rated	228 (30%)	6 (15%)	563 (27%)	221 (30%)	11 (14%)	565 (27%)
Second highest rated	331 (43%)	11 (28%)	720 (35%)	307 (42%)	37 (46%)	718 (34%)
Mixed effects	8 (1%)	5 (13%)	30 (1%)	6 (1%)	5 (6%)	32 (2%)
No effects	57 (7%)	6 (15%)	125 (6%)	47 (6%)	14 (17%)	127 (6%)
Negative effects	1 (0%)	4 (10%)	3 (0%)	1 (0%)	4 (5%)	3 (0%)
Insufficient evidence	144 (19%)	8 (20%)	643 (31%)	145 (20%)	10 (12%)	640 (31%)

Source: Pew Charitable Trusts Results First Clearinghouse and author coding by ideological category.

therapies, university efforts, charitable groups, nondescript public health campaigns, and messages delivered via phone, mail, or the Internet in the non-ideological category. Many of these programs nonetheless require government staff or funding support and are not costless to implement. In addition, I did not code efforts such as separate court systems as ideological, though they may also require extra resources. Even the non-ideological policy interventions and programs may thus raise conservative ire.

The small number of conservative policies and programs in the database were concentrated in criminal justice and education, whereas the liberal efforts – in addition to those categories – were broadly distributed across family support, public health, and mental health. These policy and programmatic efforts tend to target vulnerable populations such as the poor, children, prisoners, and those with health problems, as policy tends to be directed toward difficult-to-solve social problems. Conservative policy efforts are simply less extensive in these areas.

According to either categorization, the small number of conservative programs and policies assessed are associated with less research support. Programs and policies not easily categorized ideologically had a record somewhere between clearly liberal and conservative approaches, with more of them rated as having insufficient evidence to reach any conclusion. By social science standards, all of these policy and program evaluations look wildly optimistic, suggesting many fewer cases of mixed, null, or negative effects than would be expected to occur by chance. This means evidence of effectiveness may only be selectively revealed or published. Even so, by either measure, conservative policies account for only 1 percent of the highest-rated policies and a striking 50 percent of the small number of policies rated as having negative effects (such as trying juveniles as adults in criminal law). Even accounting for substantial researcher and practitioner bias, this suggests that conservatives often pursue the same ideologically driven approaches rather than tracking and scaling up the most successful efforts (which usually involve more government intervention, or at least non-profit and institutional programming that requires public resources and support).

Many of the most effective programs are comprehensive efforts that involve public institutions such as schools, in addition to social workers and academic or public health professionals, as well as cooperation from business, non-profits, and unorganized community groups.

They are often tailored to particular populations via culturally specific and place-based programming. They also tend to target the most difficult cases, including poor and minority populations already attached to the health, social welfare, and criminal justice systems, or already experiencing trauma or challenges in school. The Harlem Children's Zone, for example, includes everything from schools to parenting and health services focused in the poorest section of the community. Although conservative approaches to these problems and populations do exist (in fact, the Zone includes charter schools, coded as having conservative support), they are generally not the focus of conservative visions of policy. Many of the proponents of these policies and programs tout their potential to reduce costs over the long term by diverting populations from courts, prisons, hospitals, and social welfare programs. This, however, does not mean such policies and programs are cost-free or will immediately reduce government expenditure. Most involve large up-front investments, ongoing government support, and active participation by mostly liberal professionals in mostly liberal locales.

Conservative policymakers could, of course, still use this evidence base to their advantage. There are myriad programs established or funded by states without significant research support, so a closer look at the evidence might justify a scaling back of the role of government in society. There are certainly many programs that no not live up to the hopes of their liberal supporters once they are put into practice. But this still puts Republican state legislative majorities and governors in a more difficult situation than Democrats. Across the policy spectrum, Democrats can argue that there are hundreds of policies with good evidence to support them that could be funded at higher levels, or that work elsewhere and could be adapted in their states. If one program does not have enough evidence to support it, Democrats can simply respond that state efforts should be redirected toward those government interventions that do work, with governments running grant programs to reward those with the most evidence of success.

Republicans, meanwhile, are put in the position of arguing that some programs should be discontinued, even those where participants might believe they have benefited (despite a lack of research evidence confirming this). Conservatives can also argue that state funds are being wasted on ineffective programs, perhaps justifying a wider skepticism of proposed but unproven liberal efforts. However, this argument is hardly equivalent to having an alternative menu of policy proposals that comply with conservative principles and also have research evidence supporting their application. Even the traditional conservative argument that charities better deliver services than government – which could be advanced with reference to successful non-profit programs – now usually runs up against requests by such non-profit organizations for direct government support, integration with public services, and public-condoned coordination across the public, non-profit, and private sectors. Even George W. Bush's faith-based initiatives, for example, directed more resources from governments at all levels to non-profit ventures; the church-based programs then requested further government assistance and integrated themselves with public service provision.

Some readers might interpret this evidence as an indictment of conservatism: compared to liberals, conservatives lack evidence-supported policies derived from their ideological principles. However, the evidence can also be read as somewhat supportive of conservative ideas about the difficulty of demonstrating clear gains from government-supported programs, and could justify opposing liberal tendencies to try various policies before conclusively demonstrating their effectiveness. Conservatives might also argue that liberal foundations or scholars have gone out of their way to assess more liberal ideas or proposals, while downgrading conservative options. While appreciating such general concern about liberal bias in policy research, I did not see much evidence that it was impacting case selection or measured outcomes in my review. Instead, I think the explanation is simpler: most policy and program ideas are about new approaches or efforts, which usually entail more funding or government action. Liberals will always be able to find programs to build or scale up in areas that make a difference on some outcome. If one program does not work, they can propose a reform or adaptation, a more comprehensive effort, or an alternative. Conservatives are instead stuck arguing that the aggregate evidence still does not support an ever-expanding government effort to solve social problems, even while many seemingly worthy efforts are fighting for support.

Big Picture Evidence of Republican Policy Effects

Rather than assess the effects of each policy separately, some researchers have sought global evidence of Republicans' collective impact on the states. Political Scientist Jacob Grumbach followed up on the social effects of policy in several issue areas where he saw increasing state policy polarization.[61] He finds that health insurance coverage is now more widespread in Democratic states, although it began rising to a lesser extent in Republican states as well (following passage of the Affordable Care Act). Grumbach finds little or no differences in incarceration rates between Republican and Democratic states, noting that Democratic states also passed tough-on-crime policies in the 1980s and 1990s until criminal justice reform became more popular nationwide. On education, he finds that Republican states previously had higher rates of high school graduation, but Democratic states have subsequently matched them; Republican states have slightly higher charter enrollment rates, but it is increasing in Democratic states as well. He also finds limited differences in carbon emissions. Grumbach claims the results show that where the parties are polarizing, the outcomes are also moving apart. Even so, all of the impacts demonstrated seem quite modest, with the biggest effect (health insurance rates) likely driven by Democratic states' adoptions of more extensive Medicaid expansions – another example of an impact due to less Republican action.

As Grumbach has shown, it is certainly possible to find areas of policy where Democrats and Republicans diverge – and even some proximate outcomes that may be associated with such divergences. But new policy tends to be more liberal than conservative, both more expansive than contractionary and more accepting of social change over time, meaning that most policy areas trend leftward. Conservatives have had successes, without achieving their aspiration to disrupt the wider scope of liberalizing policy trends.

Given the overwhelming state gains made by Republicans, which came at the same time as the party was becoming increasingly conservative, it would stand to reason that a windfall of policy gains achieving their broader objectives (or, if skeptical Democrats were correct, leading to detrimental outcomes) would have resulted. But Republicans faced constraints at each step: from control of government to policy outputs, and then from policy outputs to social and economic effects. Republican leadership led to some considerable changes in policy, but they were unable to reverse the broad build-up of state governments that had already taken place across all states, setting them on different liberal and conservative pathways. Conservative policies have had some important direct effects, such as reduced public sector union involvement in politics on behalf of their opponents. Even so,

Table 5.3 *Outcomes of partisan governance*

	Association with democratic control	Difference-in-differences causal estimate	Regression discontinuity causal estimate
Voter turnout	–	0	0
Felons ineligible to vote	0	0	0
Violent crime rate	+	0	0
Robbery rate	0	0	0
Rape rate	0	0	0
Property crime rate	+	0	0
Murder rate	+	0	0
Car theft rate	+	0	0
Value added by agriculture	0	0	0
Unemployment rate	+	0	0
Top 1% share of income	–	0	0
Top 0.1% share of income	–	0	0
Consumer price index	–	0	0
Real per capita income	–	0	0
Population growth	0	0	0
Housing price index	–	0	0
Gross state product per capita	–	0	0
High school graduation rate	–	0	0
School attendance rate	+	0	0
Residential sector energy price	0	0	0
CO_2 emissions	0	0	0
Commercial energy consumed	+	0	0
New Green Card holders	0	0	0
Health spending per capita	0	0	0
Divorce rate	+	0	0
Birth rate	–	0	0
Abortion rate	+	0	0

Source: From Holbein and Dynes (2018). + and – indicate positive or negative relationships with full Democratic control of state government. Zeros indicate no statistically significant relationship.

given the myriad factors affecting social outcomes, many of their policy outputs may not have driven broad real-world results.

Researchers (and especially partisan activists who deploy research) tend to selectively choose to study or highlight the outcomes that are the most likely to show differences. In a new research paper, political scientists John Holbein and Adam Dynes counteract these difficulties by looking at many categories of outcomes (economics, education, crime, family, the environment, and health), which could conceivably be related to policy differences across Democratic and Republican states.[62] Table 5.3 lists the individual outcomes tracked, with all statistically significant relationships listed: + indicates that full Democratic control is associated with a higher estimate for that variable, − indicates a lower estimate, and zero indicates no clear relationship.

The first column lists the bivariate association in state-years between each outcome and Democratic control (including analyses from 1961 to 2012, though not all variables are measured in all years). Across 27 diverse outcomes, they find that most are associated with contemporaneous Democratic and Republican partisan control of states. That is, if you look simply at which party controls which states, you will find different outcomes. Unemployment, energy consumption, divorce, abortion, as well as murder and crime rates are higher in states under Democratic control, while income, graduation rate, economic growth, income, and birth rate are lower. This appears to make for a devastating review of Democratic governance, appropriate for a Republican campaign commercial. Democrats are left to argue that their governed states have lower prices, cheaper housing, better school attendance, and a lower share of income going to the richest earners.

However, these estimates are all quite misleading. When Holbein and Dynes systematically look at differences over time and place, removing associations that are the result of constant state-level factors and nationwide year-level factors, they find no evidence of large or systematic differences for any measure (as visible in the second column of Table 5.3). Zero of the 27 outcomes show significant associations with partisan control, regardless of whether it is the governor, house chamber, or senate chamber that is in different partisan hands, or all three at once. In fact, there are fewer partisan differences than should be expected based purely on chance, given the number of different outcomes. The third column of Table 5.3, based on regression discontinuity estimates, again finds no evidence of differences due to Democratic or Republican control. Recall that this procedure takes advantages of differences around close gubernatorial elections and closely split legislative chambers to make better causal inferences. Even when looking for long-term impacts, they find no evidence of differences driven by sustained Democratic or Republican control. It is another sign that correlation may not equal causation: what looks like a clear pattern may turn out to be a product of reverse causality (for example, Democrats may come to power in states with more social and economic difficulties) or due to other coinciding variables (for example, Democratic states may be more diverse or well-educated).

The research by Holbein and Dynes does track party influence on hard-to-move outcomes such as population and economic growth but does not require Republican or Democratic control to move these broader social or economic trends. Even quite-proximate-to-policy outcomes such as the abortion rate, school attendance rate, the top 1 percent share of income, the number of felons ineligible to vote, and energy prices, are unaffected by party control of state government. Despite changes in abortion law, education policy, tax rates, and voting rights, therefore, there is little evidence that the underlying outcomes of these policies have been significantly affected by policy changes made possible by party control of government. Since the research looked separately for changes due to state house control, state senate control, and gubernatorial partisanship, any shifts are unlikely to be due to policy changes under the control of one branch. Also, since they investigated relationships over two and four years, as well as more extended periods, but again found no clear evidence of short- or long-term influence, it cannot be chalked up to, say, abortion policies taking a long time to go into effect or tax rates being later reversed. Holbein and Dynes were expecting to find some relationships, perhaps even clear trade-offs between Republican and Democratic governance that voters could use to evaluate the parties, but instead they found no systematic effects at all.

Some of the results may seem to conflict with those based on research on the outcomes of specific policies. For example, some abortion restrictions may reduce the abortion rate, but Republican control does not seem to do so. Although there is always the possibility that one of the results is wrong, I would offer an alternative reconciliation. The path from party to outcome runs through policy differences, meaning that parties have to effect consequential policies enough to matter. Policy-specific studies are able to compare the most restrictive policies with the least restrictive, showing that they produce different outcomes. But that is a long way from demonstrating that the kinds of policies enacted when a state moves from Republican to Democratic control are consequential enough to have those same outcomes, especially after courts, administrators, and non-governmental actors have a chance to shape the policy as enacted on the ground.

When data and research are deployed in state political or journalistic discussions, it usually looks more like the first column in

Table 5.3 than either of the latter two columns. But quick summaries of Red and Blue state averages can be deceiving. The research shows it is not hard to produce op-eds with descriptive evidence that Republican or Democratic governance brings more benefits, especially when outcomes can be picked from several options in order to support a partisan spin. However, consistent relationships that account for state differences and incorporate broader trends over time (that happen to be correlated with state partisanship) are much harder to come by.

This research concerns the overall effect of parties on social and economic outcomes and does not foreclose the possibility that particular Republican-adopted policies have had important outcomes. The effects of policies could, of course, cancel one another out if outcomes move in different directions. It might also be that policies are not adopted in a widespread enough manner or to a broad enough degree to produce consistent differences in outcome based on party. Even so, this literature should give pause to both triumphant and dystopian views of the potential impact of Republican gains. Even if Red and Blue states are now differing more in their policies, it does not imply that their socio-economic trends (good or bad) are a product of those policy differences.

Prior research results may help explain the unexpected findings of Holbein and Dynes: that there is insufficient evidence to conclude that party control of government has produced *any* changes in state social and economic outcomes. The path from partisan change to policy outputs remains long and obstructed, as does the path from policy outputs to social and economic change. As Caughey and Warshaw show, partisan control of government has only recently been associated with policy outputs, and partisanship still does not overwhelm other state differences. Policy had also nationalized, with periodic efforts to revive state decision-making still tending to entail more reliance on federal decisions. In this sense, the lack of overwhelming social and economic effects should be less surprising. The policy consequences, just like the policy output effects, were real but not overwhelming.

The Influence of Historical Policy Choices

Even if recent policies driven by changes in state partisanship have not made discernable changes to state economies or societies, policy choices taken in less polarized eras may still have been important.

Political scientists Gerald Gamm and Thad Kousser have tracked state policies and their relationships to critical outcomes, such as life expectancy and incomes, over more than a century (from 1880 to 2010).[63] They focus on high levels of two-party competition in state politics as the essential factor, the critical mechanism being that competitive states produce higher social spending. States with highly competitive party systems spent more and spent earlier, especially on education and health, with spending leading to longer lives and higher incomes. The South, as is typical, stands out as low in competition, spending, and socio-economic outcomes.

These findings show outcomes that are more consequential, but also point to limits to conservative policy action. Most obviously, Republicans who win close political competition have (according to their data) traditionally followed Democrats in dedicating more funds to social spending on liberal priorities, in order to appeal to constituents. Given that the impacts are from spending, changes in the size and scope of government (which are harder to achieve) may also be a prerequisite for major socio-economic impact. The overall pattern of state spending, with all states vastly increasing spending for most of the twentieth century, may also be a sign that the major gains were achieved by spending on low-hanging fruit such as sanitation and making basic education available (possibly with diminishing returns as those public goods increased in cost). Since historical decisions in a less polarized era (and the path dependence that followed) put states on different spending trajectories, polarized parties and increasing Republican control may have arrived too late in state development to move these indicators. Similarly, another analysis finds that unions historically contributed to strong employment law protections, with states retaining different policies decades later based on early union density, even in the face of political decline.[64] The results are yet another sign that public policy can have important outcomes, without implying that the most recent differences in policies due to partisan control will be the driving force of future success or failure.

What Can Republicans Tout and Democrats Bemoan?

This review does not suggest that much confidence should be placed in broad-brush comparisons of Red and Blue states, particularly those where politicians and voters stereotype large, diverse states such as Texas and California – even proposing that people move between them. Many state policies do have identifiable impacts on important outcomes, but at the scale they are usually enacted, such effects are often conditional and muted (charter school enrollment increases at a higher rate based on more welcoming policies, for instance, but mostly follows national trends and never becomes the dominant form of education). If policy trajectories are sustained and well-calibrated to their states' conditions, they may be able to move the needle – but this is not at all the same as declaring Red or Blue state policies nationally superior.

If you wanted to build a case in favor of Democratic policy, the results provide a few building blocks. Basic redistributive economic policies tend to have their intended direct effects: providing resources to the poor increases their relative economic standing, whereas taxing the poor diminishes it. Straightforward Democratic policies such as social benefits at least increase the economic outcomes of the beneficiaries, while occasionally directly addressing the policy concern by stimulating improvements in areas such as educational achievement, environmental damage, and public health. Some of the theorized downsides to these approaches, such as reduced economic activity due to over-taxation or overregulation, do not materialize or may be smaller than feared. This means Blue states may not be near the upper limits of their abilities to pursue greater redistribution, targeted regulation, and more spending, while avoiding major economic consequences.

Yet recall that these are the kinds of policies that tend to liberalize slowly over time, without overwhelming differences across Red or Blue states. This means there may be big differences between the socioeconomic effects of the current policies put in place by, say, Alabama and Massachusetts, without it necessarily implying that recent policy trends in each state add up to meaningful differences in impact. Long-term differences can be deceiving, acting more as causes rather than consequences of political trends.

What about the Republican case? Here the evidence is limited. There are some marginally but directly effective policies that successfully target outcomes such as union political activity and welfare rolls. However, with even direct interventions to increase gun ownership or reduce abortion difficult to make effective, broader conservative goals may be hard to reach. If one intrinsically prefers conservative policy for increasing freedom, or decreasing the role of the public over the private sector, it might be interpreted as good news that policies reducing regulation have limited effects on economic outcomes. There is even evidence for direct business and individual benefits from lower taxation. But the evidence supporting the claim that Republican approaches to business development and employment produce big gains for the general population is simply not apparent. Also, given that Republicans' ability to shift the overall state tax and regulation burden is considerably more limited than assumed, their impact may in fact be greater in social policy areas where more laws have passed with their imprint (the same cases where real-world outcomes have been harder to budge).

Republicans may dismiss this evidence as primarily originating in liberal academic circles. While I am sympathetic to the fear that political ideology influences policy studies by changing the questions asked, the measures used, and the framing and interpretation of results, I have sought out studies of Republican-initiated policy changes without finding many that confirm broad effects. The studies I have looked at do not seem obviously designed to make Republican policies look bad, only to assess their effects on commonly cited outcomes.

Most studies did not find broad negative effects of conservative policies or Republican control either, suggesting that the disconnect was in the breadth of policy effects rather than in the helpful or unhelpful direction of change. Particular conservative policies that do have broad effects may not have been implemented widely enough to systematically produce those outcomes across Republican states. Republicans may also be able to argue that their states selected the best of the Democratic-supported programs to emulate while avoiding the broadest government roles, such that Red states did not suffer any consequences for not moving as fast in changing policy as Blue states.

Even when policies have clear effects, however, we cannot necessarily credit state partisanship for their effects. The policies may not in fact be as associated with changing the party in control of government; other policies enacted by the parties may counteract the effects of the policies under focus; or the effects may be too small to register in wider-scale investigations. This is also why the broader study of the consequences of parties in government is valuable, despite it putting the mechanisms of policy influence in a black box to look purely at partisan inputs and socio-economic outputs. Here the picture is less complicated: outcomes that might initially appear to be correlated to party governance are not robustly predicted once studies take account of changes over time and persistent state differences. This explains why commentators can be misled: in any given year, judged on a variety of outcomes, Red and Blue states will look different, regardless of whether control of government was an underlying cause. Certain types of states may generate Republican or Democratic governance, but new parties in power do not bring clear benefits or costs – even if they retain power over an extended period. Thus, the results neither validate Republicans' aspirations nor confirm Democrats' fears. Instead, they suggest that partisan policy deserves neither the credit nor the blame it usually receives for the positive and negative features of Red and Blue states.

Notes

1 National Public Radio. "Texas Becoming a Magnet for Conservatives Fleeing Liberal States Like California." Available at: www.npr.org/2017/ 08/27/546391430/texas-becoming-a-magnet-for-conservatives-fleeing-liberal-states-like-california.

2 Texas seemed to have the upper hand in this particular comparison until recent years, when California has been making economic gains. See Lydia Phillis. 2017. "In the Texas vs. California Rivalry, California is Winning." *Houston Chronicle.* Available at: www.houstonchronicle.com/business/ texanomics/article/Gov-Abbott-keeps-bashing-California-but-Texas-11202452.php.

3 See John Schoen. 2015. "Are Red or Blue States Better Job Creators?" CNBC. Available at: www.cnbc.com/2015/08/13/are-red-or-blue-states-better-job-creators.html; and Irina Ivanova. 2017. "Inequality between Red and Blue States Persists Despite Booming Economy." CBS MoneyWatch. Available at: www.cbsnews.com/news/another-type-of-economic-inequality-the-red-blue-state-divide/.

4 See Richard Florida. 2015. "Is Life Better in America's Red States?" *New York Times.* Available at: www.nytimes.com/2015/01/04/opinion/ sunday/is-life-better-in-americas-red-states.html; and Nicholas Kristof. 2017. "Blue States Practice the Family Values Red States Preach." *New York Times.* Available at: www.nytimes.com/2017/11/18/opinion/sunday/blue-states-red-states-values.html.

5 Artz et al. (2016).

6   Jacob S. Hacker and Paul Pierson. 2016. "The Path to Prosperity is Blue." *New York Times*. Available at: www.nytimes.com/2016/07/31/opinion/campaign-stops/the-path-to-prosperity-is-blue.html.

7   Rickman and Wang (2018).

8   For the federal literature, see Bartels (2016) and Potrafke (2018).

9   Potrafke (2018).

10 Widestrom, Hayes, and Dennis (2018).

11 Cahan and Potrafke (2017).

12 Potrafke (2018), citing Beland and Boucher (2015).

13 Beland (2015).

14 Cestau (2018).

15 Bergquist (2018).

16 Bruno et al. (2015); Collins (2012); Eisenach (2015); Eren and Ozbeklik (2016); Feigenbaum, Fouirnaies, and Hall (2017); Hoxie et al. (2017); Jordan et al. (2016); Kalenkoski and Lacombe (2006); Kogan (2017); Minor (2012); Roberts and Habans (2015); Stevans (2009).

17 Eidlin (2018); Farber et al. (2018).

18 Bitler and Hoynes (2010); De Jong et al. (2006); Grogger (2003); Kaushal and Kaestner (2001); Mazzeo, Rab, and Eachus (2003); McKernan and Ratcliffe (2006); Nathan and Gais (2001); Schoeni and Blank (2000).

19 Meyer and Wu (2018); O'Brien and Travis (2018).

20 Low et al. (2018).

21 Andrés and Hempstead (2011); Barati (2016); Crandall et al. (2016); Fleegler et al. (2013); Gius (2014); Grambsch (2008); Kovandzic, Marvell, and Vieraitis (2005); Lee et al. (2013); Rand Corporation (2018); Sen and Panjamapirom (2012); Siegel, Ross, and King (2013); Siegel et al. (2017); Smith and Spiegler (In Press); Webster, Crifasi, and Vernick (2014).

22 Bitler and Zavodny (2001); Felkey and Lybecker (2014, 2018); Grossman et al. (2014); Jones and Jerman (2014, 2017); Joyce et al. (2009); Medoff (2007); New (2011); Sen (2007).

23 Gale, Krupkin, and Rueben (2015); Goff, Lebedinsky, and Lile (2012); Holcombe and Lacombe (2004); Reed and Rogers (2004).

24 For a review of the most recent changes, see https://files.taxfoundation.org/20171213151239/Tax-Foundation-FF568.pdf.

25 Shuai and Chmura (2013).

26 Serrato and Zidar (2016).

27 Nallareddy, Rouen, and Serrato (2018).

28 See Jensen and Malesky (2018).

29 Lindsey and Teles (2017).

30 Redbird (2017).

31 Hayes and Medina (2015).

32 Hatch and Rigby (2015).

33 Wolfson and Belman (2016).
34 See Henig (2009). A Mathematica research summary with negative results is available at www.mathematica-mpr.com/our-publications-and-findings/ projects/charter-schools-are-they-effective. A CREDO study that finds more positive results is available at http://credo.stanford.edu/documents/ NCSS%202013%20Final%20Draft.pdf.
35 National Center for Education Statistics. Available at: https://nces.ed.gov/ programs/coe/indicator_cgb.asp.
36 For a negative review of the main two positive studies, see https://nepc .colorado.edu/thinktank/review-meta-analysis.
37 National Association of Secondary School Principals. Available at: www .nassp.org/policy-advocacy-center/nassp-position-statements/private-school-vouchers/.
38 Jackson, Johnson, and Persico (2016).
39 The Nation's Report Card, a product of the National Assessment of Educational Progress, regularly ranks states (available at: www .nationsreportcard.gov). The National Education Association teachers' union also ranks states (available at: www.nea.org/assets/docs/180413-Rankings_And_Estimates_Report_2018.pdf), as does *Forbes Magazine* (available at: www.forbes.com/sites/karstenstrauss/2018/02/01/the-most-and-least-educated-states-in-the-u-s-in-2018/#3bb7886351e1) with surprisingly similar results.
40 Paglayan (2019).
41 Flavin (2018).
42 Jacoby and Schneider (2001).
43 For an updated review, see www.kff.org/medicaid/issue-brief/the-effects-of-medicaid-expansion-under-the-aca-updated-findings-from-a-literature-review-march-2018/. The research is supported by the Kaiser Family Foundation, which has been an advocate of expansion, though the report does not leave out any significant findings in the recent literature.
44 Duggan, Gupta, and Jackson (2019).
45 Randomized lotteries for Medicaid did produce changes in access, but not most health outcomes. The results of the lottery study differ from those of observational research. For a review of the Oregon Health Insurance Experiment and a full list of studies, see www.nber.org/oregon/1.home .html.
46 Michener (2018).
47 For a review, see AARP Policy Institute coverage, available at: www.aarp .org/content/dam/aarp/ppi/2017-01/experience-has-taught-us-that-high-risk-pools-do-not-serve-consumers-well.pdf.
48 Barry and Busch (2006).
49 Heaton (2015).

50 Waxman et al. (2014).
51 Galasso and Luo (2016).
52 See Elango et al. (2015).
53 See Roman (2013).
54 See Brookings Institution report, available at: www.brookings.edu/research/the-costs-opportunities-and-limitations-of-the-expansion-of-529-education-savings-accounts/.
55 Newman and O'Brien (2011).
56 Franko and Witko (2017).
57 Bucci (2018).
58 Kelly and Witko (2014).
59 Kelly and Witko (2012).
60 The Pew Charitable Trusts. 2017. "How States Engage in Evidence-Based Policymaking." Available at: www.pewtrusts.org/-/media/assets/2017/01/how_states_engage_in_evidence_based_policymaking.pdf.
61 Grumbach (2018a).
62 Holbein and Dynes (2018).
63 Gamm and Kousser (2017).
64 Galvin (2019).

6 THE ELUSIVE RED STATE MODEL

When the US Supreme Court ruled that the individual mandate in the Affordable Care Act was constitutional, liberals breathed a sigh of relief at having escaped a 5–4 decision that might have overturned the entirety of the law. But two liberal justices, Elena Kagan and Stephen Breyer, actually joined John Roberts and conservatives in objecting to the law's take-it-or-leave-it offer to the states on Medicaid expansion. Although the original law would have given states the near-illusory choice of either accepting the expansion or eliminating federal support for their full Medicaid program, the court ruling now gave states the choice of opting out of the expansion with no penalty.

Since the case against the Act was brought with the support of many Republican attorneys general, it set the stage for Republican activists and legislators to prove their conservative bona fides by blocking the expansion. Yet as governors know well, Medicaid is a popular program, and cutting it leads to declines in incumbent governor vote share.[1] On the one hand, what followed was among the clearest examples of the policy impact of partisan control of the states: many Red states refused or delayed the relatively generous federal offer paying for nearly all the initial expansion costs, instead standing up for the principle of limited government (or, depending on your perspective, sticking it to both largely-Democratic constituencies and Obama himself). On the other hand, even in a period of unprecedented conservative rule, 36 states doubled the size of their largest program. This was driven by federal expansion under a Democratic president, but often supported by Republican governors. Increased Republican control of state governments has thus had real consequences for health care recipients, but even so has not fully disrupted the liberal direction of policy change nationwide.

Republicans have more often stuck to professed policy commitments when it comes to abortion law, though this has actually meant support for greater government regulation. Increases in Republican control brought forth numerous additional abortion laws. Today, 27 states have mandated counseling and a waiting period, including several that mandate the specific (and purposely frightening) content of the counseling; 22 states have limits on late-term abortions; 38 states require parental notice or consent for minors; 26 states require surgical center standards for abortion clinics; 12 states require ultrasounds prior to abortion; and 8 states are trying to require that abortion doctors have hospital admission privileges. More than 288 restrictions on abortion were enacted in the states just in the period of 2011 to 2015.[2]

Alongside these restrictions, US abortions have been falling. The rate reached 188 abortions per 1,000 live births in 2015 (the latest available data), down from 233 per 1,000 in the same jurisdictions in 2006, and down from an overall high of 359 per 1,000 in 1980.[3] However, a closer look makes it more difficult to draw a direct line from policy to outcomes. Abortions have been falling across both Red and Blue states and have been part of a much broader decline in pregnancy (especially in teenage years), driven principally by increased access to contraceptives and a decline in unintended pregnancies. The largest declines were among young people and racial minorities, with most remaining abortions occurring early in pregnancies among the young and unmarried. It is possible that state policy contributed to relative abortion rates by making abortion harder to obtain in some states. Conversely, efforts to make it easier to obtain in other states, especially through funding (including via the Medicaid expansion) may also be influential. But, of course, abortion is still legal nationwide and numerous other factors associated with state partisanship, such as religiosity and demographics, impact abortion rates. Courts have limited the ability of legislatures to change abortion laws in ways that actually change behavior on the ground, with implemented policies differing less across states following court actions (compared to when they were initially passed).[4] States can try to limit abortions to only the early months of pregnancies (which, if implemented, might meaningfully change their abortion rate), but be constrained by courts to only ban those just before birth without a medical rationale (which has far less impact because it does not address most abortion circumstances). Overall, the more common abortion clinic access and licensing laws seem to have little effect (or, depending on the law, indiscernible effects) on abortion rates, though increased funding for abortion services may have greater effects.[5]

These two examples show real and considerable policy effects partially attributable to Republican control of American state governments. As I have demonstrated, such effects are not generally clear across the policy spectrum and are often less extensive in areas other than abortion and Medicaid. But even in these two cases of policy change (successful, from a Republican point of view), the impact on socio-economic outcomes has been more limited than publicly perceived. In the Medicaid case, classic policy liberalism continued its expansion in the face of conservative opposition (though poor and minority constituents in non-expanding states bore the brunt).[6] In the abortion case, policies marginally helped along social trends that had already been reducing long-term abortion rates, but wide availability was still the norm based on federal and legal constraints.

Neither example, nor the book's larger premises or evidence, should be taken to mean that there are no partisan effects on state policy or (more nihilistically) that nothing matters for social outcomes. Indeed, Republican control of state government has produced real policy differences, perhaps even more so than in prior eras when ideology and party were less closely aligned. Even so, these examples do illustrate the extent to which the path from party control to policy change to social outcomes is a tortuous one, with particular barriers for conservatives attempting to roll back the power of government. Eliminating or reducing the scope of government programs or the scale of intervention in the economy is an uphill battle; moreover, even when put into action, policies that slow the growth of spending or regulation do not usually have the effects on state economies or societies that proponents or opponents anticipate. When Republicans have moved policy substantially, it has most often been in relatively symbolic areas (like gun control) where the states they controlled had already adopted conservative stances. Thus, many of these changes have had limited effects.

What do Republicans Have to Show for Their Revolution?

I am hopeful that the triangulating approach pursued in this book can add to the current research literature as well as public understanding of the policy impact of party politics. Narrative histories demonstrate that Republican state officials are often consumed with the same budgetary politics as their predecessors. They can quite often be successful, but usually in concert with other factors such as interest groups and public opinion, and not always by sticking to their hand-picked policy agenda. My quantitative models of policymaking added two important findings. First, that even when Republican control is influential, conservatives are often fighting an uphill battle against rising liberalism, and, second, that change is usually modest and long-term, rather than immediate and transformative. In addition, issue-specific quantitative studies show that state partisanship influenced some policy adoptions, but the findings were often conditional, with some issue-specific factors and path-dependent histories also playing important roles.

My reviews of social and economic outcomes associated with Republican policy success also flagged important considerations for those who would tout a Red state model for social and economic success or failure. Many policies have important effects, but the size of the effects on proximate outcomes are usually smaller than anticipated (right-to-work laws, for example, only slowly accelerated the nationwide trend toward lower unionization rates), and the effects on broader outcomes often fail to materialize altogether (visions of economic revitalization or greater employment based on right-to-work laws, for example, did not match reality). Simplistic comparisons of one-year differences in Red and Blue states do not tell policymakers or citizens much about the effects of party-preferred policies. Even scholars may fall victim to picking a few outcomes most likely to show effects, and thereby failing to learn from what the lack of evidence says about other relationships between policy and outcomes.

Though American state governments do bear the marks of a quarter-century of increasing Republican rule, they still largely take on the same functions and pursue the same goals as they did previously. There is considerable variation across the states, though only part of this is due to partisanship. The 2018 election brought at least a temporary end to increasing Republican rule, so the period since 1992 may come to be seen as a relative high point in both Republican electoral success and their policy impact. But the Republican revolution has been less transformational than advertised. Despite protestations, there is no Red state model of policies with predictable socio-economic outcomes that Republicans can tout and bring to other states. Most state differences are not due to current politics or policies, with true policy effects varied and multi-directional. The Red state model is, in practice, mostly a slower and less active version of what is on offer in Blue states, with policies and outcomes much closer to contemporary neighbors from either party than to Red states of the past.

Implications from Varied Evidence

This book's compilation of prior research and varied original studies has uncovered both common patterns and differences across the policy spectrum. To review, Table 6.1 summarizes the conclusions and takeaways from each form of evidence. From research using broad metrics to judge the policy outputs of Republican governance, we learned that Red states produce relatively more conservative policies while policy as a whole trends leftward. This suggests conservatives can slow, but not redirect, the advance of government into new social roles. From interviews and books covering policymaking in each state, we learned that budgetary politics still dominate, with most Republican governors constrained by the economy and the math and most Republican legislatures lacking a sustained menu of policies to pursue. Social issue trends may be most visible, but the hard problems of government require less ideologically consistent solutions. In studies of policymaking in specific issue areas, we noticed that Republican gains were most striking where the party had a direct political interest in the outcome or, alternatively, where they found Democrats or the federal government moving in the same direction. As the book moved to the effects of policy, issue-specific and broader research again contributed separate insights. Policy evaluations of specific changes showed smaller-than-expected but real effects on outcomes with obvious policy levers (taxes affect incomes, for example) but much less movement on broader metrics (like economic growth). The broadest studies linking partisan control to socio-economic outcomes put even these policy effects in context. The policies consistently implemented in Red and Blue states

Table 6.1 *Conclusions and implications of the book's evidence*

Type of evidence	Findings	Takeaway
Quantitative studies of policy output under Republican control	Significant Red/Blue state differences in relative conservatism, but liberal absolute trends in policy	Conservatives can slow the growth of liberalism, but not alter the direction of policy
Qualitative research on Republican policymaking	Governors' agendas are budget focused and dependent; Republican legislatures have narrower agendas	Social issue trends do not encompass more central and less ideological policymaking
Issue-specific studies of the policy outputs of Republican control	Largest policy moves come when direct political gains are at stake or when Republicans have liberal and federal allies	Republicans unite more for partisan gains; substantive policy is more bipartisan
Policy-specific studies of policy outcomes	Easier, but still difficult, to move proximate outcomes; much harder to move broad socio-economic state features	Policy matters for specific outcomes, with smaller effects than anticipated
Broad studies of Republican policy outcomes	Despite associations, no systematic differences between the socio-economic outcomes of Red and Blue states	Policies with most influence are not enacted broadly enough to move the needle

may not be consequential enough to change the relative standing of the states on key socio-economic outcomes.

Given the issue-area variation, the book also provides some issue-specific lessons for policymakers and scholars. With example policies, I have summarized these implications in Table 6.2. Partisan influence may be strongest when it comes to the rules of political competition, where party interests are directly at stake (though the courts still have a role in limiting how much parties can rig the process to their benefit). When an issue area has somehow been dislodged from conventional left–right ideological conflict, there is also room for large movements in policy. In these circumstances, federal and subnational policy often move together while conservative movement figures seek to find new allies and redefine what constitutes the conservative viewpoint (as in the case of criminal justice). Even when it comes to polarizing issues that divide liberals and conservatives, we still saw differences between the social and economic issue spheres. In social issues, Red and Blue states moved far apart in some areas (guns and

Table 6.2 *Lessons for policy*

Type of policy	Examples	Findings
Political reforms	Redistricting; voter identification; early voting	Real partisan influence with court constraints
Consensus policy	Criminal justice reform; charter schools; pre-K education	Can move left or right with broad coalition and opportune political timing
Ideological social issues	Abortion; guns; immigration; gay rights; drugs	Polarizing partisan influence but liberal social trends; harder to move outcomes
Ideological economic issues	Taxes, spending, regulation	Marginal redistribution possible; backlash when cut size or scope of government

abortion) while initial division gave way to liberal advance in others (gay rights). But social outcomes seemed limited in the polarizing cases, perhaps because federal policy limited the range of state variation. On economic policy, conservatives faced their traditional global difficulty: the size and scope of government remained difficult to contract.

Combined, these findings add perspective to popular debate on partisanship and policymaking and add context to other research. Focusing on the most high-profile states or the most divisive issue areas at any given moment can paint a distorted picture of policy action in the states. Immigration policies may well spread quickly across the states accompanied by televised protest, for example, while early childhood education slowly expands without much notice. Voter identification laws designed to benefit Republicans may generate the most national concern, even if research shows limited effects. Meanwhile, technical changes to local government sales and property tax powers (beyond our notice) may end up profoundly affecting the incomes of the poor. Understanding state policymaking requires attention to the mundane and the divisive, the blatantly partisan along with the subtle and distinct.

What the Results Mean for Conservative Parties

The book's analyses were specific to recent trends in state partisanship and policy in American state governments. Nonetheless, they contain several empirical regularities that match prior studies of politics and policy across time and countries. First, government's liberal bias limits the scope of conservative policy impact and determines its character. Since government tends to grow in size and scope over time, a party that seeks to counteract those trends is liable to face considerable challenges. It may have occasional successes in reducing government's role, but they are often fleeting rather than permanent, or counteracted by expansions elsewhere. This means the conservative parties' greatest impacts may come from blocking government expansions proposed by liberals, rather than innovating on their own. The Republican Party has been influential in maintaining America's more limited social welfare policies and (by global standards) its laissez-faire approach, meaning its contribution to policy has been quite consequential. However, within the context of a conservative national government moving in a liberal direction, Republicans took control of state governments that had already taken on an expansive scope. Their largest impact came in slowing or preventing continued expansion but viewed through the lens of historical political development or long-standing inter-state differences such impacts were limited.

Second, Republican influence can be greater when the party prioritizes policies not on the conventional government expansion–contraction continuum or when it embraces changes already in motion. Where both increased availability of contraception and restrictive policies emerged alongside reduced abortion funding, they could collectively further the decline in abortions. Where unions were already declining as a share of the workforce and becoming increasingly concentrated in the public sector, Republican policies could further weaken their role (especially in politics). When they took on charter school expansion, traditionally a Democratic alternative to voucher-based private school choice, Republicans could help expand the number of children served by those schools and help stimulate many new school reform proposals. When they linked a Democratic effort to reduce punitiveness with a conservative effort to limit prison expansion, Republicans could help reverse the direction of a generation's worth of policy on criminal justice. Conservative policies that try to block social changes in progress, such as increasing acceptance of gay rights, were much less successful.

Third, the effects of conservative party control often look more substantial at first glance than when they are explored in greater depth.

Given the many descriptive associations between party control and state outcomes such as economic growth, employment, and population growth, there will usually be a partisan story of success or failure available for those motivated to tell it. Given the parties' regional patterns of support and governance, each party's supporters will be able to look at the other's states as backward-looking, culturally distant, or perpetually downtrodden. With an expanding political industry, increased election advertising, constant public relations campaigning, ever-growing and nationalized polarization, and rising partisan and online media outlets, there will continue to be lots of actors with incentives to highlight state differences they say are attributable to the parties. Given that many of these professed outcomes can be causes of state partisanship, as well as potential outcomes, and because partisanship is now correlated with nearly every social and economic attribute of states and individuals, these arguments can be superficially convincing and hard to counter. But the evidence here, which separates the effects of permanent state differences from changes in partisanship, finds limited systematic associations.

Fourth, and more troubling for Democrats, conservative parties can maintain a successful electoral coalition despite modest policy results. Republican Party politicians, activists, and voters are happier with a slower pace of policymaking than the Democratic coalition and seem less motivated to be the first state to try new approaches. Even when Republicans came to power with an extensive agenda that had been blocked by years of prior Democratic rule, the energy for overwhelming change tended to dissipate after a few sessions. Like Democrats, however, Republicans can selectively use the tools of government to reward their supporters; they have even increased reliance on sales taxes over progressive property taxes. Republicans are also quite effective at narrow institutional policy changes designed to benefit the party electorally. They have used redistricting processes to the full extent possible, enacted numerous restrictions aimed at Democratic voters, and limited the power of Democratic governors. The party that is less concerned with democratizing reforms and fairness for its own sake may therefore benefit from playing the political game, first and foremost, to win elections and maintain power.

A study of one period in recent American political history cannot, of course, be the final verdict on the impact of parties or the limits of conservatism. A party's agenda, capacity, or strategy changes across time, level of government, and place; even within the time period reviewed here, there is evidence that Republicans took greater conservative steps during the Obama administration compared to the Clinton and Bush administrations. Republicans might also have had greater impact in states such as Wisconsin, where they had more of a progressive legacy to counteract, than in states such as Alabama, where policy already matched their preferred contours.

Nonetheless, the evidence presented here is also not easy to dismiss. I chose a case that seemed ripe for conservative success: a large and sustained shift in state power coinciding with a clear ideological agenda and a party moving rightward. Conditions may change, but Republican control of the states in the 1990s, 2000s, and 2010s offered a reasonable test of their ability to transform government and society. Rather than proving an exception to the international and historical limits to conservative governance, the outcomes reflected these same limitations.

Alternative Interpretations

This review does not foreclose other interpretations of the evidence, which might lead to a more expansive view of the success of the Republican revolution in American state politics. First, it is reasonable to ask about the counterfactual of Democratic control. Do Republican accomplishments look more significant when compared against what Democrats might have achieved? If Republican gains in the states since the 1990s had instead been replaced by Democratic gains, this would have made more of a difference to the shape of state governments. Even based on my cautious interpretation of the evidence, it suggests that – in this alternative story of Democratic dominance – state government would take up a greater share of the economy, and numerous state policies would have moved further leftward. Given that Democratic governments are more active than Republican ones, we would likely have seen many more policy innovations, as well as new programs spread more widely across the nation. It is reasonable to think more states would look like California and less like Texas, at least in policy.

That said, a few qualifications are in order. Many of the California–Texas differences were already set in place. Some conservative trends, such as those in education policy, have seen nationwide growth and might not have been stopped even in this scenario; while many liberal trends have continued across states even without Democratic control. It is also worth asking what would have needed to happen in order to generate this level of Democratic dominance. The scenario would likely have included sustained Republican presidencies moving federal policy rightward, and perhaps a less liberal Democratic party highly compromised on racial and social issues. The counterfactual assumes all else would be held constant, which would not be true in practice. If the trade-off was more state control in exchange for six equivalents of the Trump administration, I doubt many Democrats would take the bargain.

A second critique might be that I have downplayed the stakes of the policy changes that Republicans have achieved. If access to abortion is a fundamental right in many Democrats' eyes, any restriction on its availability could be judged disastrous. If you are a potential Medicaid recipient left off the expansion in a Red state, party control certainly makes a difference to you. If climate change requires immediate nationwide action to avert catastrophe, then many states dragging their heels could be judged in apocalyptic terms. If union resilience is seen as the main possibility for stemming the tide of rising inequality, recent Republican gains might have been enough (in some eyes) to leave us forever unequal. Alternatively, Republicans may believe that doing all they can to reduce abortions is morally equivalent to stopping murders midstream, in which case stopping even a few is of the upmost importance. If high taxes constitute theft or high regulation is judged the first step on the road to tyranny, modest policy changes could likewise be seen as critical. Given such beliefs and attitudes, nothing I have uncovered detracts from these interpretations of the policies Republicans have enacted. I do consider these changes consequential, but believe they are still limited in comparison with the more dramatic over-time trends in policy across states and the remaining state-specific differences that did not shift with party control.

Third, an alternative view could focus on the cold mechanics of power politics above and beyond policy and social outcomes. As I have said, Republicans have been effective at staying in power – and they have drawn district boundaries in a way that has increased Republican advantage. For some models of politics that view politicians as single-minded seekers of re-election – and even some definitions of parties as inherently coalitions of politicians seeking power – this is enough to declare victory on the central mission.[7] Even those who view parties as primarily coalitions of benefit-seeking interest groups might see a few successful redistributions of benefits from Democratic to Republican constituencies as the name of the game. I see parties as also interested in policy gains and as (at least a little) sincere in their relative emphasis on different values and ideological convictions. By these standards, Republicans have been less successful at translating their recent electoral gains to substantive victories.

A fourth interpretation might quibble with my standard of success. Perhaps the focus should be on whether the Republican Party has actually moved policy more than would be expected, given the changes in state public opinion and the voices of voters as expressed in elections. According to this view, by achieving rule changes and successfully controlling redistricting, Republicans have counteracted the public's ideas and interests. Despite declining public support, they stayed in power in states such as North Carolina, Wisconsin, and Michigan in 2018, and then used their (in this view ill-gotten) power to further entrench themselves. To the extent that this is a moral argument, my results do not address it. But the book's quantitative models and qualitative reviews both seek to assess whether Republican control mattered independently of nationwide or state-specific trends in public opinion. Perhaps any additional gains made that do not represent public opinion change could be judged unfair, but the results show that party-driven changes are small relative to broader trends in public opinion and long-standing state cultural differences.

A fifth, related, objection might point to the overwhelming support for liberal policy positions across states and districts. Indeed, public officials misjudge the extent to which the American public holds liberal policy positions on a broad range of issues, with even Democratic officials underestimating support for their party's preferred policies.[8] To take one example, regardless of state, the public prefers a higher minimum wage to that which is on offer – even though policymakers raise the minimum wage more in states that prefer a higher wage, every state undershoots public preferences (by an average of $2).[9] The American public, however, has also long held conservative predispositions on broader values and ideological conceptualizations, even while many gravitate toward liberal policy positions. The Republican Party represents the public's broader endorsements of limited government, traditional values, and national identity, where on a worldwide scale the American public stands out as particularly conservative despite their support for liberal policy.[10] Republicans win elections among publics that do not support their policy positions, in part because the public's reaction to too much liberal policy being enacted in one swoop is to become more conservative. In slowing liberalism, rather than retracting the role of state governments, Republicans are perhaps enacting this conservative side of public opinion: the public's long-standing skepticism toward big government.

A final objection might be that I have told another story of American politics that, like many prior studies of electoral and institutional politics, is largely specific to the unique South. It is true that nearly every pattern in the book applies disproportionately in that region. In the South, Republicans have won and sustained control of state governments more than they have in any other region. They have also inherited more governments that were already conservative leaning and that thus required fewer changes. Although the patterns that I have documented hold up nationwide, one could argue that state politics outside of the South fit a more traditional thermostatic pattern: Republicans and Democrats have exchanged control of states in the Midwest, for example, each enacting only a few priority items before their party control is counteracted. It is true that the Southern states have showed more permanent electoral change and less policy change. But Southern regional influence has been quite broad, encompassing non-confederate neighboring states that had less conservative governments, such as Oklahoma, Missouri, Kentucky, and West Virginia. Moreover, even states with Southern cultural regions, such as Ohio and Indiana, have become less competitive for Democrats without fundamentally changing their governments' characters.

Even so, I do endorse seeing part of the story told here as an aspect of the Southern realignment, if for no other reason than it helps correct misperceptions. Public observers tend to assume that Southern states went Republican when they moved in presidential voting, but the state-level trends are actually quite recent. Republican gains were delayed in Southern state legislatures because older conservative voters stuck with the Democrats throughout their voting lives, in part because the party ran conservative state candidates that matched their legislative districts.[11] As happened in Congress, Republican gains came mostly at the expense of the most conservative politicians in the Democratic

Party. This not only increased polarization but also meant that changes in policymaker opinion and political culture were not as extreme as may have been assumed from changing election outcomes. As it did under Democratic control, the South still stands out as a region with distinctive policies and a slow ascension to national political trends.

Conservatism as an Unachievable Ideal?

Given this book's largely skeptical account of Republicans' ability to translate their ideological goals into policy outputs and desirable social outcomes – and its equation of that record with endemic difficulties of government retrenchment – one reading would suggest a severe rebuttal of conservatism's potential. Even when given power in the form of one-party rule by the world's most consistently conservative party, conservatives are unable to achieve their stated objectives. A less charitable view might suggest that it is all a farce, with conservative branding merely serving as a smokescreen for power-hungry politicians uninterested in policy. Even a sympathetic review might suggest that the conservative project is not sustainable as a governing vision, with built-in tendencies to support what conservative critics label "Democrat-light" or "Republican in Name Only" policies. If viewed as a project to reduce the role of government in society, return America to its foundational roots, and shrink public service provision and redistributive efforts, conservatism is indeed a perennial failure.

However, conservatism has always functioned more as a set of skeptical predispositions – with reminders of traditional strengths and warnings of quickening change and widening scope – rather than as a menu of concrete and immutable policy positions. Conservatism, from this perspective, functions primarily as a break on liberalism that raises the standards for adopting new government functions, forces policy concessions that decentralize and marketize implementation, and asks policymakers to honor prior social arrangements and voluntary action. Even in this sense, it is still fighting a losing battle over time, as societies evolve toward new social norms and governments take on more problems and invent new policy tools. This does not, however, mean it lacks impact: conservatism accounts in part for distinctive American approaches to policy and government and keeps states changing at different speeds without ultimate convergence.

Conservative movement leaders can also take heed of my results. The Republican state takeover was their most ambitious project, set off by devolution and the investment of substantial movement resources to reinvigorate federalism and limit the budding welfare state. Organizing in the states, from grassroots organizations to think tanks – and authoring model bills to share and implement nationally – has been successful in conventional terms: it has developed many new state experts, provided activist support for conservative policy goals, and resulted in quite a few bills being passed. But its failures signal that the tendency for government to grow in size and scope (and for social liberalism to advance over time) was not due to insufficient conservative organizing, uncommitted politicians, or a leftward-moving Overton Window. Instead, the challenges are inherent to the infeasibility of achieving a conservative restoration, as well as the unpopularity of the conservative vision when put into practice (especially where benefits are revoked). Even Tea Party governors are forced to balance budgets while caring for and educating citizens. The most successful conservative movement in the industrialized world passed a lot of legislation and won a lot of elections but was still unable to adjust the main duties of American state governments, or their size and scope. If that is a permanent limitation, it might make more sense to concentrate on improving the efficiency of existing institutions and limiting further expansion.

To provide inspiration for future efforts, Republicans may also want to reflect on where they were able to move policy and shift social outcomes. One place to look is taking opportunities to join Democrats in the early stages of nationwide shifts. Republicans initially treated calls for public charter schools as efforts to exclude religious and private schools from parental choice, but eventually came to see them as a challenge to unionized and bureaucratic school districts. Republican states even joined forces with the Obama administration to align state policies on charter schools, standardized testing, and teacher evaluation with administration priorities in an effort to win federal grant funding, in the process making education the only major issue area where states collectively moved rightward during an era of Republican dominance. On criminal justice, Republicans abandoned some initial electorally beneficial aims (known colloquially as "lock em up" crime policy) in favor of less punitive policies that drew from other conservative principles (such as less prison spending and government expansion). Mainstream conservative institutions such as ALEC and the Koch network joined liberal foundations and civil rights advocates in championing the shift toward criminal justice reform, which started in conservative states and has now become national. Adopting a flexible conservatism that looks for victories and liberal allies can thus be a path to significant policy gains in state and national policy.

The limits of the Republican revolution in the states can also impart lessons for federal politics. The nationalization of state politics, especially in the American political system based on geographic representation, has largely helped Republicans win power in conservative states. But state gains, like federal gains, have often not translated into conservative policy practice. At the federal level, Republicans have also failed to shrink government or restore traditional values, but they at least have had more success, with gains in areas such as cutting taxes and restoring defense spending. State Republican politicians mostly lack those options, with less deficit financing to fall back on and no category of spending they are committed to expand. The problems of the national Republican Party, in full control of the federal government for the 115th Congress and yet able to pass only one major conservative priority (tax cuts), may thus not be specific to the Trump administration or the constraints of federal power. Republicans have more options in national government, where debt financing awaits and national security priorities remain. The increasing distance between Republican campaign rhetoric and their efforts in governance should also not be seen as a Trump creation. The limits of conservatism are clear at all levels of government, even where Republicans maintain full control and no executive has led them off message or toward a new agenda. Despite plenty of competent and committed conservative governors, Republican policy results have also been limited in the states.

Although left-wing activists often envy conservative organizing in the states – believing that it has succeeded in moving the Overton Window (the realm of acceptable policy) rightward, I find the evidence less convincing. If we credit conservatives with normalizing the right-wing options in issue areas like education and labor (where many states have moved rightward), do we not also need to credit liberals with moving the acceptable range of policy options leftward on campaign finance, civil rights, the environment, health care, gay rights, drug policy, taxes, and convenience voting (where states have collectively moved leftward even in a period of rising Republican rule)?

It is fair for liberals to lament that the United States remains, in international terms, a country with relatively conservative policies at all levels of government (and perhaps to credit the conservative movement for maintaining that US social and economic system). It is less reasonable, however, to declare the conservative project to shift the policy conversation rightward an unmitigated success. Conservatives have won some battles and reshaped some conversations, but policy often moves leftward anyway.

Democrats' Road Forward

The results of this book also give Democrats concerns to ponder. The 2018 elections gave the party its best results in a generation, yet they failed to regain the ground they had lost in state governments. Increasing geographic polarization, nationally and within states, and the relative concentration of Democrats in urban and coastal areas, mean there are no obvious solutions to their lack of competitiveness in many states where they regularly used to have a chance at winning statewide races and legislative seats. Although Republicans can be blamed for gerrymandering and electoral rules changes, much of the lack of competitiveness stems from an inability to compete in Southern and rural areas, and from the related downsides of a national liberal party. Democrats can, of course, retreat to California and other states where they have increasing power and a broad policy agenda. In some ways, this book's focus on control of most states and most state policies is misleading, given that so many more people are affected by California's policies and programs than those of other states. Perhaps control of the Metropolitan Water District of Southern California is worth more than control of some states, given it affects more people and has more resources. But such an account understates the extent to which states matter permanently in America's political system, where they will continue to hold the most prominent subnational place in the Constitution and nearly all policy regimes.

The nationalization of state politics also makes a voter backlash specific to state political outcomes less likely over time. Although there are cases, such as Kansas under Brownback or Wisconsin under Walker, where state policy direction becomes salient, most of the time voters barely register what is happening in state capitols. Overall, public approval is just as high for polarized legislatures led by more extreme parties as for consensus legislatures run by moderates; the main predictor of one's legislative approval is simply whether one's partisan side is in control.[12] Voters are judging by national standards; when it comes to voting for the state legislature, presidential approval has three times the impact of state legislative approval![13] Democratic state legislators, no matter what they were doing, were seen as representatives of Obama under his administration, just as Republican legislators are now tied to Trump in voters' minds. Although local newspapers and television are still covering state politics, citizens are moving away from these sources in favor of national outlets. As a result, fewer people now know the name of their governor, despite knowing the names of national leaders such as the vice president.[14] For a few reasons, Democrats have fared poorly from this nationalization: first, their party was historically more reliant on local, party-distinct candidate reputations; second, Democratic policymaking has historically been more tied to bringing home visible benefits to districts; and third, representation systems built on geography hurt the more spatially concentrated party.[15] That disadvantage is unlikely to change.

Democrats can be heartened to learn that liberal policies are more abundant than conservative ones, that their policies are more likely to make lists of evidence-based solutions, and that their myriad programs and regulatory approaches are largely stable once implemented. Like Republican control of government, however, Democratic control of state government did not fundamentally reorient government and failed to produce large changes in states' major socio-economic conditions. Thus, while Democrats can pass more policies and support a broader range of government endeavors, this does not demonstrate that a Blue state model is well-honed, consequential, and available to apply anywhere. Instead, Democrats govern many states with clear socio-economic challenges that they have proven no more able to solve than Republicans.

The liberal policy solutions that do have evidence of success tend to be straightforward: giving resources to constituents in need helps them, as does coordinating services and targeting the neediest populations. Although a reasonable policy approach, it does not always add up to a saleable public agenda. It does not address fundamental challenges such as market inequality or climate change. Democratic states prove early to adopt new ideas, a sometimes-enviable approach, but one that can mean a "Let's do something" approach to addressing problems even before the dust has settled on the workability of initial efforts. Scaling up small successful programs for statewide reach has been a consistent challenge, with state-level results often failing to match optimistic extrapolations from early trials. Democrats should not be spared criticism of the tendency of states to pass symbolic social issue policies, rather than focusing on the most difficult problems. Neither party has proved able to raise their states' relative standing on educational quality, public health, or economic strength. For both sides, it is much easier to continue fighting the culture wars than to take on perennial struggles.

Partisanship, Innovation, and Change

The United States has a stable two-party system, with more entrenched state-level party dominance and more ideological and uncooperative parties than it had a generation ago. The conservative revolution in the states coincided with a further nationalization and polarization of American politics, meaning state elections are now often treated as referenda on national politics and the president. This despite many problems still being addressed mainly at lower levels. Even in a nationalized era, constituents can still occasionally get animated about local schools or town ordinances, but state politics (the middle level of governance) has mostly lost its resonance. It has become a venue for national parties and interest groups to pursue their agendas, while not carrying independent weight in the minds of most citizens.

We should not expect these features of state politics and policy to change anytime soon. The parties have their agendas, the states have their partisan leans, and the common state programs and responsibilities are here to stay. Yet every day, a state legislator still works on consequential legislation and a governor still decides the fate of a program or policy. And nearly every day, some of those decisions and efforts make a difference to some constituents. The fact that changes in state partisan control are not enough to explain policy differences or outcomes across states is not evidence that they do not matter. Instead, it is a sign that the daily work of government is still consequential – despite the partisan theatre – even when it is not about one side winning a battle. Increased conservative power does not foreclose the possibility that a liberal or non-partisan effort will gain steam nationally, or that a state will choose an independent path on a state-specific challenge. Since state governments are not losing their traditional responsibilities or consolidating all of their operations, bureaucrats and policy experts still have many tools for making a difference and many avenues for pursuing change.

Charitable foundations have, as of late, been asking their grant recipients to articulate a "theory of change" for their organizational missions. As the Annie E. Casey Foundation puts it: "A theory of change outlines how to create [community] change ... by showing the relationships between outcomes, assumptions, strategies and results."[16] The idea is that participants in public-oriented work should have an understanding of how their individual efforts contribute to the broader good. The ask implies that lasting and effective action cannot stem from service work alone, but requires building coalitions, coordinating efforts, and attending to opportunities. Politics cannot be avoided in these discussions, as it is the means by which societies make broad-scale changes, usually through public programs and policies. Among politically minded advocacy groups, these theories of change sometimes end up quite partisan and ideological (with the necessity of Democratic ascension assumed). But even ostensibly apolitical groups tend to rely on change scenarios that might only come with a broad leftward or rightward national shift. Although foundations and civic groups, like individuals, are more often oriented to the local or national level than the state level, many of the challenges they seek to address necessitate aligned state policy.

The states may no longer serve as independent "laboratories of democracy" that, as Louis Brandeis stressed, "try novel social and economic experiments." However, in a wide range of issue areas, they are still our primary means for innovating new policies and enacting our collective visions of the good society.[17] Today, such battles often take the form of partisan competition over staid liberal or conservative ideas. But the stalling of the conservative movement has shown that there is more to state politics than party control of government and the general ideological direction of policy. There is no off-the-shelf Red state model to achieve a conservative or just society. At the same time, there remain plenty of non-partisan policy innovations, nationwide political trends, state-specific and regional exceptions, and everyday government decisions that impact lives beyond partisan political winds. More theories of change should acknowledge the important role of state policy in social advancement, but fewer should rely on the perennial theory that all that is required is a final vanquishing of one's partisan opponents.

Notes

1 Kogan (2018).
2 Abortion restriction information originates from the Guttmacher Institute, with updates available at www.guttmacher.org/united-states/abortion/state-policies-abortion; mapped summaries of policy differences are available via FiveThirtyEight at https://fivethirtyeight.com/features/maps-of-access-to-abortion-by-state/.
3 Centers for Disease Control. 2018. Abortion Surveillance – United States, 2015. Available at: www.cdc.gov/mmwr/volumes/67/ss/ss6713a1.htm?s_cid=ss6713a1_w.
4 Kastellec (2018).
5 Austin and Harper (2018); Jones and Jerman (2017); Medoff (2015). But some studies do find larger impacts, especially those associated with mass clinic closures in Texas; see Fischer, Royer, and White (2017). The largest effects seem to come from access to abortion funding, already limited in Red states prior to the latest wave of anti-abortion policies. In 2019, several states tried to nearly eliminate abortions, in an attempt to force the US Supreme Court to revisit *Roe v. Wade*. Were that effort to succeed, it would make state action much more influential.
6 Medicaid decisions exacerbated existing racial and class inequalities across states. See Michener (2018).
7 See Aldrich (2011) for that conception of parties and Mayhew (2004) for that view of legislators.
8 Broockman and Skovron (2018).
9 Simonovits, Guess, and Nagler (2019).
10 See Ellis and Stimson (2012); Grossmann and Hopkins (2016).
11 Myers (2016).
12 Richardson and Milyo (2017).
13 Rogers (2016).
14 Hopkins (2018).
15 Grossmann and Hopkins (2016); Hopkins (2018).
16 See Annie E. Casey Foundation. "Theory of Change." Available at: www.aecf.org/resources/theory-of-change/.
17 *New State Ice Co. v. Liebmann*, 285 U.S. 262 (1932).

REFERENCES

Adolph, Christopher, Christian Breunig, and Chris Koski. In Press. "The Political Economy of Budget Trade-Offs." *Journal of Public Policy*, 1–26.

Alberty, E. M. 2014. "The Spread of Charter School Legislation among the States: An Application of Policy Diffusion Theory to Education Policy." Dissertation. Retrieved from ProQuest Database (Accession No. 1557451).

Aldrich, John. 2011. *Why Parties? A Second Look*. Chicago: University of Chicago Press.

Alexander, Michelle. 2010. *The New Jim Crow: Mass Incarceration in the Age of Colorblindness*. New York: The New Press.

Allan, James P., and Lyle Scruggs. 2004. "Political Partisanship and Welfare State Reform in Advanced Industrial Societies." *American Journal of Political Science* 48(3): 496–512.

Amidon, Ethan. 2018. "Politics and the Death Penalty: 1930–2010." *American Journal of Criminal Justice* 43(4): 831–860.

Andrés, Antonio Rodríguez, and Katherine Hempstead. 2011. "Gun Control and Suicide: The Impact of State Firearm Regulations in the United States, 1995–2004." *Health Policy* 101: 95–103.

Anzia, Sarah, and Terry Moe. 2016. "Do Politicians Use Policy to Make Politics? The Case of Public-Sector Labor Laws." *American Political Science Review* 110(4): 763–777.

Arceneaux, Kevin. 2002. "Direct Democracy and the Link between Public Opinion and State Abortion Policy." *State Politics and Policy Quarterly* 2(4): 372–387.

Armingeon, Klaus, Kai Guthmann, and David Weisstanner. 2015. "Choosing the Path of Austerity: How Parties and Policy Coalitions Influence Welfare

State Retrenchment in Periods of Fiscal Consolidation." *West European Politics* 39(4): 628–647.

Artz, Georgeanne M., Kevin D. Duncan, Arthur P. Hall, and Peter F. Orazem. 2016. "Do State Business Climate Indicators Explain Relative Economic Growth at State Borders?" *Regional Science* 56(3): 395–419.

Austin, Nichole, and Sam Harper. 2018. "Assessing the Impact of TRAP Laws on Abortion and Women's Health in the USA: A Systematic Review." *BMJ Sexual and Reproductive Health* 44: 128–134.

Barati, Mehdi. 2016. "New Evidence on the Impact of Concealed Carry Weapon Laws on Crime." *International Review of Law and Economics* 47: 76–83.

Barrilleaux, Charles. 2006. "Ideological Cleavage, Political Competition, and Policy Making in the American States." In *Public Opinion in State Politics*, ed. Jeffrey Cohen, 121–141. Stanford: Stanford University Press.

Barry, Colleen L., and Susan H. Busch. 2006. "Do State Parity Laws Reduce the Financial Burden on Families of Children with Mental Health Care Needs?" *Health Services Research* 42(3): 1061–1084.

Bartels, Larry M. 2016. *Unequal Democracy: The Political Economy of the New Gilded Age.* Princeton: Princeton University Press.

Baskaran, Thushyanthan. 2011. "Fiscal Decentralization, Ideology, and the Size of the Public Sector." *European Journal of Political Economy* 27(3): 485–506.

Beland, Louis-Philippe. 2015. "Political Parties and Labor-Market Outcomes: Evidence from US States." *American Economic Journal: Applied Economics* 7(4): 198–220.

Beland, Louis-Philippe, and Vincent Boucher. 2015. "Polluting Politics." CRREP Working Paper No. 2015-05.

2017. "Party Affiliation and Public Spending: Evidence from U.S. Governors." *Economic Inquiry* 55(2): 982–995.

Benoit, Kenneth, and Michael Laver. 2007. "Estimating Party Policy Positions: Comparing Expert Surveys and Hand-Coded Content Analysis." *Electoral Studies* 26: 90–107.

Bergquist, Parrish. 2018. "Controlling the Regulators: How Party Control of Government Shapes Environmental Regulation in the 21st Century." Working Paper. Available at: http://parrishb.mit.edu/sites/default/files/images/Bergquist_sample_180913.pdf.

Biggers, Daniel R., and Michael J. Hanmer. 2017. "Understanding the Adoption of Voter Identification Laws in the American States." *American Politics Research* 45(4): 560–588.

Bitler, Marianne, and Hilary W. Hoynes. 2010. "The State of the Safety Net in the Post-Welfare Reform Era." Federal Reserve Bank of San Francisco Working Paper No. 2010-31.

Bitler, Marianne, and Madeline Zavodny. 2001. "The Effect of Abortion Restrictions on the Timing of Abortions." *Journal of Health Economics* 20: 1011–1032.

Bjorklund, Eric. In Press. "Out of the Many, One? U.S. Sub-National Political-Economies in the Post-Welfare Reform Era." *Socio-Economic Review*.

Bjørnskov, Christian, and Niklas Potrafke. 2013. "The Size and Scope of Government in the US States: Does Party Ideology Matter?" *International Tax and Public Finance* 20(4): 687–714.

Blair, Diane, and Jay Barth. 2005. *Arkansas Politics and Government*, Second Edition. Lincoln: University of Nebraska Press.

Blais, Andre, Donald Blake, and Stephane Dion. 1993. "Do Parties Make a Difference? Parties and the Size of Government in Liberal Democracies." *American Journal of Political Science* 37(1): 40–62.

Boehmke, Frederick J., Mark Brockway, Bruce Desmarais, Jeffrey J. Harden, Scott LaCombe, Fridolin Linder, and Hanna Wallach. 2018. "State Policy Innovation and Diffusion (SPID) Database v1.0." Available at: https://doi. org/10.7910/DVN/CVYSR7.

Bonica, Adam, and Maya Sen. 2017. "The Politics of Selecting the Bench from the Bar: The Legal Profession and Partisan Incentives to Introduce Ideology into Judicial Selection." *Journal of Law and Economics* 60(4): 559–595.

Bove, Vincenzo, Georgios Efthyvoulou, and Antonio Navas. 2017. "Political Cycles in Public Expenditure: Butter vs Guns." *Journal of Comparative Economics* 45(3): 582–604.

Boyer, William, and Edward Ratledge. 2009. *Delaware Politics and Government*. Lincoln: University of Nebraska Press.

Breznau, Nate. 2015. "The Missing Main Effect of Welfare State Regimes." *Sociological Science* 2: 420–441.

Bromley-Trujillo, Rebecca, and John Poe. In Press. "The Importance of Salience: Public Opinion and State Policy Action on Climate Change." *Journal of Public Policy*.

Broockman, David E., and Christopher Skovron. 2018. "Bias in Perceptions of Public Opinion among Political Elites." *American Political Science Review* 112(3): 542–563.

Broockman, David E., and Matthew Tyler. 2018. "Uncovering Agenda-Driven Congressional Responsiveness With Multi-Session Ideal Points." Working Paper.

Brooks, Clem, and Jeff Manza. 2006. "Why do Welfare States Persist?" *Journal of Politics* 68(4): 816–827.

Bruno, Robert, Roland Zullo, Frank Manzo IV, and Alison Dickson. 2015. "The Economic Effects of Adopting a Right-to-Work Law: Implications for Illinois." *Labor Studies Journal* 40(4): 319–361.

Bucci, Laura. 2018. "Organized Labor's Check on Rising Economic Inequality in the U.S. States." *State Politics and Policy Quarterly* 18(2): 148–173.

Cahan, Dodge, and Niklas Potrafke. 2017. "The Democratic-Republican Presidential Growth Gap and the Partisan Balance of the State Governments." CESifo Working Paper Series No. 6517.

Caldarone, Richard P., Brandice Canes-Wrone, and Tom S. Clark. 2009. "Partisan Labels and Democratic Accountability: An Analysis of State Supreme Court Abortion Decisions." *Journal of Politics* 71(2): 560–573.

Castles, Francis G., and Herbert Obinger. 2008. "Worlds, Families, Regimes: Country Clusters in European and OECD Area Public Policy." *West European Politics* 31(1): 321–344.

Castro, Vítor, and Rodrigo Martins. 2017. "Politically Driven Cycles in Fiscal Policy: In Depth Analysis of the Functional Components of Government Expenditures." *European Journal of Political Economy* 55(3): 44–64.

Caughey, Devin, and Jasjeet Sekhon. 2011. "Elections and the Regression Discontinuity Design: Lessons from Close U.S. House Races, 1942–2008." *Political Analysis* 19: 385–408.

Caughey, Devin, and Christopher Warshaw. 2016. "The Dynamics of State Policy Liberalism, 1936–2012." *American Journal of Political Science* 60(4): 899–913.

2018. "Policy Preferences and Policy Change: Dynamic Responsiveness in the American States, 1936–2014." *American Political Science Review* 112(2): 249–266.

Caughey, Devin, Yiqing Xu, and Christopher Warshaw. 2017. "Incremental Democracy: The Policy Effects of Partisan Control of State Government." *Journal of Politics* 79(4): 1342–1358.

Cestau, Darío. 2018. "The Political Affiliation Effect on State Credit Risk." *Public Choice* 175(1–2): 135–154.

Chatterji, Aaron K., Joowon Kim, and Ryan C. McDevitt. 2018. "School Spirit: Legislator School Ties and State Funding for Higher Education." NBER Working Paper No. 24818.

Chernick, Howard. 2005. "On the Determinants of Subnational Tax Progressivity in the U.S." *National Tax Journal* 58(1): 93–112.

Clingermayer, James, and B. Dan Wood. 1995. "Disentangling Patterns of State Debt Financing." *American Political Science Review* 89(1): 108–120.

Clinton, Joshua, and Mark D. Richardson. 2019. "Lawmaking in American Legislatures: An Empirical Investigation." *Journal of Public Policy* 39(1): 143–175.

Collingwood, Loren, Stephen Omar El-Khatib, and Benjamin Gonzalez O'Brien. In Press. "Sustained Organizational Influence: American Legislative

Exchange Council and the Diffusion of Anti-Sanctuary Policy." *Policy Studies Journal*.

Collins, Benjamin. 2012. "Right to Work Laws: Legislative Background and Empirical Research." Congressional Research Service. Available at: https://fas.org/sgp/crs/misc/R42575.pdf.

Conant, James K. 2006. *Wisconsin Politics and Government: America's Laboratory of Democracy*. Lincoln: University of Nebraska Press.

Cramer, Katherine. 2016. *The Politics of Resentment: Rural Consciousness in Wisconsin and the Rise of Scott Walker*. Chicago: University of Chicago Press.

Crandall, Marie, Alexander Eastman, Pina Violano et al. 2016. "Prevention of Firearm-Related Injuries with Restrictive Licensing and Concealed Carry Laws: An Eastern Association for the Surgery of Trauma Systematic Review." *Journal of Trauma and Acute Care Surgery* 81(5): 952–960.

Cronin, Thomas, and Robert Loevy. 1993. *Colorado Politics and Policy: Governing the Centennial State*. Lincoln: University of Nebraska Press.

2012. *Colorado Politics and Policy: Governing a Purple State*. Lincoln: University of Nebraska Press

Crosson, Jesse. 2019. "Stalemate in the States: Agenda Control Rules and Policy Output in American Legislatures." *Legislative Studies Quarterly* 44(1): 3–33.

Dagan, David, and Steven Teles. 2016. *Prison Break: Conservatives Turned Against Mass Incarceration*. New York: Oxford University Press.

De Jong, Gordon F., Deborah Roempke, Shelley K. Irving, and Tanja St. Pierre. 2006. "Measuring State TANF Policy Variations and Change After Reform." *Social Science Quarterly* 87(4): 755–781.

Dennis, Christopher, William S. Moore, and Tracey Somerville. 2007. "The Impact of Political Parties on the Distribution of State and Local Tax Burdens." *The Social Science Journal* 44(2): 339–347.

DiSalvo, Daniel, and Jeffrey Kucik. 2018. "Unions, Parties, and the Politics of State Government Legacy Cost." *Policy Studies Journal* 46(3): 573–597.

Duggan, Mark, Atul Gupta, and Emilie Jackson. 2019. "The Impact of the Affordable Care Act: Evidence from California's Hospital Sector." National Bureau of Economic Research Working Paper No. 25488. Available at: www.nber.org/papers/w25488.

Egan, Patrick J. 2013. *Partisan Priorities: How Issue Ownership Drives and Distorts American Politics*. New York: Cambridge University Press.

Eidlin, Barry. 2018. *Labor and the Class Idea in the United States and Canada*. New York: Cambridge University Press.

Eisenach, Jeffrey A. 2015. "Right-to-Work Laws: The Economic Evidence." NERA Economic Consulting. Available at: www.nera.com/content/dam/nera/publications/2015/PUB_Right_to_Work_Laws_0615.pdf.

Elango, Sneha, Jorge Luis Garcia, James J. Heckman, and Andres Hojman. "Early Childhood Education." National Bureau of Economic Research. Available at: www.nber.org/papers/w21766.

Elkjaer, Mads Andreas, and Torben Iversen. 2018. "The Political Representation of Economic Interest." Working Paper. Available at: www.people.fas.harvard.edu/~iversen/PDFfiles/Elkjaer&Iversen2018.pdf.

Ellis, Christopher, and James Stimson. 2012. *Ideology in America*. New York: Cambridge University Press.

Enns, Peter K. 2016. *Incarceration Nation: How the United States Became the Most Punitive Democracy in the World*. New York: Cambridge University Press.

Eren, Ozkan, and Serkan Ozbeklik. 2016. "What Do Right-to-Work Laws Do? Evidence from a Synthetic Control Method Analysis." *Journal of Policy Analysis and Management* 35(1): 173–194.

Erikson, Robert S., Michael B. MacKuen, and James A. Stimson. 2002. *The Macro Polity*. New York: Cambridge University Press.

Erikson, Robert S., Gerald C. Wright, and John P. McIver. 1993. *Statehouse Democracy: Public Opinion and Policy in the American States*. New York: Cambridge University Press.

2006. "Public Opinion in the States: A Quarter Century of Change and Stability." In *Public Opinion in State Politics*, ed. Jeffrey E. Cohen, 229–253. Palo Alto: Stanford University Press.

Eriksson, Kimmo, and Pontus Strimling. 2015. "Group Differences in Broadness of Values may Drive Dynamics of Public Opinion on Moral Issues." *Mathematical Social Sciences* 77: 1–8.

Esping-Andersen, Gøsta. 1990. *The Three Worlds of Welfare Capitalism*. Oxford: Oxford University Press.

Farber, Henry S., Daniel Herbst, Ilyana Kuziemko, and Suresh Naidu. 2018. "Unions and Inequality Over the Twentieth Century: New Evidence from Survey Data." NBER Working Paper No. 24587.

Feigenbaum, James, Alexander Fouirnaies, and Andrew Hall. 2017. "The Majority-Party Disadvantage: Revising Theories of Legislative Organization." *Quarterly Journal of Political Science* 12(3): 269–300.

Felkey, Amanda J., and Kristina M. Lybecker. 2014. "Utilization of Oral Contraception: The Impact of Direct and Indirect Restrictions on Access to Abortion." *The Social Science Journal* 51: 44–56.

2018. "Do Restrictions Beget Responsibility? The Case of U.S. Abortion Legislation." *The American Economist* 63(1): 59–70.

Finger, Leslie K. 2018. "Vested Interests and the Diffusion of Education Reform across the States." *Policy Studies Journal* 46(2): 378–401.

Fischer, Stefanie, Heather Royer, and Corey White. 2017. "The Impacts of Reduced Access to Abortion and Family Planning Services on Abortion, Births, and Contraceptive Purchases." National Bureau of Economic Research Working Paper No. 23634.

Flavin, Patrick. 2018. "State Government Public Goods Spending and Citizens' Quality of Life." *Social Science Research* 78(1): 28–40.

Fleegler, Eric W., Lois K. Lee, Michael C. Monuteaux, David Hemenway, and Rebekah Mannix. 2013. "Firearm Legislation and Firearm-Related Fatalities in the United States." *Journal of the American Medical Association: Internal Medicine* 173(9): 732–740.

Forman Jr., James. 2017. *Locking Up Our Own: Crime and Punishment in Black America*. New York: Farrar, Straus and Giroux.

Franko, William, and Christopher Witko. 2017. *The New Economic Populism: How States Respond to Economic Inequality*. New York: Oxford University Press.

Galasso, Alberto, and Hong Luo. 2016. "Tort Reform and Innovation." Working Paper. Available at: www.law.northwestern.edu/research-faculty/searlecenter/events/innovation/documents/GalassoLuo_10June16.pdf.

Galasso, Vincenzo. 2014. "The Role of Political Partisanship during Economic Crises." *Public Choice* 158(1–2): 143–165.

Gale, William G., Aaron Krupkin, and Kim Rueben. 2015. "The Relationship Between Taxes and Growth at the State Level: New Evidence." *National Tax Journal* 68(4): 919–942.

Galvin, Daniel. 2019. "Labor's Legacy: The Construction of Subnational Work Regulation." Institute for Policy Research, Northwestern University. Working Paper.

Gamm, Gerald, and Thad Kousser. 2017. "Life, Literacy, and The Pursuit of Prosperity: Party Competition and Policy Outcomes in 50 States." Paper presented at the State Politics and Policy Conference, St. Louis, MO.

Garfinkel, Irwin, Lee Rainwater, and Timothy Smeeding. 2010. *Wealth and Welfare States*. New York: Oxford University Press.

Garmann, Sebastian. 2014. "Do Government Ideology and Fragmentation Matter for Reducing CO_2 Emissions?" *Ecological Economics* 105: 1–10.

Gius, Mark. 2014. "An Examination of the Effects of Concealed Weapons Laws and Assault Weapons Bans on State-Level Murder Rates." *Applied Economics Letters* 21(4): 265–267.

Goff, Brian, Alex Lebedinsky, and Stephen Lile. 2012. "A Matched Pair Analysis of State Growth Differences." *Contemporary Economic Policy* 30(2): 293–305.

Grambsch, Patricia. 2008. "Regression to the Mean, Murder Rates, and Shall Issue Laws." *The American Statistician* 62(4): 289–295.

Gray, Virginia, and Russell Hanson. 2004. *Politics in the American States: A Comparative Analysis*, Eighth Edition. Washington, DC: CQ Press.

Grogger, Jeffrey. 2003. "The Effects of Time Limits, the EITC, and Other Policy Changes on Welfare Use, Work, and Income among Female-Headed Families." *The Review of Economics and Statistics* 85(2): 394–408.

Grossman, Daniel, Sarah Baum, Liza Fuentes, Kari White, Kristine Hopkins, Amanda Stevenson, and Joseph E. Potter. 2014. "Change in Abortion Services after Implementation of a Restrictive Law in Texas." *American Journal of Obstetrics and Gynecology* 90: 496–501.

Grossmann, Matt. 2014. *Artists of the Possible: Governing Networks and American Policy Change Since 1945.* New York: Oxford University Press.

Grossmann, Matt, and David A. Hopkins. 2016. *Asymmetric Politics: Ideological Republicans and Group Interest Democrats.* New York: Oxford University Press.

Grumbach, Jacob M. 2018a. "From Backwaters to Major Policymakers: Policy Polarization in the States, 1970–2014." *Perspectives on Politics* 16(2): 416–435.

　2018b. "Polarized Federalism: Activists, Voters, and the Resurgence of State Policy in the U.S." Dissertation. University of California, Berkeley.

　2018c. "How Should We Measure Ideal Points for Policy Outcomes?" Working Paper.

Hall, Peter A., and David Soskice. 2001. *Varieties of Capitalism: The Institutional Foundations of Comparative Advantage.* Oxford: Oxford University Press.

Hansen, Eric, Caroline Carlson, and Virginia Gray. 2017. "Interest Group Density and Policy Change in the States." Working Paper. Available at: http://hansen.web.unc.edu/files/2014/12/ig_policy_change.pdf.

Hardy, Richard, Richard Dohm, and David A. Leuthold. 1995. *Missouri Government and Politics.* Columbia: University of Missouri Press.

Hare, Christopher, and James Monogan. In Press. "The Democratic Deficit on Salient Issues: Immigration and Healthcare in the States." *Journal of Public Policy.*

Harris, Michael, and Rhonda Kinney, eds. 2003. *Innovation and Entrepreneurship in State and Local Governments.* Lanham: Lexington Books.

Hartmann, Sebastian. 2015. *Partisan Policy-Making in Western Europe.* Wiesbaden: Springer.

Hartney, Michael, and Patrick Flavin. 2011. "From the Schoolhouse to the Statehouse: Teacher Union Political Activism and U.S. State Education Reform Policy." *State Politics and Policy Quarterly* 11(3): 251–268.

Hatch, Megan, and Elizabeth Rigby. 2015. "Laboratories of (In)equality? Redistributive Policy and Income Inequality in the American States." *Policy Studies Journal* 43(2): 163–187.

Hayes, Thomas, and D. Xavier Medina. 2015. "Fiscal Policy and Economic Inequality in the U.S. States: Taxing and Spending from 1976 to 2006." *Political Research Quarterly* 68(2): 392–407.

Heaton, Paul. 2015. "How Does Tort Law Affect Consumer Auto Insurance Costs?" *Journal of Risk and Insurance* 84(2): 691–715.

Henig, Jeffrey R. 2009. *Spin Cycle: How Research Gets Used in Policy Debates: The Case of Charter Schools*. New York: Russell Sage Foundation.

Hertel-Fernandez, Alexander. 2018. *State Capture: How Conservative Activists, Big Businesses, and Wealthy Donors Reshaped the American States – and the Nation*. New York: Oxford University Press.

Herwartz, Helmut, and Bernd Theilen. 2017. "Ideology and Redistribution through Public Spending." *European Journal of Political Economy* 46(3): 74–90.

Higgs, Robert. 2004. *Against Leviathan: Government Power and a Free Society*. Oakland: Independent Institute.

  2015. "The Ongoing Growth of Government in the Economically Advanced Countries." In *The Dynamics of Intervention: Regulation and Redistribution in the Mixed Economy*, 279–300. Bingley: Emerald Publishing Group.

Hill, Andrew J., and Daniel B. Jones. 2017. "Does Partisan Affiliation Impact the Distribution of Spending? Evidence from State Governments' Expenditures on Education." *Journal of Economic Behavior and Organization* 143: 58–77.

Hoffer, Katherine. 2018. "Policy Innovation and Change: The Diffusion and Modification of the Renewable Portfolio Standard, 1994–2014." Doctoral dissertation. Colorado State University.

Holbein, John B., and Adam Dynes. 2018. "Noisy Retrospection: Does the Political Party in Power Affect Policy Outcomes?" Working Paper.

Holcombe, Randall G., and Donald J. Lacombe. 2004. "The Effect of State Income Taxation on Per Capita Income Growth." *Public Finance Review* 32(3): 292–312.

Holyoke, Thomas, and Heath Brown. 2019. "After the Punctuation: Competition, Uncertainty, and Convergent State Policy Change." *State Politics and Policy Quarterly* 19(1): 3–28.

Hopkins, Dan. 2018. *The Increasingly United States*. Chicago: University of Chicago Press.

Howell, William G., and Asya Magazinnik. 2017. "Presidential Prescriptions for State Policy: Obama's Race to the Top Initiative." *Journal of Policy Analysis and Management* 36(3): 502–531.

Hoxie, Philip G., Michael R. O'Herron, Matthew L. Floyd, Aidan C. McLaughlin, and Paul M. Sommers. 2017. "The Labor Market Effects of Right-to-Work Laws, 2010–2014." *Open Journal of Social Sciences* 5: 1–6.

Hübscher, Evelyne. 2016. "The Politics of Fiscal Consolidation Revisited." *Journal of Public Policy* 36(4): 573–601.

Imbeau, Louis M., François Pétry, and Moktar Lamari. 2001. "Left-Right Party Ideology and Government Policies." *European Journal of Political Research* 40(1): 1–29.

Iversen, Torben. 2001. "The Dynamics of Welfare State Expansion." In *The New Politics of the Welfare State*, ed. Paul Pierson. New York: Oxford University Press.

Jackson, C. Kirabo, Rucker C. Johnson, and Claudia Persico. 2016. "The Effects of School Spending on Educational and Economic Outcomes: Evidence from School Finance Reforms." *Quarterly Journal of Economics* 131(1): 157–218.

Jackson, Joshua Conrad, Michele Gelfand, Soham De, and Amber Fox. 2019. "The Loosening of American Culture over 200 Years is Associated with a Creativity-Order Trade-Off." *Nature Human Behavior*. Online First. Available at: www.nature.com/articles/s41562-018-0516-z.

Jacobs, Anna W. 2017. "Greasing the Skids: How Corporate Elite Campaign Donations Shape State-Level Collective Bargaining Legislation." Dissertation. Vanderbilt University.

Jacobs, David, and Ronald Helms. 2001. "Racial Politics and Redistribution: Isolating the Contingent Influence of Civil Rights, Riots, and Crime on Tax Progressivity." *Social Forces* 80(1): 91–121.

Jacoby, William, and Saundra Schneider. 2001. "Variability in State Policy Priorities: An Empirical Analysis." *Journal of Politics* 63(2): 544–568.

Jäger, Kai. 2017. "Economic Freedom in the Early 21st Century: Government Ideology Still Matters." *Kyklos* 70(2): 256–277.

Jenkins, Shannon. 2016. *The Context of Legislating: Constraints on the Legislative Process in the United States*. New York: Routledge.

Jensen, Carsten. 2010. "Issue Compensation and Right-Wing Government Social Spending." *European Journal of Political Research* 49(2): 282–299.

—— 2011. "Determinants of Welfare Service Provision after the Golden Age." *International Journal of Social Welfare* 20(2): 125–134.

—— 2014. *The Right and the Welfare State*. Oxford: Oxford University Press.

Jensen, Carsten, and Henrik Bech Seeberg. 2015. "The Power of Talk and the Welfare State: Evidence from 23 Countries on an Asymmetric Opposition-Government Response Mechanism." *Socio-Economic Review* 13(2): 215–233.

Jensen, Jennifer. 2017. "Governors and Partisan Polarization in the Federal Arena." *Publius: The Journal of Federalism* 47(3): 314–341.

Jensen, Nathan, and Edmund Malesky. 2018. *Incentives to Pander: Why Politicians Use Corporate Welfare for Political Gain.* New York: Cambridge University Press.

Jilson, Cal. 2015. *Texas Politics: Governing the Lone Star State,* Fifth Edition. New York: Routledge.

Jones, Rachel K., and Jenna Jerman. 2014. "Abortion Incidence and Service Availability in the United States, 2011." *Perspectives on Sexual and Reproductive Health* 46(1): 3–14.

2017. "Abortion Incidence and Service Availability in the United States, 2014." *Perspectives on Sexual and Reproductive Health* 49(1): 17–27.

Jordan, Jeffrey L., Aparna Mathur, Abdul Munasib, and Devesh Roy. 2016. "Did Right-to-Work Laws Impact Income Inequality? Evidence from U.S. States using the Synthetic Control Method." American Enterprise Institute (AEI). Available at: www.aei.org/publication/did-right-to-work-laws-impact-income-inequality-evidence-from-u-s-states-using-the-synthetic-control-method/.

Jordan, Marty P., and Matt Grossmann. 2018. *The Correlates of State Policy Project v.2.1.* East Lansing: Institute for Public Policy and Social Research.

Joshi, Nayan Krishna. 2015. "Party Politics, Governors, and Healthcare Expenditures." *Economics and Politics* 27(1): 53–77.

Jost, Kenneth. 1996. "The States and Federalism." *CQ Researcher* 6: 793–816.

Joyce, Theodore J., Stanley K. Henshaw, Amanda Dennis, Lawrence B. Finer, and Kelly Blanchard. 2009. "The Impact of State Mandatory Counseling and Waiting Period Laws on Abortion: A Literature Review." Guttmacher Institute. Available at: www.guttmacher.org/report/impact-state-mandatory-counseling-and-waiting-period-laws-abortion-literature-review.

Kalenkoski, Charlene M., and Donald J. Lacombe. 2006. "Right-to-Work Laws and Manufacturing Employment: The Importance of Spatial Dependence." *Southern Economic Journal* 73(2): 402–418.

Karch, Andrew, Sean C. Nicholson-Crotty, Neal D. Woods, and Ann O'M. Bowman. 2016. "Policy Diffusion and the Pro-Innovation Bias." *Political Research Quarterly* 69(2): 83–95.

Kastellec, Jonathan P. 2018. "How Courts Structure State-Level Representation." *State Politics and Policy Quarterly* 18(1): 27–60.

Kaufman, Dan. 2018. *The Fall of Wisconsin: The Conservative Conquest of a Progressive Bastion and the Future of American Politics.* New York: W. W. Norton & Company.

Kaushal, Neeraj, and Robert Kaestner. 2001. "From Welfare to Work: Has Welfare Reform Worked?" *Journal of Policy Analysis and Management* 20(4): 699–719.

Kausser, Thad, and Justin Phillips. 2012. *The Power of American Governors.* New York: Cambridge University Press.

Kelly, Nathan J., and Christopher Witko. 2012. "Federalism and American Inequality." *Journal of Politics* 74(2): 414–426.

2014. "Government Ideology and Unemployment in the U.S. States." *State Politics and Policy Quarterly* 14(4): 389–413.

Kersbergen, Kees van, and Barbara Vis. 2013. *Comparative Welfare State Politics: Development, Opportunities and Reform.* Cambridge: Cambridge University Press.

Kincaid, John. 2019. "Dynamic De/Centralization in the United States, 1790–2010." *Publius: The Journal of Federalism* 49(1): 166–193.

Kogan, Vladimir. 2017. "Do Anti-Union Policies Increase Inequality? Evidence from State Adoption of Right-to-Work Laws." *State Politics and Policy Quarterly* 17(2): 180–200.

2018. "The Political Fallout from Tennessee's Mass Medicaid Disenrollment." Working Paper. Available at: https://papers.ssrn.com/sol3/papers.cfm?abstract_id=3184345.

Kosack, Stephen, Michele Coscia, Evann Smith, Kim Albrecht, Albert-László Barabási, and Ricardo Hausmann. 2018. "Functional Structures of US State Governments." *Proceedings of the National Academy of Sciences* 115(46): 11748–11753.

Kovandzic, Tomislav V., Thomas B. Marvell, and Lynne M. Vieraitis. 2005. "The Impact of Shall-Issue Concealed Handgun Laws on Violent Crime Rates: Evidence From Panel Data for Large Urban Cities." *Homicide Studies* 9(4): 292–323.

Kreitzer, Rebecca J. 2015. "Politics and Morality in State Abortion Policy." *State Politics and Policy Quarterly* 15(1): 41–66.

Kroeger, Mary. 2018. "Bureaucrats Writing Bills." Working Paper. Available at: https://sites.google.com/view/maryakroeger/research?authuser=0.

Lee, Justin, Kevin P. Moriarty, David B. Tashjian, and Lisa A. Patterson. 2013. "Guns and States: Pediatric Firearm Injury." *Journal of Trauma and Acute Care Surgery* 75(1): 50–53.

Lee, Soomi. 2018. "Do States Circumvent Constitutional Supermajority Voting Requirements to Raise Taxes?" *State Politics and Policy Quarterly* 18(4): 417–440.

Leeson, Peter, Matt Ryan, and Claudia Williamson. 2012. "Think Tanks." *Journal of Comparative Economics* 40(1): 62–77.

Leigh, Andrew. 2008. "Estimating the Impact of Gubernatorial Partisanship on Policy Settings and Economic Outcomes: A Regression Discontinuity Approach." *European Journal of Political Economy* 24(1): 256–268.

Lezar, Tex, ed. 1994. *Making Government Work: A Conservative Agenda for the States.* Washington, DC: Regnery.

Linder, Fridolin, Bruce Desmarais, Matthew Burgess, and Eugenia Giraudy. In Press. "Text as Policy: Measuring Policy Similarity through Bill Text Reuse." *Policy Studies Journal.*

Lindsey, Brink, and Steven Teles. 2017. *The Captured Economy: How the Powerful Enrich Themselves, Slow Down Growth, and Increase Inequality*. New York: Oxford University Press.

Little, Thomas H. 1998. "On the Coattails of a Contract: RNC Activities and Republican Gains in the 1994 State Legislative Elections." *Political Research Quarterly* 51(1): 173–190.

Low, Hamish, Costas Meghir, Luigi Pistaferri, and Alessandra Voena. 2018. "Marriage, Labor Supply and the Dynamics of the Social Safety Net." NBER Working Paper No. 24356.

Lyons, William, John Scheb, and Billy Star. 2001. *Government and Politics in Tennessee*. Knoxville: University of Tennessee Press.

Mariani, Giulia. 2019. "Religious Diversity and Party Control in the States: Explaining Adoptions of Same-Sex Marriage Laws." *Sexuality Research and Social Policy*. Online First. Available at: https://link.springer .com/article/10.1007/s13178-019-0379-8.

Masugi, Ken, and Brian Janiskee. 2011. *Democracy in California: Politics and Government in the Golden State*. Lanham, MD: Rowman and Littlefield.

Mayhew, David. 2004. *Congress: The Electoral Connection*, Second Edition. New Haven: Yale University Press.

Mazzeo, Christopher, Sara Rab, and Susan Eachus. 2003. "Work-First or Work-Only: Welfare Reform, State Policy, and Access to Postsecondary Education." *The Annals of the American Academy of Political and Social Science* 586: 144–171.

McCann, Pamela Clouser. 2016. *The Federal Design Dilemma: Congress and Intergovernmental Delegation*. New York: Cambridge University Press.

McKernan, Signe-Mary, and Caroline Ratcliffe. 2006. "The Effect of Specific Welfare Policies on Poverty." The Urban Institute. Available at: www .urban.org/research/publication/effect-specific-welfare-policies-poverty.

Medoff, Marshall H. 2007. "Price, Restrictions and Abortion Demand." *Journal of Family and Economic Issues* 28(4): 583–599.
  2015. "The Impact of State Abortion Policy on the Price of an Abortion." *Behavior and Social Issues* 24: 56–67.

Meyer, Bruce D., and Derek Wu. 2018. "The Poverty Reduction of Social Security and Means-Tested Transfers." National Bureau of Economic Research Working Paper No. 24567. Available at: www.nber.org/papers/ w24567.

Meyer-Gutbrod, Joshua. 2018. "American Federalism and Partisan Resistance in an Age of Polarization." Dissertation. Cornell University.

Michener, Jamila. 2018. *Fragmented Democracy: Medicaid, Federalism, and Unequal Politics*. New York: Cambridge University Press.

Miller, Penny M. 1994. *Kentucky Politics and Government*. Lincoln: University of Nebraska Press.

Minor, Darrell. 2012. "Poverty, Productivity, and Public Health: The Effects of Right to Work Laws on Key Standards of Living." *The NEA Higher Education Journal*. Available at: www.nea.org/assets/docs/PovertyProductivityAndPublicHealth.pdf.

Miras, Nicholas, and Stella Rouse. 2018. "The Effects of Misalignment and the Pursuit of a Counter-Partisan Agenda: How National Politics Conditions State Policymaking." Working Paper. Available at: https://gvpt.umd.edu/sites/gvpt.umd.edu/files/Miras%20and%20Rouse%20_AP%20Workshop%20Paper.pdf.

Morehouse, Sarah McCally, and Malcolm Jewell. 2003. *State Politics, Parties, and Policy*. Lanham, MD: Rowman and Littlefield.

Myers, Adam. 2016. "Electoral Incongruence and Delayed Republican Gains in Southern State Legislatures." *American Review of Politics* 35(2): 73–102.

Nallareddy, Suresh, Ethan Rouen, and Juan Carlos Suárez Serrato. 2018. "Do Corporate Tax Cuts Increase Income Inequality?" NBER Working Paper No. 24598.

Nathan, Richard P., and Thomas L. Gais. 2001. "Is Devolution Working? Federal and State Roles in Welfare." Brookings Institution. Available at: www.brookings.edu/articles/is-devolution-working-federal-and-state-roles-in-welfare/.

New, Michael J. 2011. "Analyzing the Effect of Anti-Abortion U.S. State Legislation in the Post-Casey Era." *State Politics and Policy Quarterly* 11(1): 28–47.

Newman, Katherine S., and Rourke O'Brien. 2011. *Taxing the Poor: Doing Damage to the Truly Disadvantaged*. Berkeley: University of California Press.

Norrander, B., and C. Wilcox. 1999. "Public Opinion and Policymaking in the States: The Case of Post-Roe Abortion Policy." *Policy Studies Journal* 27: 707–722.

Nowlan, James D. 2010. *Illinois Politics: A Citizen's Guide*. Champaign: University of Illinois Press.

O'Brien, Rourke L., and Adam Travis. 2018. "Income Inequality and Tax Policy: Evidence from U.S. States 1980–2010." Working Paper.

Paglayan, Agustina. 2019. "Public-Sector Unions and the Size of Government." *American Journal of Political Science* 63(1): 21–36.

Parry, Janine A., and Richard P. Wang. 2009. *Readings in Arkansas Politics and Government*. Fayetteville: University of Arkansas Press.

Pickering, Andrew, and James Rockey. 2011. "Ideology and the Growth of Government." *The Review of Economics and Statistics* 93(3): 907–919.

Pierson, Paul. 1994. *Dismantling the Welfare State? Reagan, Thatcher, and the Politics of Retrenchment*. New York: Cambridge University Press.

2001. *The New Politics of the Welfare State*. New York: Oxford University Press.

Potrafke, Niklas. 2011. "Does Government Ideology Influence Budget Composition? Empirical Evidence from OECD Countries." *Economics of Governance* 12(2): 101–134.

2017. "Partisan Politics: The Empirical Evidence from OECD Panel Studies." *Journal of Comparative Economics* 45(4): 712–750.

2018. "Government Ideology and Economic Policy-Making in the United States: A Survey." *Public Choice* 174(1): 145–207.

Prothero, Stephen. 2017. *Why Liberals Win (Even When They Lose Elections): How America's Raucous, Nasty, and Mean Culture Wars Make for a More Inclusive Nation*. New York: Harper.

Rand Corporation. 2018. "Gun Policy in America." Report. Available at: www .rand.org/research/gun-policy.html.

Rasess, Damian, and Jonas Pontusson. 2015. "The Politics of Fiscal Policy during Economic Downturns, 1981–2010." *European Journal of Political Research* 51(1): 1–22.

Reckhow, Sarah. 2012. *Follow the Money: How Foundation Dollars Change Public School Politics*. New York: Oxford University Press.

Redbird, Beth. 2017. "The New Closed Shop? The Economic and Structural Effects of Occupational Licensure." *American Sociological Review* 83(3): 600–624.

Reed, W. Robert. 2006. "Democrats, Republicans, and Taxes: Evidence that Political Parties Matter." *Journal of Public Economics* 90(4–5): 725–750.

Reed, W. Robert, and Cynthia L. Rogers. 2004. "Tax Cuts and Employment in New Jersey: Lessons From a Regional Analysis." *Public Finance Review* 32(3): 269–291.

Reich, Gary. 2018. "Hitting a Wall? The Trump Administration Meets Immigration Federalism." *Publius: The Journal of Federalism* 48(3): 372–395.

In Press. "One Model Does Not Fit All: The Varied Politics of State Immigrant Policies, 2005–16." *Policy Studies Journal*.

Renzulli, Linda A., and Vincent J. Roscigno. 2005. "Charter School Policy, Implementation, and Diffusion Across the United States." *Sociology of Education* 78(4): 344–366.

Richardson, Lilliard, and Jeffrey Milyo. 2017. "Giving the People What They Want? Legislative Polarization and Public Approval of State Legislatures." *State and Local Government Review* 48(4): 270–281.

Rickman, Dan, and Hongbo Wang. 2018. "Two Tales of Two U.S. States: Regional Fiscal Austerity and Economic Performance." *Regional Science and Urban Economics* 68: 46–55.

Riech, Gary, and Jay Barth. 2017. "Planting in Fertile Soil: The National Rifle Association and State Firearms Legislation." *Social Science Quarterly* 98(2): 485–499.

Riverstone-Newell, Lori. 2017. "The Rise of State Preemption Laws in Response to Local Policy Innovation." *Publius: The Journal of Federalism* 47(3): 403–425.

Roberts, Anthony J., and Robert A. Habans. 2015. "Exploring the Effects of Right-to-Work Laws on Private Wages." UCLA Institute for Research on Labor and Employment Working Paper. Available at: https://escholarship .org/uc/item/5n091465.

Roberts, Barbara M., and Muhammad A. Saeed. 2012. "Privatizations around the World: Economic or Political Determinants?" *Economics and Politics* 24(1): 47–71.

Rogers, Diane Lim, and John Rogers. 2000. "Political Competition and State Government: Do Tighter Elections Produce Looser Budgets." *Public Choice* 105: 1–21.

Rogers, Steven. 2016. "National Forces in State Legislative Elections." *Annals of the American Academy of Political and Social Science* 667(1): 207–225.

Roman, John. 2013. "Cost Benefit Analysis of Criminal Justice Reforms." *National Institute of Justice Journal* 272: 31–38.

Rosenthal, Alan. 2009. *Engines of Democracy: Politics and Policymaking in State Legislatures.* Washington, DC: CQ Press.

Schmitt, Carina. 2015. "Panel Data Analysis and Partisan Variables: How Periodization does Influence Partisan Effects." *Journal of European Public Policy* 23(10): 1442–1459.

Schneier, Edward V., and Brian Murtaugh. 2009. *New York Politics: A Tale of Two States.* New York: Routledge.

Schoeni, Robert F., and Rebecca M. Blank. 2000. "What Has Welfare Reform Accomplished? Impacts on Welfare Participation, Employment, Income, Poverty, and Family Structure." National Bureau of Economic Research Working Paper No. 7627.

Seeleib-Kaiser, Martin, Silke Van Dyke, and Martin Roggenkamp. 2008. *Party Politics and Social Welfare.* Cheltenham: Edward Elgar.

Sen, Bisakha. 2007. "State Abortion Restrictions and Child Fatal-Injury: An Exploratory Study." *Southern Economic Journal* 73(3): 553–574.

Sen, Bisakha, and Anantachai Panjamapirom. 2012. "State Background Checks for Gun Purchase and Firearm Deaths: An Exploratory Study." *Preventative Medicine* 55: 346–350.

Serrato, Juan Carlos Suarez, and Own Zidar. 2016. "Who Benefits from State Corporate Tax Cuts? A Local Labor Markets Approach with Heterogenous Firms." *American Economic Review* 106(9): 2582–2624.

Shor, Boris, and Nolan McCarty. 2011. "The Ideological Mapping of American Legislatures." *American Political Science Review* 105(3): 530–551.

Shuai, Xiaobing, and Christine Chmura. 2013. "The Effect of State Corporate Income Tax Rate Cuts on Job Creation." *Business Economics* 48(3): 183–193.

Siegel, Michael, Craig S. Ross, and Charles King III. 2013. "The Relationship Between Gun Ownership and Firearm Homicide Rates in the United States, 1981–2010." *American Journal of Public Health* 103(11): 2098–2105.

Siegel, Michael, Ziming Xuan, Craig S. Ross, Sandro Galea, Bindu Kalesan, Eric Fleegler, and Kristin A. Goss. 2017. "Easiness of Legal Access to Concealed Firearm Permits and Homicide Rates in the United States." *American Journal of Public Health* 107(12): 1923–1929.

Simonovits, Gabor, Andrew Guess, and Jonathan Nagler. 2019. "Responsiveness without Representation: Evidence from Minimum Wage Laws in U.S. States." *American Journal of Political Science* 63(2): 401–410.

Smith, Jacob, and Jonathan Spiegler. In Press. "Explaining Gun Deaths: Gun Control, Mental Illness, and Policymaking in the American States." *Policy Studies Journal*.

Sorens, Jason, Fait Muedini, and William Ruger. 2008. "U.S. State and Local Public Policies in 2006: A New Database." *State Politics and Public Policy Quarterly* 8(3): 309–326.

Squire, Peverill, and Keith Hamm. 2005. *101 Chambers: Congress, State Legislatures, and the Future of Legislative Studies*. Columbus: The Ohio State University Press.

Squire, Peverill, and Gary Moncrief. 2015. *State Legislatures Today: Politics Under the Domes*. Lanham, MD: Rowman and Littlefield.

Stevans, Lonnie K. 2009. "The Effect of Endogenous Right-to-Work Laws on Business and Economic Conditions in the United States: A Multivariate Approach." *Review of Law and Economics* 5(1): 595–614.

Stewart, William. 2016. *Alabama Politics in the Twenty-First Century*. Tuscaloosa: University of Alabama Press.

Sutton, Lenford C., and Richard A. King. 2013. "Financial Crisis Not Wasted: Shift in State Power and Voucher Expansion." *Journal of Education Finance* 38(4): 283–303.

Tanzi, Vito, and Ludger Schuknecht. 2000. *Public Spending in the 20th Century: A Global Perspective*. New York: Cambridge University Press.

Thom, Michael. 2017. "The Drivers of Public Sector Pension Reform Across the U.S. States." *American Review of Public Administration* 47(4): 431–442.

Thomas, Clive S., and Laura Savatgy. 2016. *Alaska Politics and Public Policy: The Dynamics of Beliefs, Institutions, Personalities, and Power*. Fairbanks: University of Alaska Press.

Van Horn, Carl. 2006. *State of the States*, Fourth Edition. Washington, DC: CQ Press.

Vogel, Steven Kent. 1998. *Freer Markets, More Rules: Regulatory Reform in Advanced Industrial Countries*. Ithaca: Cornell University Press.

2018. *Marketcraft: How Governments Make Markets Work*. New York: Oxford University Press.

Wade, Magic. 2015. "Labor's Last Stand? The Great Recession and Public Sector Collective Bargaining Reform in the American States." Dissertation. University of Minnesota. Available at: http://hdl.handle.net/11299/175360.

2018. "Targeting Teachers while Shielding Cops? The Politics of Punishing Enemies and Rewarding Friends in American State Collective Bargaining Reform Agendas." *Journal of Labor and Society* 21(2): 137–157.

Waxman, Daniel A., Michael D. Greenberg, M. Susan Ridgely, Arthur L. Kellermann, and Paul Heaton. 2014. "The Effect of Malpractice Reform on Emergency Department Care." *New England Journal of Medicine* 371(16): 1518–1525.

Weatherby, James B., and Randy Stapilus. 2011. *Governing Idaho: Politics, People, and Power*. Caldwell: Caxton Press.

Webster, Daniel, Cassandra Kercher Crifasi, and Jon S. Vernick. 2014. "Effects of the Repeal of Missouri's Handgun Purchaser Licensing Law on Homicides." *Journal of Urban Health* 91(2): 293–302.

Widestrom, Amy, Thomas Hayes, and Christopher Dennis. 2018. "The Effect of Political Parties on the Distribution of Income in the American States: 1917–2011." *Social Science Quarterly* 99(3): 895–914.

Wlezien, Christopher. 1995. "The Public as a Thermostat: Dynamics of Preferences for Spending." *American Journal of Political Science* 39(4): 981–1000.

Wolfson, Paul J., and Dale Belman. 2016. "15 Years of Research on U.S. Employment and the Minimum Wage." Tuck School of Business Working Paper No. 2705499. Available at: https://papers.ssrn.com/sol3/papers.cfm?abstract_id=2705499.

Wong, Kenneth K., and Warren E. Langevin. 2007. "Policy Expansion of School Choice in the American States." *Peabody Journal of Education* 82(2–3): 440–472.

Wong, Kenneth, and Francis X. Shen. 2002. "Politics of State-Led Reform in Education: Market Competition and Electoral Dynamics." *Educational Policy* 16(1): 161–192.

Yu, Jinhai, Edward Jennnings, and J. S. Butler. 2019. "Dividing the Pie: Parties, Institutional Limits, and State Budget Trade-Offs." *State Politics and Policy Quarterly*. Online First. Available at: https://journals.sagepub.com/doi/abs/10.1177/1532440018822469.

Zimmerman, Joseph. 2010. *Congress: Facilitator of State Action*. Albany: State University of New York Press.

INDEX

abortion, 102, 132, 153–154, 162
   policy effects, 123, 126–127, 159
Affordable Care Act, 9, 129, 130, 152
Alabama, 91, 93, 95, 96, 97, 146, 161
ALEC (American Legislative Exchange
   Council), 95, 100, 104–105, 106,
   107, 167
Arizona, 1, 92, 94, 97

Blue states, 6, 24–25, 40, 78, 118, 119,
   120–123, 145–146, 148, 169
   partisan effects, 157
   policy effects, 155, 156
   see also Democratic states
Boehmke, Frederick J., 68, 80
Brockway, Mark, 80
Brownback, Sam, 3, 51–52, 59, 62, 94,
   121
Bush, George W., 41, 43, 49, 106, 139

California, 6, 98, 113, 118, 168
Carter, Jimmy, 42
Caughey, Devin, 59–60, 71–75, 144
Chabot, Paul, 118
charter schools, 86, 102–103, 106, 129,
   140, 159, 166, see also education
   policies
Clinton, Bill, 3, 22, 32, 33, 42–43, 49,
   106, 133
Colorado, 1, 98
Congress, 8–9, 32, 41, 46

Connecticut, 96, 98
conservatism, 45, 47, 64, 79, 139, 165,
   167, 170, 171
conservative government, 3, 4, 5, 91–92
conservative parties, 3, 14, 19, 21,
   159–161, 166
conservative policies, 4, 26, 58–61, 62,
   67–68, 140–141, 159, 167–168
   evidence-based policies, 135–137,
   138–139
   corporate taxes, 127–128, see also
   taxation
Cowen, Tyler, 120, 121
criminal justice policies, 97, 110–111,
   131, 140, 159, 166
Cruz, Ted, 118

Dagan, David, 110
death penalty, 111
Democratic policies, 120, 146, 161–162
Democratic states, 8, 21, 22, 23, 24,
   99–100, 168
   partisan effects, 85, 86
   state policies, 24, 79, 84, 90, 91,
   112–113
Democrats, 5, 6, 22, 25, 27, 32, 43,
   168–170
   conservative policies, 67, 74–75
   liberal policies, 64, 65, 67, 71
   policy liberalism, 71, 73–74, 75, 76
   state expenditures, 54, 70

Democrats (*cont.*)
  state government, 35, 36, 37, 38–42,
    43–45, 47, 48, 49
deregulation, 16
Desmarais, Bruce, 80
drug laws, 110
Dynes, Adam, 141–144

Earned Income Tax Credit, *see* EITC
economic inequality, 16, 112, 127, 128,
    132–134
economic policies, 17, 128, 158
education policies, 1–2, 26, 86, 105–106,
    113, 128–129, 131, 140
EITC (Earned Income Tax Credit), 112
Electoral College, 108–109
  electoral rules, 107–109, *see also*
    redistricting; voter identification
    laws; voter registration laws
employees, state government, 55–56
environmental policies, 110, 113,
    140, 162
evidence-based policies, 134–139

federal government, 8–9, 15, 23, 25, 55,
    106, 111, 114, 122, 167
federal policies, 4, 8–9, 10, 167
Florida, 33, 93, 94, 95, 96, 98–99
Franko, William, 112

Gamm, Gerald, 145
gay rights policies, 86, 109–110
Georgia, 1, 92, 93, 94, 96, 97,
    107, 111
Gingrich, Newt, 3, 32
government policies, 4, 5–8, 14–15,
    16–19
  government spending, 12–13, 15–16,
    see also state expenditures
governors, 8
Grossmann, Matt, 86–90
Grumbach, Jacob, 60, 75–76, 86,
    139–140
gun control, 83–84, 105, 132
  policy effects, 123, 126

Hacker, Jacob, 121
Harden, Jeffrey J., 80
Harlem Children's Zone, 138

health policies, 9, 107, 113, 129–130,
    140, *see also* Medicaid
Hertel-Fernandez, Alexander, 3, 60–61
Higgs, Robert, 7
Holbein, John, 141–144

immigration policies, 106–107, 158
Indiana, 91, 92, 107, 121, 122, 164
interest groups, 11, 106, 111, 170

Jenkins, Emily, 86–90

Kansas, 1, 3, 51–52, 59, 62, 65, 67, 75,
    77, 91, 93, 94, 95, 96, 121
Kaufman, Dan, 100
Kentucky, 1, 33, 93, 94, 95, 96, 97, 164
Kousser, Thad, 145
Krugman, Paul, 120, 121

LaCombe, Scott, 80
liberal policies, 58–60, 62–68, 133,
    163–164, 169
  evidence-based policies, 135–137, 139
  partisan effects, 77–79
  policy liberalism, 17, 22, 56–58,
    62–64, 71–78
liberalism, 20, 21
Linder, Fridolin, 80

McCarty, Nolan, 77
Medicaid, 8, 9, 12, 54, 129–130, 140,
    152–153, 154, 162
Michigan, 41, 85, 91, 93, 95, 108
minimum wage, 18, 112, 128, 163
Minnesota, 121
Missouri, 39–40, 164
Muedini, Fait, 77

New Hampshire, 33, 37
New Jersey, 112–113
Newman, Katherine, 132, 133
No Child Left Behind Act (2001), 9
North Carolina, 1, 38–39, 41, 91, 92, 93,
    94, 96, 97
North Dakota, 40

Obama, Barack, 22, 32, 35, 42, 43, 49,
    106, 107, 166, 169
O'Brien, Rourke, 132, 133

occupational licensing, 128
Ohio, 93, 94–95, 96, 164
Oklahoma, 1, 38, 77, 93, 95, 96, 97,
    111, 164

partisan effects, 11, 15, 16–19, 48,
    58–62, 84–86, 122–123, 141–144,
    154, 155, 157–158, 170–172
  Democratic states, 85, 86
  policy liberalism, 77–79
  Republican states, 48, 84, 85, 86
  state policies, 43, 87–88, 159–160
Personal Responsibility and Work
    Opportunity Act (1996), 9
Pew Charitable Trusts, 134–135
Pierson, Paul, 16, 121
  policies, 26, 43, see also Democrat
    policies; Republican policies;
    state policies
policy effects, 123, 125–127, 141–145,
    147–148, 154, 155, 156–157
policy liberalism, 17, 22, 56–58, 62–64,
    71–78
pre-emption laws, 106
pre-kindergarten education, 83, 97, 98
professionalization, 10
public opinion, 59
  partisan effects, 15, 21, 43
  policy liberalism, 58, 59, 75, 77
public policies, 134–139

Red states, 1, 6, 24–25, 40, 78, 118, 119,
    120–123, 145–146, 148
  partisan effects, 157
  policy effects, 155, 156
  see also Republican states
redistricting, 39, 40–41, 43, 107–108,
    160, 162, 163
Republican government, 11, 12
Republican policies, 22–23, 26–27,
    102, 104, 114–115, 118–120, 132,
    146–147, 162–163, 166–167
  liberal policies, 163–164
  policy effects, 123, 125–127, 155, 156,
    159, 160
  reform, 24
Republican states, 3, 8, 22–23, 24, 25,
    48, 99–100
  partisan effects, 48, 84, 85, 86

state policies, 14, 24, 79, 84, 89, 90,
    91, 92–93
Republicans, 1, 2–4, 5–6, 14, 15, 22–23,
    25–26, 27, 32–33, 39, 43, 49
  conservative policies, 67, 78
  liberal policies, 62, 64–65, 67, 71, 78,
    79
  policy liberalism, 71, 76, 77, 78, 79
  state expenditures, 54, 70, 71
  state government, 13, 26, 33–36,
    37–38, 39, 40–41, 44, 45–49
right-to-work laws, 104
  policy effects, 123, 125
Robare, Iris, 86–90

Shor, Boris, 77
Skocpol, Theda, 3
social programs, 7–8
Sorens, Jason, 77
Soroka, Stuart, 43
South Carolina, 91, 92, 93, 95,
    96, 97
South Dakota, 1, 33, 91, 92, 93, 95,
    97, 98
Southern states, 13, 33, 37–38, 92,
    132–133
state capitol reporters, 90–99
state expenditures, 52–55, 68–71, 145
  Democrats, 54, 70
  Republicans, 54, 70, 71
  see also government spending
state government, 4, 10–12, 13, 19, 26,
    32, 33, 37, 42, 48, 52, 164–165
  Democrats, 35, 36, 37, 38–42, 43–45,
    47, 48, 49
  employees, 55–56
  Republicans, 13, 26, 33–36, 37–38, 39,
    40–41, 44, 45–49
state policies, 4, 5–6, 9–10, 13, 19–22,
    23–24, 52, 56–58, 84–85, 86–90,
    99–100, 114–115, 120, 131–132,
    155–156, 158, 168–172
  Democrats, 24, 79, 84, 90, 91,
    112–113
  partisan effects, 43, 84–86,
    159–160
  reform, 24
  Republican states, 14, 24, 79, 84, 89,
    90, 91, 92–93

tax policies, 103, 121, 162
taxation
    policy effects, 123, 125, 127, 132–133
    tax cuts, 123, 125, 127
teachers, 1–2, 26, 97–98, 129
Teles, Steven, 110
Texas, 6, 33, 37, 111, 118, 119
tort reforms, 130
Trump, Donald, 27, 43, 45, 49, 107, 111, 113, 167, 169

unionization, 1, 101, 104, 133
unions, 104, 129, 145, 162
    United States government, see federal government
Utah, 33, 91, 92, 93, 94, 95, 96

voter identification laws, 107, 158
voter registration laws, 108, 113

Wagner, Adolph, 6–7
Wagner's Law, 6–7
Walker, Scott, 3, 100, 101, 104, 109
Wallach, Hanna, 80
Warshaw, Christopher, 59–60, 71–75, 144
welfare reforms, 132
    policy effects, 123, 125–126
welfare states, 14–16
West Virginia, 1, 164
Wisconsin, 3, 41, 91, 100–101, 109, 121, 161
Witko, Christopher, 112
Wlezien, Christopher, 43